IDEAS AND DEBATES IN FAMILY LAW

Ideas and Debates in Family Law is written for family law students, at undergraduate level and beyond, who are looking for less orthodox ideas about family law. The book's first section looks at themes in family law, addressing challenges facing the family justice system, rights and responsibilities, and the internationalisation of the law regulating families. The second section is focused on adult relationships: it suggests new ways for the law to allocate legal consequences for families, debates the consequences of the 'contractualisation' of marriage, and explores the value of 'fairness' in family finances. The third section is about children, discussing the welfare principle, parental responsibility and practical parenting. Although these issues sound common enough in a family law book, the discussions found here are far from common. Useful by itself or alongside a textbook, *Ideas and Debates in Family Law* offers new and thought-provoking perspectives on family law issues.

Ideas and Debates in Family Law

Rob George

·H A R T·
PUBLISHING

OXFORD AND PORTLAND, OREGON
2012

Published in the United Kingdom by Hart Publishing Ltd
16C Worcester Place, Oxford, OX1 2JW
Telephone: +44 (0)1865 517530
Fax: +44 (0)1865 510710
E-mail: mail@hartpub.co.uk
Website: http://www.hartpub.co.uk

Published in North America (US and Canada) by
Hart Publishing
c/o International Specialized Book Services
920 NE 58th Avenue, Suite 300
Portland, OR 97213-3786
USA
Tel: +1 503 287 3093 or toll-free: (1) 800 944 6190
Fax: +1 503 280 8832
E-mail: orders@isbs.com
Website: http://www.isbs.com

British Library Cataloguing in Publication Data
Data Available

ISBN: 978-1-84946-254-9

Typeset by Hope Services, Abingdon
Printed and bound in Great Britain by
TJ International Ltd, Padstow, Cornwall

Foreword

Clifford Geertz, the anthropologist of law, once said that a society's laws are as much a part of its culture as are its language or its poetry. We should acknowledge and appreciate the way that family law in England and Wales has, up until now, been much admired in other countries for the expertise of its judges and lawyers, for the level of access to legal help, and above all for the child-centred pragmatic and comprehensive provisions of the Children Act 1989.[1] But we are entering a time of great uncertainty for Family Law and Family Justice. Following the thoughtful and comprehensive independent Family Justice Review chaired by David Norgrove, published by the Ministry of Justice in November 2011, there were high hopes for more effective organisational structures, more specialist higher profile judges working in better managed courts, resting firmly on continuing support for the established legal framework set out in the Children Act. But the wide-ranging cuts in legal aid expected to follow the passing of the Legal Aid, Sentencing and Punishment of Offenders Bill in Parliament at the time of writing, which will effectively remove private family law from the scope of legal aid funding, are a cause for serious concern about the ability of the system to maintain not just family law but access to family justice. *Ideas and Debates in Family Law* sets out the key questions facing those who work on these matters whether as lawyers or social scientists, as practitioners or scholars. It would have been useful and thought provoking at any time. As we enter this period of austerity, though, it will be more than useful: it will be a key tool in the hands of the next generation of students of family law and family policy, enabling them to ask tough questions, seek effective answers, and defend and develop that part of the legal system which protects the vulnerable and seeks fair outcomes for those engaged in family change or dispute.

The book looks first at the overarching issues of defining and using the concepts of justice, rights and responsibilities, and what happens when family matters cross geographical borders. It then turns to the ways in which intimate adult relationships are regulated and managed, followed by a closer focus on marriage and how it can be ended without unfairness. The final two chapters look at how the law supports children, taking a critical look at the welfare principle which guides all decision making in the courts on child-related matters under the Children Act, and at day-to-day issues of parenting when parents cannot agree. Every chapter moves easily from legal philosophy

---

[1] See M Maclean et al, 'Family Justice in Hard Times' [2011] *Journal of Social Welfare and Family Law* 319.

to empirical data, across jurisdictions and over time. The erudition is worn lightly, and the language used avoids intimidating technicality or legal jargon.

The author has studied and taught in Oxford, and is a valued member of an interdisciplinary group researching and writing about family law, the Oxford Centre for Family Law and Policy (OXFLAP). His colleagues welcome and congratulate him on this book. Even the most cursory glance at the bibliography will show his debt to John Eekelaar in particular, and his familiarity not only with legal scholars but also with social scientists, demographers and policy analysts working on family issues and with practitioners. The interdisciplinary approach sits well with the international points of reference also. *Ideas and Debates in Family Law* embodies the essential elements of socio-legal studies or empirical legal studies or the sociology of law, whichever term is preferred. The common core is represented by the ability to embrace not only the lawyer's search for an answer but also the social scientist's search for the next question. This book asks good questions, and invites answers. But the questions are so good that it is to be hoped that they will lead not only to today's answers but to the next generation of questions also.

Rob George has recently organised a series of seminars for law students on Family Law and Family Policy. They have attended in unprecedented numbers, together with members of the Law Faculty and visitors from other universities both in the UK and beyond. The meetings were lively, well attended, and set in motion by Rob George with a little background information and a couple of deceptively simple-sounding but sharp, far-reaching and stimulating questions, often accompanied by comment from a visiting expert. The result without exception was fast-moving, intellectually stimulating and original debate. The seminars were so successful that the process is now developed here in book form, retaining the accessibility and freshness of a face-to-face meeting, but adding further materials and examples. I am sure that this exciting and informative account of current questions in family law and policy will be read and enjoyed not only by students of law, but by all those concerned about how we deal with family problems where law has a part to play.

Mavis Maclean

Acknowledgements

Ideas and Debates in Family Law started life as a series of undergraduate seminars in the Law Faculty of Oxford University which ran between 2006 and 2011. I am grateful for the enthusiasm of the students who attended, as well as for the thoughtful comments of my guest speakers, who were: Nicholas Bamforth, Julia Brophy, Alison Diduck, John Eekelaar, Peter Graham Harris, John Haskey, Jonathan Herring, Joan Hunt, Craig Lind, Mavis Maclean, Julie McCandless and Carol Sanger.

Thanks to Richard Hart and Rachel Turner at Hart Publishing for supporting me in this project and for their guidance as it has developed. Parts of *Ideas and Debates in Family Law* draw on my doctoral thesis,[2] and consequently I owe thanks to the Arts and Humanities Research Council for funding that research (Grant no 135597) and to Mavis Maclean for supervising me while I did it. My understanding of trusts of the family home, discussed in chapter six, improved greatly due to conversations with Michael Ashdown, though he bears no responsibility for my views. Parts of chapters five, six and eight draw inspiration from a number of articles which I co-authored with Peter Graham Harris and Jonathan Herring;[3] thanks to my colleagues for their help and to Jordan Publishing for permission to reproduce some of that material here. I have been grateful for constructive feedback on draft chapters from Mavis Maclean, John Eekelaar and Peter Graham Harris.

Special thanks, finally, to Mavis Maclean and John Eekelaar, who encouraged me to write this book and guided me in developing the ideas contained in it. I cannot imagine more generous mentors, and I am grateful for all that they have done to help me.

Rob George
University College, Oxford
January 2012

[2] R George, 'Reassessing Relocation: A Comparative Analysis of Legal Approaches to Disputes over Family Migration after Parental Separation in England and New Zealand' (unpublished DPhil thesis, University of Oxford: 2010).

[3] R George, P Harris and J Herring, 'Pre-Nuptial Agreements: For Better or For Worse?' [2009] *Family Law* 934; P Harris and R George, 'Parental Responsibility and Shared Residence Orders: Parliamentary Intentions and Judicial Interpretations' [2010] *Child and Family Law Quarterly* 151; P Harris, R George and J Herring, 'With this Ring I Thee Wed (Terms and Conditions Apply)' [2011] *Family Law* 367; J Herring, P Harris and R George, 'Ante-Nuptial Agreements: Fairness, Equality, and Presumptions' (2011) 127 *Law Quarterly Review* 335.

Contents

Table of Cases

European Court of Human Rights

European Union

New Zealand

United States of America

Table of Legislation

United Kingdom

Statutory Instruments

Australia

European Union

Regulations

France

New Zealand

Introduction

Ideas and Debates in Family Law

How would you end the sentence, 'Family law is . . .'? Here are some suggestions. Family law is important. Family law is exciting. Family law is interdisciplinary, complicated, fast-moving and challenging. Family law is part of a bigger picture – it is part of the broad web of the law in general, interacting with property law, criminal law, contract law and administrative law amongst many others; but it is also part of a bigger debate which goes beyond the law and into policy. *Ideas and Debates in Family Law* is designed to help you move from learning about family law as it is now, to thinking critically about *why* the law is like that and whether it *should* be like that.

There are many ways in which this aim could be pursued. The material contained in *Ideas and Debates in Family Law* is intended only as a start, as one way of exploring some less obvious ideas about family law and some less conventional approaches to thinking about these issues. You need some basic prior knowledge of family law before you can use this book to your best advantage, because although I have endeavoured to make it reasonably freestanding it does not contain a general statement of the law itself.[1] You will also find that the topics chosen for discussion are sometimes quite narrow, and so it will help you if you know enough about the law to be able to place

---

[1] Good family law textbooks include: A Diduck and F Kaganas, *Family Law, Gender and the State*, 3rd edn (Oxford, Hart Publishing, 2012); J Herring, *Family Law*, 5th edn (Harlow, Longman, 2011); N Lowe and G Douglas, *Bromley's Family Law*, 10th edn (Oxford, Oxford University Press, 2007); B Hale, D Pearl, E Cooke and D Monk, *The Family, Law and Society*, 6th edn (Oxford, Oxford University Press, 2009); S Harris-Short and J Miles, *Family Law: Text, Cases and Materials*, 2nd edn (Oxford, Oxford University Press, 2011); J Masson, R Bailey-Harris and R Probert, *Cretney's Principles of Family Law*, 8th edn (London, Sweet and Maxwell, 2008).

these ideas in context. The aim of the book is to help you to start thinking critically about family law, not to offer you easy answers. In fact, I offer few 'answers' at all here. This is a book of questions, not a book of answers.

Some of the ideas in the book may seem odd – for example, chapter five introduces the idea of a 'fixed-term marriage', and chapter seven suggests that the main aim of the welfare principle in child law[2] might be to make parents argue about better things, rather than to make the outcomes for children better. These are not the conventional ways in which family law issues are debated. When you read them, I suggest that you take nothing at face value, and keep in mind two points. First, the ideas in this book are not 'suggestions', and it is important to note that I do not agree with all of the opinions expressed here. (This is not my vision for family law!) But second, there is a reason why I have focused on the issues addressed here, and each chapter is designed to illustrate an idea. Often, my examples are a little 'tongue in cheek', intended to highlight concerns about family law issues by pushing apparently sensible arguments to their (il)logical conclusions. So, while the points which I am making are serious, the examples given are not always made seriously.

Because the aim is to help you to think about issues, I ask a lot of questions. Some are purely rhetorical, but most are worthy of thought. Many of them are questions to which I do not have any ready answers, and it should not concern you if you find them hard – they *are* hard! As with many things, the answer which you ultimately reach is probably less important than what you learnt along the way by asking the question in the first place.

Ideas and Debates in Family Law is written in three broad sections. The first three chapters are about *overarching themes* which affect all of family law in one way or another. Chapter one ('Family Law and Family Justice') is about the idea of justice in the family context, and the vision of family justice presented in that chapter is something of a recurring theme as the book goes on. Chapter two ('Rights and Responsibilities') is the most jurisprudential chapter in the book, asking about the role of rights and responsibilities in families and in family law disputes. The increasing internationalisation of family law is addressed in Chapter three ('International Family Law'), which considers the ways in which family life and family law are becoming increasingly regulated at a supra-national level.

The second section of the book is about the *regulation of adult relationships*. Chapter four ('Regulating Adult Relationships') is about the ways in which the law regulates different types of intimate adult relationships in general, while Chapter five ('The Meanings of Marriage') is about marriage specifically, asking what marriage is and whether it should be re-conceptualised. Financial orders in the event of relationship breakdown are the subject of

---

[2] Children Act 1989, s 1(1): 'When a court determines any question with respect to the upbringing of a child . . . the child's welfare shall be the court's paramount consideration.'

Chapter six ('Fairness in Family Finances'), where we deconstruct the increasingly prevalent focus on 'fairness'.

The final two chapters of the book focus on the *law relating to children*. Chapter seven ('The Values of Welfare') is about the welfare principle, discussing the varied ways in which that principle might be interpreted and offering a defence (of sorts) of its continued use. The book closes, in chapter eight ('Parental Responsibility, Parenting and Status'), with discussion of parental responsibility and court orders about children's residence.

It is obvious that many important family law issues are not covered in any of these chapters. Discussions of public family law, to do with the protection of children from abuse or neglect,[3] and of domestic violence,[4] are the most obvious omissions. The reason for omitting these topics is primarily that, although they are clearly parts of family law – and important parts at that – they are also different from much of family law, in that they interact to a great extent with criminal law, tort law and public law more generally.[5] That is, of course, not a reason to ignore child protection or domestic violence, but it may be a reason to think about them slightly differently from the way I approach the family law topics which are addressed in this book.

Leaving those topics aside, it will also become clear that the topics which are covered in *Ideas and Debates in Family Law* could have included a number of sub-issues which are either omitted entirely, or which receive only passing mention. For example, an important issue relating to 'marriage' in the UK is whether same-sex couples should be able to marry (specifically) or whether civil partnerships are a sufficient equivalent. I have views on that question,[6] but it is not an area that I focus on. The reason for their omission is simple enough: this is a small book, and there is not room for everything, so in general I have tried to focus on issues which are less frequently addressed elsewhere. Moreover, the approaches suggested in this book should help you to think about all issues of family law critically, so the fact that a topic is not covered here specifically does not mean that it cannot be thought about in similar ways.

The illustrations and case authorities cited in the book are primarily drawn from the legal jurisdiction of England and Wales. From time to time, I give examples from other jurisdictions for comparison, and a fair amount of the secondary literature used is not from England and Wales. Despite this focus, most of the ideas discussed are not specific to any one jurisdiction, and I

---

[3] See, eg, L Hoyano and C Keenan, *Child Abuse: Law and Policy Across Boundaries* (Oxford, Oxford University Press, 2007).

[4] See, eg, *Yemshaw v London Borough of Hounslow* [2011] UKSC 3, [2011] 2 FLR 1614; J Herring, 'The Meaning of Domestic Violence' [2011] *Journal of Social Welfare and Family Law* 297.

[5] For example, in L Hoyano and C Keenan, *Child Abuse: Law and Policy Across Boundaries* (Oxford, Oxford University Press, 2007), only around 100 of the 934 pages of text are about family law; the rest of the book is about criminal law, tort law, human rights and civil procedure.

[6] See ch 5 below, 'The Meanings of Marriage', n 2.

hope that they will be of interest to students and scholars of family law far beyond the borders of the English and Welsh legal system.

Finally, for the avoidance of doubt, I do not anywhere purport to set out 'the law' on any of the topics discussed, even though I sometimes give brief introductory overviews. However, insofar as it is relevant, I have endeavoured to make any references to the law accurate as at 1 January 2012.

Family Law and Family Justice

> **Key Questions**
>
> What is family law?
>
> What is the family justice system, and how do courts and lawyers work to implement family law?
>
> Why is it important to see family law as a matter of justice?

Family law is important. It facilitates *adjustments* to people's family relationships, it *protects* vulnerable adults and children within families, and it *supports* families and their familial roles in society.[1] The family justice system administers these functions as a forum for enforcing people's rights; protecting them from harassment, bullying and abuse of power within families; and promoting values like welfare, fairness, equality and justice. These things are of fundamental importance.

Probably no country's family law or its administration of family justice are perfect. Certainly few people in any country would suggest that the detail of family law or of the family justice system could not be improved, and much of this book presents ideas about ways in which the law could (or occasionally should) be changed. However, before getting to detailed discussion about the law, it is first necessary to understand why there should be something called 'family law' and a family justice system in which family disputes are resolved at all.

In the first part of this chapter, a basic overview of the world of family law and of the family justice system is offered, so that the arena for the ideas and

---

[1] J Eekelaar, *Family Law and Social Policy*, 2nd edn (London, Weidenfeld and Nicolson, 1984).

debates in this book can be clearly delineated. In the second section, we look at some of the arguments which might be presented 'against' family law. These arguments give the opportunity, in the third section, to ask some fundamental questions about the nature and purpose of family law, and to make the argument 'for' family law.

THE WORLD OF FAMILY LAW

The first question to ask is simply this: what is family law about?

There are two basic ways in which this question could be answered. The first is a *descriptive* answer, which will be given in this section. The second answer is a more adventurous *philosophical* one, which we come to in the final part of this chapter. However, even the descriptive answer offers enough challenges for now.

A number of ideas can be offered about the core *theme* of family law. Jonathan Herring suggests that family law is 'the law governing the relationships between children and parents, and between adults in close emotional relationships', though he also notes that there are somewhat arbitrary 'conventions' about which sub-issues within those categories are usually thought of as the domain of family law.[2] As Alison Diduck and Felicity Kaganas explain, these conventions continue to focus on 'the monogamous sexual relationship (either actually or symbolically) between a man and a woman'.[3] Elsewhere, Diduck describes family law as 'the body of law that defines and regulates the family, family relationships and family responsibilities'.[4]

In general, the following basic issues are usually seen to be within the remit of family law (though some also appear in other areas of the law, such as criminal law and property law):

- **The regulation of intimate adult relationships:** traditionally, this includes the formation and dissolution of formal relationships (primarily marriage), together with related issues affecting non-formal relationships,[5] as well as some discussion of the regulation of on-going relationships (such as protection from domestic violence).

---

[2] J Herring, *Family Law*, 5th edn (Harlow, Pearson, 2011) 15.

[3] A Diduck and F Kaganas, *Family Law, Gender and the State*, 3rd edn (Oxford, Hart Publishing, 2012) 3.

[4] A Diduck, 'Family Law and Family Responsibility' in J Bridgeman, H Keating and C Lind (eds), *Responsibility, Law and the Family* (Aldershot, Ashgate, 2008) 262.

[5] In the UK, people in these relationships are usually termed 'cohabitants', but other terms are used elsewhere, such as New Zealand's 'de facto couples'.

- **The regulation of family finances and property:** the focus here is usually on property and financial arrangements in the event of relationship breakdown, but there is also discussion of finances and property within families and, occasionally, between generations.
- **The regulation of parents and children:** four primary issues come in here – the law's regulation of who is a parent; children's rights; disputes between parents about their children's upbringing; and the protection of children from abuse and neglect by their parents.

These 'core issues' are supplemented in some books by discussion of connected topics, such as the law relating to older people,[6] child support and state welfare provisions,[7] or the legal consequences of death in families.[8] However, some issues which affect families – sometimes in profound ways – are rarely considered to be part of family law: examples include immigration law[9] and the parts of employment law concerning families.[10]

It is difficult to think of family law in isolation. Not only does it interrelate with many other areas of the law,[11] but also with other academic disciplines,[12] and with social policy more broadly. Social policy is about the ways in which societies are organised, about the relationship between the individual, the state, and other social actors (like religious organisations, charities, unions – in the UK coalition government's terminology, *the big society*). Social policy can be broken down into subsections which focus on particular aspects of that organisation. So, for example, education policy is about the provision of schooling and other education, and normally focuses on the state's involvement with, and role in the organisation of, nurseries, schools, colleges and universities.

Family policy is about the organisation and regulation of social functions which either are or could be performed by families in our communities. While there are some issues which are purely about families, many issues of family policy interact with other parts of social policy. For example, if the state provides nurseries for children aged 3 to 5 as part of its education policy, that impacts on how families with young children are able to organise themselves.[13]

Not all parts of family policy are of direct relevance to family law. Family law is only one way in which a state's family policies are articulated, and in

[6] Herring, *Family Law*, ch 12.
[7] B Hale, D Pearl, E Cooke and D Monk, *The Family, Law and Society*, 6th edn (Oxford, Oxford University Press, 2009) ch 3.
[8] N Lowe and G Douglas, *Bromley's Family Law*, 10th edn (Oxford, Oxford University Press, 2007) ch 19.
[9] B Hale, 'Families and the Law: The Forgotten International Dimension' [2009] *Child and Family Law Quarterly* 413; see also ch 3 below, 'International Family Law'.
[10] See, eg, the Work and Families Act 2006.
[11] Think about the links between family law and i) criminal law, ii) tort law, iii) contract law, iv) land law, v) trusts, vi) public law, vii) EU law and viii) private international law, just for starters.
[12] Especially psychology and sociology, but also economics, politics and others.
[13] See, eg, M Daly and K Rake, *Gender and the Welfare State: Care, Work and Welfare in Europe and the USA* (Cambridge, Polity Press, 2003) ch 4.

particular 'family law [is] the family policy most concerned with family formation, structure and dissolution'.[14] When looking at questions of family law,
though, it is worth thinking about how those questions relate to broader
issues of family policy. For example, when thinking about children's residence
arrangements after parental separation, the viability of shared residence
arrangements is not a purely legal question. There are broader issues. One
issue would be to ask about the research evidence (psychological, sociological, socio-legal) about how children react to splitting their time between two
homes.[15] Another is about the ability of the family to provide two physical
homes for their children – and if the family's resources cannot manage this,
whether the state ought to assist them by providing housing.[16] These are
not all legal questions, but they are important issues for family lawyers to
consider, because family law cannot be detached from its social and policy
contexts.

If that is the core substance of family law, what about the structures within
which it is implemented? In terms of the courts, the system in England and
Wales is far from straightforward.[17] Family cases can start in front of any of
four different levels of judge in several different courts,[18] depending primarily
on the complexity of the issues.[19] The simplest cases are heard by district
judges or magistrates sitting in Family Proceedings Courts, while the most
complex cases usually start before a High Court judge.[20] In between are circuit judges and district judges sitting in the County Courts, as well as district
judges of the High Court and district judges of the Principal Registry of the
Family Division.

Circuit judges also hear appeals from the Family Proceedings Courts and
from district judges in the County Courts, while High Court judges hear

---

[14] S Kamerman and A Kahn, *Family Change and Family Policies in Great Britain, Canada, New Zealand and the United States.* (Oxford, Clarendon Press, 1998) 17.

[15] See, eg, E Trinder, 'Shared Residence: A Review of Recent Evidence' [2010] *Family Law* 1192; B Fehlberg, B Smyth, M Maclean and C Roberts, 'Legislating for Shared Time Parenting After Separation: A Research Review' [2011] *International Journal of Law, Policy and the Family* 318.

[16] If you think that sounds like a purely theoretical question, see *Holmes-Moorhouse v Richmond-upon-Thames LBC* [2009] UKHL 7, [2009] 1 FLR 904.

[17] See Practice Direction 30A, [2.1], which supplements the Family Procedure Rules 2010, part 30. The summary given here is rather simplified, but suffices for our purposes. *cf* the simple system in New Zealand under the Family Courts Act 1980 (New Zealand): virtually all family cases start in the Family Court; first appeals go to the High Court, with further appeals to the Court of Appeal and then the Supreme Court.

[18] It is said that these courts have 'original jurisdiction', ie cases can originate there. The argu-
ments in favour of a single family court, put forward but rejected in the UK in the 1980s, have recently been revived: see D Norgrove (chair), *Family Justice Review: Final Report* (London, HMSO, 2011) [hereafter, *Family Justice Review*] [2.158] ff.

[19] Some types of case are assumed to be complex, and must be filed in the High Court, such as international child abduction cases, but many types of case can start in any of the courts, and it is down to the lawyers and judges to try to match the complexity of the case to the appropriate level of court.

[20] This is usually a judge of the Family Division of the High Court, but some property cases are heard in the Chancery Division, and a few cases might go to the Queen's Bench Division.

appeals from district judges of the High Court and from the Principal
Registry. Decisions of High Court judges and of circuit judges (whether at
first instance or on appeal) can be appealed to the Court of Appeal, and
Court of Appeal decisions can, in turn, be appealed to the Supreme Court.
(High Court cases can also 'leapfrog' straight to the Supreme Court in limited
circumstances.[21]) This less-than-obvious structure is illustrated in Box 1.1.

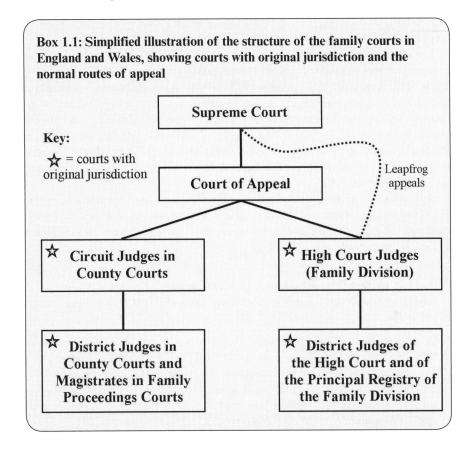

**Box 1.1: Simplified illustration of the structure of the family courts in
England and Wales, showing courts with original jurisdiction and the
normal routes of appeal**

However, as well as understanding the structure of the courts, it is important
to appreciate the role that the courts play in family cases. While the image of
a court is of a place where opposing litigants fight while a judge referees the
battle and then decides the outcome, very few family disputes are like that.
For example, research into the work of divorce lawyers shows clearly that
courts play a small part of the overall divorce process, and that getting a final
decision from a judge (rather than simply directions about how to proceed) is

---

[21] Administration of Justice Act 1969, ss 12–16.

very rare.[22] Some cases are resolved entirely independently by the parties, and some are resolved following mediation or counselling. Most, though, are settled with the assistance of solicitors, sometimes aided by barristers, but with relatively little interaction with the court. Research in the late 1990s showed that many cases went to court briefly to get guidance (known as 'directions') from a judge, but 'results might be better defined as . . . agreement or compromise between the parties following some guidance from the court rather than any formal adjudication'.[23] As this research highlighted, the family court 'provides a framework within which compromises can be made'.[24]

The key players in most family cases are therefore the lawyers. While there is some overlap, the role of solicitors and barristers in family law work varies. Both have been studied by Mavis Maclean and John Eekelaar, who explain that the aim of both halves of the profession is to minimise conflict and work towards a fair, sustainable settlement which is 'the best deal for their clients *within the normative standards of the law*'.[25] In other words, the law provides the background against which lawyers help their clients to reach agreements, with the lawyers' experience of judicial decision-making used to cross-check and guide their advice.

Solicitors do the bulk of the work in family cases, and normally see a client's case through from beginning to end. The work involved is well explained by Eekelaar, Maclean and Beinart, whose references to 'lawyers' in the extract in Box 1.2 mean solicitors specifically.

Box 1.2: extract from J Eekelaar, M Maclean and S Beinart, *Family Lawyers: The Divorce Work of Solicitors* (Oxford, Hart Publishing, 2000) 184

Of course lawyers bargained, and sometimes put pressure on the other side, but that does not amount to 'scoring points and settling wrongs, real or imagined'. . . . We have shown abundantly that the lawyer's role is not confined to merely giving legal advice. It extends to providing reassurance and practical support for many clients during a particularly stressful period. It often extends to dealing with third parties. . . . [L]awyers standardly encouraged clients to discuss matters between themselves, especially those concerning children and the household contents, although they did tend to warn clients against entering into agreements with the other party over finances unless they checked with the

---

[22] G Davis, S Cretney and J Collins, *Simple Quarrels: Negotiating Money and Property Disputes on Divorce* (Oxford, Clarendon Press, 1994) 253; see also R Ingleby, *Solicitors and Divorce* (Oxford, Oxford University Press, 1992); J Eekelaar, M Maclean and S Beinart, *Family Lawyers: The Divorce Work of Solicitors* (Oxford, Hart Publishing, 2000).

[23] S Maclean, *Legal Aid and the Family Justice System* (London, Legal Aid Board Research Unit, 1998) 101.

[24] Ibid, 97.

[25] Eekelaar, Maclean and Beinart, *Family Lawyers*, 185.

solicitor. There were moreover a number of cases where the parties were only able to communicate *through* the solicitor, so in those circumstances the lawyer was the only channel of communication which worked. . . . Our evidence does, however, show the lawyers consciously taking many measures to try to *reduce* tension. . . . In view of the often highly emotional state which many of their clients were experiencing when they came to see the lawyer, it is difficult to see how the lawyers could have worked with the clients at all unless they succeeded in reducing the level of distress. The extent to which negotiation through lawyers results in settlement is perhaps testament to their success.

Barristers usually become involved in family cases for relatively short periods. Sometimes they advise on a point of law (on paper or at a client conference), but more often they join a case when the solicitors are unable to negotiate a settlement and litigation looks likely. Even then, though, their aim is to negotiate. Barristers talk convincingly about how a judge is likely to view the case, and much of their work with the client is done outside the courtroom, in a meeting room or in the corridor. The barristers often go in and out of court several times over the course of a morning, updating the judge and asking for more time to negotiate.[26] As Maclean and Eekelaar note from their study of the family bar, few cases end up being formally adjudicated by the judge. Despite the public image of the barrister as a litigator, in family cases 'counsel find standing up in court stressful. If this point is reached they have lost control. They are in the hands of a judge'.[27]

A better way to understand the family barrister's role is therefore as a mentor and guide for their client, as Maclean and Eekelaar explain in the extract in Box 1.3, which gives an overview of the barrister's role.

Box 1.3: extract from M Maclean and J Eekelaar, *Family Law Advocacy: How Barristers Help the Victims of Family Failure* (Oxford, Hart Publishing, 2009) 121

What has been achieved [through the barrister's involvement in a case]? A dispute has been managed, pro tem. The available information has been rigorously tested, and hopefully this injection of reality has led to a settlement, though agreement may be too strong a word. . . . A sometimes bewildered client has had the goings-on explained, been comforted, been protected from hostility and, perhaps most important, had his or her viewpoint represented. Given that any case which reaches a barrister, other than those where counsel is being used only for advice or

---

[26] M Maclean and J Eekelaar, *Family Law Advocacy: How Barristers Help the Victims of Family Failure* (Oxford, Hart Publishing, 2009) 120.

[27] Ibid, 120.

> settlement in conference, is deeply conflicted and entrenched, or, in a public law setting, has set up state bureaucracy against an often vulnerable individual, this is an impressive result.

This role is a far cry from the adversarial, antagonistic image of lawyers put forward by some, especially government policy-makers,[28] who tend to contrast lawyers unfavourably with mediators and other forms of alternative dispute resolution. Mediation is said to be more cost-effective and 'to be in the best interest of those involved' compared with seeing a lawyer and, by implication, litigating.[29] However, while it is widely recognised that privately arranged settlements, reached without significant judicial intervention, are often beneficial, two important points need to be understood.

First, family lawyers spend the bulk of their time negotiating and mediating, both formally and informally, with their own clients and with 'the other side'. There is not a binary choice between lawyers on the one side and mediators on the other side. Indeed family solicitors' work is such a mixture of negotiation and litigation that the term 'litigotiation' seems appropriate to describe it.[30] Second, there is reason to be cautious about the claim that mediation is suitable for most cases which presently end up being resolved by lawyers (with or without going to court). A good summary of these concerns is given by Diduck and Kaganas in the extract in Box 1.4.

Box 1.4: extract from A Diduck and F Kaganas, *Family Law, Gender and the State*, 3rd edn (Oxford, Hart Publishing, 2012) 743

While private ordering enables parties to avoid the stress and expense of litigation and while it may often enable parties to retain some measure of autonomy, it may be a far from perfect solution in some cases of family break-up. To speak of family privacy and family autonomy is to assume that the family is capable of making decisions as a unit. However, the interests and desires of different family members may be very different and may even be irreconcilable. To contain decision-making and dispute resolution in the private sphere means that the formal safeguards designed to ensure that each party's case is heard are absent. Imbalances of power may be left unredressed and a party unable to articulate his or her point of view is disadvantaged. In addition, a party may 'agree' out of fear or exhaustion to arrangements that could be damaging.

---

[28] See, eg, Lord Chancellor's Department, *Looking to the Future: Mediation and the Ground for Divorce, A Consultation Paper* (London, HMSO, 1993).

[29] Ministry of Justice, *Proposals for the Reform of Legal Aid in England and Wales: Consultation Paper 12/10* (London, HMSO, 2010) [hereafter, MoJ, *Consultation Paper*], [4.69] ff.

[30] M Galanter, 'Worlds of Deals: Using Negotiation to Teach about Legal Process' (1984) 34 *Journal of Legal Education* 268; more generally, see R Mnookin and L Kornhauser, 'Bargaining in the Shadow of the Law: The Case of Divorce' (1979) 88 *Yale Law Journal* 950.

So, this gives some indication of what the world of family law is about. In the next section, we look in more detail at some of the arguments 'against' family law and the use of lawyers to resolve family disputes.

ARGUMENTS AGAINST FAMILY LAW

Much of the recent debate about family law has focused on legal aid.[31] Consequently, parts of this section are also about legal aid, but the issues being considered are significant for all of family law and everyone who might use the family justice system, whether they would be eligible for legal aid or not.

Looking at complaints which have been made about family law before, it is possible to see two essential arguments:[32]

- **The communitarian argument:** on this view, all of law is inherently rights-focused, and this approach is fundamentally inappropriate when resolving family disputes because rights are individualistic whereas families call for more selfless thinking.
- **The anti-legalism argument:** this approach suggests that the legal process necessitates a reduction of all issues into binary options, such as true/not true, legal/illegal or right/wrong. In the family law context, this reduction-ism demands a precision of evidence which is unrealistic, and imposes win/lose outcomes which make conflicts worse rather than better.

The current complaints against family law seem to straddle both arguments, though neither approach is adopted explicitly.[33] So what are the present arguments? The position can be best found in the UK coalition government's Consultation Paper regarding proposed cuts to legal aid,[34] supplemented by other documents.[35]

When it came to power in May 2010, the government set about reducing the UK's budget deficit, primarily by cutting public spending. One source of

[31] The Legal Aid, Sentencing and Punishment of Offenders Bill was awaiting Royal assent when this book went to press.

[32] J Eekelaar, 'Family Justice: Ideal or Illusion?' (1995) 48(2) *Current Legal Problems* 191, 194–98.

[33] I am grateful to many colleagues with whom I have discussed the legal aid reforms, and especially to John Eekelaar whose analysis of the government's proposals has informed much of what follows: see J Eekelaar, '"Not of the Highest Importance": Family Justice under Threat' [2011] *Journal of Social Welfare and Family Law* 311.

[34] MoJ, *Consultation Paper*.

[35] See, eg, Ministry of Justice, *Reform of Legal Aid in England and Wales: The Government Response*, Cm 8072 (London, HMSO, 2011) [hereafter, MoJ, *Government Response*]; *Family Justice Review*.

potential 'saving' which the government identified was the legal aid budget for family law. The total spent on legal aid in 2009 was just over £2bn,[36] which the government noted with apparent embarrassment made it 'one of the most comprehensive, and expensive, legal aid provisions in the world'.[37] Of this £2bn, around £660m was spent on 'representation' in civil and family cases.[38] Most of that £660m was allocated to family law, and something like two thirds of the family law budget was allocated to public law cases concerning allegations of neglect or abuse of children.

Changes were proposed through the Legal Aid, Sentencing and Punishment of Offenders Bill 2012, aimed at reducing the overall legal aid bill by £350m,[39] mostly from the family law budget. Two justifications were offered by the government for the cuts to family legal aid:

- **The financial justification:** the government points out that there is a general need to reduce public spending in order to bring the budget deficit down, and family legal aid needs to be cut as part of that overall agenda.
- **The ideological justification:** the government considers that the law is an inappropriate way for family problems to be resolved, and so wishes people to take 'personal responsibility for their problems', problems which 'very often result from litigants' own decisions in their personal lives'.[40]

These two points call on entirely different arguments, either of which could be made without the other. While many would take issue with the validity of the financial justification,[41] the more fundamental challenge for the family lawyer comes from the ideological justification.

The government's case against family law proceeds on the basis that family problems are private problems, best kept out of the public sphere entirely and, in particular, best kept out of court. The government makes numerous references to 'unnecessary litigation', saying, for example, that its reforms are guided by 'the desire to stop the encroachment of unnecessary litigation into

---

[36] MoJ, *Consultation Paper*, [2.9].

[37] MoJ, *Government Response*, [2.3]; see also MoJ, *Consultation Paper*, [2.9]. It seems not to have occurred to anyone in government that having one of the most comprehensive legal aid schemes in the world might be seen as a source of pride.

[38] MoJ, *Consultation Paper*, 29 (Table 1). A further £260m is spent on 'help' with civil and family matters, which one assumes to be funding for Citizens Advice Bureaux, Community Legal Centres, etc (though the Consultation Paper does not specify what 'help' or 'representation' mean), while nearly £1.2bn was spent on criminal legal aid. This high cost of criminal legal aid is largely caused by the massive increase in the number and complexity of criminal offences introduced since the mid-990s: see generally I Loader and R Sparks, *Public Criminology? Studying Crime and Society in the Twenty-First Century* (Abingdon, Routledge, 2010).

[39] MoJ, *Consultation Paper*, [2.4].

[40] MoJ, *Consultation Paper*, [2.11] and [4.19].

[41] It is at least arguable that money spent on legal aid for family problems saves money overall, because the involvement of lawyers and the legal resolution of problems reduces the extent to which families and individuals call on other state-funded services, including health and social care, education, police, housing and benefits: see Z Williams, 'So We Can't Afford Legal Aid? Look at the Costs Without It', *The Guardian* (23 June 2011).

society by encouraging people to take greater personal responsibility for their problems'.[42] This view is bolstered by the government's claim that this 'unnecessary litigation' has been brought about by a combination of people's personal choices and lawyers' interference:

[T]here is a range of other cases which can very often result from a litigant's own decisions in their personal life. . . . Where the issue is one which arises from the litigant's own personal choices, we are less likely to consider that these cases concern issues of the highest importance.[43]

We are concerned that the provision of legal aid in this area is creating unnecessary litigation and encouraging long, drawn-out and acrimonious cases . . .[44]

Legal aid funding can be used to support lengthy and intractable family cases which may be resolved out of court if funding were not available. In such cases, we would like to move to a position where parties are encouraged to settle using mediation, rather than protracting disputes unnecessarily by having a lawyer paid for by legal aid.[45]

So, family cases are said to reflect 'choices' about people's 'personal lives', and providing legal aid encourages 'long, drawn-out and acrimonious cases', thus 'protracting disputes unnecessarily by having a lawyer' when, if only people would mediate instead, these 'intractable disputes' would be 'resolved out of court'.

Now, it could be pointed out that the quotations here relate only to legal aid provision in family cases. However, the government clearly takes the same view regardless of who is to pay, as can be seen from three of the 'guiding principles' set out in the terms of reference for the Family Justice Review:

The court's role should be focused on protecting the vulnerable from abuse, victimisation and exploitation and should avoid intervening in family life except where there is clear benefit to children or vulnerable adults in doing so.

Individuals should have the right information and support to enable them to take responsibility for the consequences of their relationship breakdown.

Mediation and similar support should be used as far as possible to support individuals themselves to reach agreement about arrangements, rather than having an arrangement imposed by the courts.[46]

The government accepts that withdrawing legal aid will not stop all cases from reaching court, and that having people representing themselves in court is likely to lead to adverse results:

We do accept . . . the likelihood of an increase in volume of litigants-in-person as a result of these reforms and thus some worse outcomes materialising. But it is not

---

[42] MoJ, *Consultation Paper*, [2.11]; see similarly [4.209], [5.6] and [5.14] and MoJ, *Government Response*, [3.15] and [3.286]; the Ministerial Forewords to both papers contain similar references.

[43] MoJ, *Consultation Paper*, [4.19].

[44] MoJ, *Consultation Paper*, [4.209].

[45] MoJ, *Consultation Paper*, [4.211].

[46] *Family Justice* Review, 182 (Annex A).

the case that everyone is entitled to legal representation, funded by the taxpayer, for any dispute or to a particular outcome in litigation.[47]

The idea that one should be unconcerned about 'worse outcomes materialising', or that one should accept that people are not entitled to 'a particular outcome' when asserting legal rights in court, is astonishing and effectively 'deprive[s] legal rights of all effect'.[48]

Overall, the government presents 'a diminished concept of what constitutes justice in regard to family matters' and, in particular, 'a startlingly limited view of the role of a court, and hence of the law which courts apply'.[49] The question is whether this is a view which one should accept. It has certainly been rejected by many commentators, with Maclean and Eekelaar saying that 'the idea that justice within families is somehow of lesser significance than elsewhere must be dispelled in the strongest terms'.[50] The final section of this chapter makes the argument for why family law needs to be recognised as a matter of justice.

FAMILY LAW AND FAMILY JUSTICE

In order to see why family disputes must be considered as a matter of justice, some thought might be given first to what is meant by 'justice'. In political philosophy, justice is explored from two core approaches:[51]

- **Transcendental institutionalism:** this approach (adopted by Hobbes, Locke, Rousseau, Kant and, to some extent, Rawls) focuses on creating the conditions for just institutions to exist (such as courts, parliaments, and so on). Some of these theorists (Kant and Rawls, for instance) also addressed the broader 'arrangements' which would be necessary for these institutions to ensure justice in society, such as how citizens would need to behave.
- **Realization-focused comparison:** those who take this approach (Adam Smith, Bentham, Wollstonecraft, Marx and JS Mill, for example) are not focused on ideal justice institutions, but rather on the removal of some particular injustice which is visible in society.

Both of these approaches might yield interesting issues for the family lawyer to consider, but since the main charge against family law seems to be the unsuitability of family disputes to resolution in court, a focus on the role of

---

[47] MoJ, *Government Response*, [3.140].
[48] Eekelaar, '"Not of the Highest Importance"', 313.
[49] Ibid, 313.
[50] M Maclean and J Eekelaar, 'Family Justice' [2011] *Family Law* 3, 3.
[51] See A Sen, *The Idea of Justice* (London, Penguin, 2010) 5–7.

institutions in promoting justice may be more pressing. The work of John Rawls, most clearly presented in his book *Justice as Fairness: A Restatement*, will be used to introduce these ideas.[52]

According to Rawls' theory, the idea of justice is most applicable to what he terms 'the basic structure (of a well-ordered society)':

> [T]he basic structure of society is the way in which the main political and social institutions of society fit together into one system of social cooperation, and the way they assign basic rights and duties and regulate the division of advantages that arise from social cooperation over time.[53]

Courts are an obvious example of the basic structure, but Rawls is clear that 'the family' (in some form or other) is also part of the basic structure, and thus 'the family [is] susceptible to the idea of justice'.[54] Consequently, although Rawls does not think that the more applied political elements of justice can be implemented within each individual family,[55] he nonetheless states that 'principles of justice still put essential restrictions on the family and all other associations'.[56] The reason why justice extends to the family is simple: all people are citizens with rights, and no association which they can form with one another can violate these rights, as explained in the extract in Box 1.5.

Box 1.5: extract from J Rawls, *Justice as Fairness: A Restatement* (London, Penguin, 2001) § 50.4

The principles defining the equal basic liberties and fair opportunities of citizens always hold in and through all so-called domains. The equal rights of women and the claims of their children as future citizens are inalienable and protect them wherever they are. . . . [G]ender distinctions limiting those rights and liberties are excluded. So the spheres of the political and the public, and the not-public and the private, take their shape from the content and application of the concept of justice and its principles. If the so-called private sphere is a place alleged to be exempt from justice, then there is no such thing.

In other words, the principles of justice apply to family life, and it is not possible to assert that these are 'private' matters if that is meant to mean that they are beyond the scope of justice, because there is no private domain in that way.

---

[52] See J Rawls, *Justice as Fairness: A Restatement* (Cambridge MA, Harvard University Press, 2001); *cf* generally N Fraser, 'Reframing Justice in a Globalising World' (2005) 36 *New Left Review* 69.

[53] Rawls, *Justice as Fairness*, § 4.1.

[54] Ibid, § 50.1.

[55] Ibid, § 50.1.

[56] Ibid, § 50.4.

So what *is* justice? For Rawls, the core of justice is having a society which involves a fair system of social cooperation over time, combined with a clear view of citizens as free and equal persons operating within a society which is regulated effectively by a public conception of fairness.[57] This vision of justice requires, as a fundamental starting point, a just basic structure which 'secures what we may call background justice'.[58] The basic structure is then responsible for removing 'bargaining advantages' which appear over time between members of any society, because if these advantages are not regularised then they will be allocated according to people's power, wealth or innate capacities, and that approach cannot achieve political justice.[59] In other words, justice demands that the *system* protect the weaker against the stronger and take some measures to equalise people's life chances. This is not a utopian vision: the aim is not to equalise people's end positions, but to ensure that the ownership of 'productive assets and human capital' (meaning education of various kinds) is widespread at the start. 'The intent is not simply to assist those who lose out through accident or misfortune (although that must be done), but rather to put all citizens in a position to manage their own affairs on a footing of a suitable degree of social and economic equality'.[60]

At various points, Rawls links his theory to the family specifically. He says, for example, that in order to ensure equality between men and women in sharing the work required by reproduction and child-raising (and, one should add, of other care-giving responsibilities), family law needs to contain special provisions to divide these burdens (more) equally between the sexes.[61] Similarly, he points out that divorce law must actively protect women from undue vulnerability, since such vulnerability will serve injustice not only on women themselves but also on children.[62]

This *vulnerability* of one person in Rawls' analysis could, conversely, be seen in terms of the *power* of another person, and the control of power is one way which some scholars conceive of the purpose of family law. Mark Henaghan, for example, says that family law should be used to regulate 'not only power as between individual family members, but power as between different ideas of what family should be'.[63] Henaghan draws on John Eekelaar's book, *Family Law and Personal Life*,[64] to argue that this power regulation is what family law is doing (or, at least, what it is aiming to do). This approach accepts that the surface of family law can appear somewhat chaotic, because

---

[57] Ibid, § 2.1.
[58] Ibid, § 4.1.
[59] Ibid, § 6.2.
[60] Ibid, § 42.3.
[61] Ibid, § 4.2.
[62] Ibid, § 50.3.
[63] M Henaghan, 'The Normal Order of Family Law' (2008) 28 *Oxford Journal of Legal Studies* 165, 166.
[64] J Eekelaar, *Family Law and Personal Life*, paperback edn (Oxford, Oxford University Press, 2007).

of the nature of the cases with which family law is concerned,[65] but argues that this *factual chaos* is not a reflection of underlying *theoretical chaos* within the law itself.[66] The law itself has a clear purpose, namely the regulation of power between individuals in their personal lives.

The family, then, must be seen to be part of life governed by the principles of justice, and one main function of family law is to regulate and control the exercise of power so as to ensure that justice is achieved. A key way in which the law controls power is though the protection of rights.[67] For Eekelaar, a right protects a valuable interest such as freedom from oppression (which can come in many guises) or the articulation of one's own view of 'the good life'.[68] Consequently, the function of family law is 'to constrain the wrongful exercise of power and leave room for individuals to make free choices in the "privileged sphere" of their intimate lives'.[69] However, since each individual's rights are to be protected from the undue influence of power by other individuals, Rawls' point that the family is not beyond the reach of justice is key:[70] as Eekelaar puts it, 'the demarcation between proper occasions for legal intervention and non-intervention is *itself a matter of law*',[71] and the line must be drawn by reference to the demands of justice itself.

Using this theory of justice and of the law's role in regulating people's personal lives, it is possible to return to the arguments made against family law and reject the limited vision of family justice envisaged therein. The legal process is a crucial way in which a person is protected against unconstrained control by a more powerful person with whom they are in an intimate relationship,[72] and any limitation within the law itself, or in access to legal advice and legal remedies, has to be seen as a denial of justice.

The government suggests that family law issues often arise from 'the litigant's own personal choices'.[73] This view simply cannot be accepted. Many family members do not 'choose' to be in an intimate relationship with one another at all:[74] a child hardly has a choice about who his or her parents are, for example. Second, even if A once chose B to be her partner, that choice cannot be said to contain an inevitable further choice to have B leave the relationship,[75] for B to refuse to pay financial contribution for A or for their

---

[65] See J Dewar, 'The Normal Chaos of Family Law' (1998) 61 *Modern Law Review* 467.

[66] See similarly A Diduck, 'Family Law and Family Responsibility' in J Bridgeman, H Keating and C Lind (eds), *Responsibility, Law and the Family* (Aldershot, Ashgate, 2008) 254–55; A Diduck, 'What is Family Law For?' (2011) 64 *Current Legal Problems* 1.

[67] See further ch 2 below, 'Rights and Responsibilities'.

[68] Eekelaar, *Family Law and Personal Life*, 137.

[69] Henaghan, 'The Normal Order of Family Law', 180.

[70] Rawls, *Justice as Fairness*, § 50.4.

[71] Eekelaar, '"Not of the Highest Importance"', 313.

[72] Eekelaar, 'Family Justice', 203–5.

[73] MoJ, *Consultation Paper*, [4.19].

[74] Eekelaar, '"Not of the Highest Importance"', 313.

[75] While starting an intimate adult relationship is (usually) a consensual act by both partners, ending one is more often a unilateral act by one partner.

child, or for B to take their child to live in another location so as to stop A from seeing the child.

These are, of course, merely examples: the point is that family law affects many people for reasons which are entirely outside their control. Moreover, even when these disputes are forced on people, most of the time 'litigation' is not the result: most family law cases are settled with the help of lawyers with little recourse to courts.[76] Given the highly personal nature of family disputes and the huge stresses of litigation, it seems most unlikely that anyone truly 'chooses' to go to court over family problems:[77] the law, as implemented by lawyers and, ultimately, by the court, is a vital arena to protect people's rights and to prevent the strong from abusing their power at the expense of the weak. This is no less important in private family law disputes than elsewhere in the law: 'power is frequently unequally divided between family disputants, and . . . [there is] gender-bias inherent in affording lower priority to the provision of legal resources in family cases than in other areas, for women constitute the largest clientele for family justice'.[78]

The government similarly says that much family litigation is 'unnecessary'.[79] One explanation for this view is that lawyers are seen as being responsible for creating family disputes; but such a view flies in the face of all available data, which clearly indicate that family lawyers successfully negotiate the vast majority of cases that come to them without litigation.[80] More damning, though, is the government's misuse of the evidence on this issue. For example, in its Consultation Paper, the government notes[81] that most children's residence and contact arrangements are made without the court being involved,[82] and that the government 'do[es] not consider that it will generally be in the best interest of the children involved for these essentially personal matters to be resolved in the adversarial forum of a court'.[83] Well, quite so, but these points say nothing whatever about what should happen to the small minority of cases which do in fact litigate. It is, of course, *generally* in children's best

[76] See above, text from n 22.

[77] In a different context, it was once said that '[t]he idle and whimsical plaintiff, a dilettante who litigates for a laugh, is a spectre which haunts the legal literature [and, one might add, the government's rhetoric], not the courtroom': K Scott, 'Standing in the Supreme Court: A Functional Analysis' (1972) 86 *Harvard Law Review* 645, 674.

[78] Eekelaar, 'Family Justice', 210; see also M Mossman, 'Gender Equality, Family Law and Access to Justice' [1994] *International Journal of Law and the Family* 357.

[79] See, eg, MoJ, *Consultation Paper*, [2.11].

[80] See above, text from n 22.

[81] MoJ, *Consultation Paper*, [4.209].

[82] However, the Consultation Paper conflates the proportion of arrangements made by *courts* with the proportion of arrangements made with the assistance of *lawyers*. Courts make orders in around 10% of residence and contact cases, whereas around 80% of separating couples consult a lawyer at some point over issues relating to the separation itself or to financial or child arrangements thereafter: see J Hunt with C Roberts, *Child Contact with Non-Resident Parents*, Family Policy Briefing Paper 3 (Oxford, University of Oxford, 2004) and H Genn, *Paths to Justice* (Oxford, Hart Publishing, 1999) 89.

[83] MoJ, *Consultation Paper*, [4.210].

interests that their living arrangements not be subjected to litigation in court; but it does not follow from this that those children whose cases do go to court are not having their best interests protected. The families which litigate are embroiled in the hardest, most entrenched disputes, where attempts by solicitors and barristers to reach a negotiated settlement have already failed.[84] Creating rules for a highly conflicted minority based on the experiences of a generally cooperative majority suggests little short of a deliberate misrepresentation of the evidence.

This point links to what Eekelaar calls a more sinister explanation for the 'unnecessary litigation' rhetoric, namely that the government does not think that family disputes involve questions of law or justice at all.[85] However, the government's view that no one is 'entitled . . . to a particular outcome' in family litigation[86] misunderstands the nature of an 'outcome' in this context. Let us take a family finance dispute following divorce as an example. It is quite true that A cannot claim to be 'entitled' to a specific sum of money from B, since there is a range of orders which could be made all of which would be reasonable.[87] So if the 'outcome' in question were a precise amount of money, then it is true that no one is entitled to it.[88] But there is an 'outcome' to which A can legitimately be said to be entitled: as the Supreme Court put it, each partner is '*entitled* to an equal share of the assets of the partnership unless there [is] good reason to the contrary' (emphasis added).[89] This 'outcome' is something to which A has a legal right. If the parties reach an agreement without legal advice which significantly under-values A's share of the assets, then A is entitled to go to court and will obtain an order increasing her share to reflect her entitlement.[90] Even a contract between the parties will not prevent A from seeking financial remedies via the court.[91] Consequently, 'to suggest that *there is no particular outcome* to which a litigant is entitled is to deprive legal rights of all effect, imply that the adjudicator may decide on a whim, and that litigation is no more than a lottery'.[92] It is true that litigation is often not needed in family disputes, but it does not follow that those cases which presently reach the courts are 'unnecessary'. Removing people's rights and their ability to protect those rights with adequate legal advice and, in some cases, litigation is to withdrawn justice from the family, and leave the weak at the mercy of the powerful.

---

[84] See above, text from n 22.

[85] Eekelaar, '"Not of the Highest Importance"', 313.

[86] MoJ, *Government Response*, [3.140].

[87] *Piglowska v Piglowski* [1999] 2 FLR 763 (HL).

[88] If this were the case, there would also be no *need* for litigation, since a good accountant would be able to calculate each person's share.

[89] *Radmacher v Granatino* [2010] UKSC 42, [2010] 2 FLR 1900, [26].

[90] *MacLeod v MacLeod* [2008] UKPC 64, [2009] 1 FLR 641.

[91] *Soulsbury v Soulsbury* [2007] EWCA Civ 969, [2008] 1 FLR 90.

[92] Eekelaar, '"Not of the Highest Importance"', 313.

CONCLUSIONS

The aim of this chapter has been to explain how the family justice system works, and to demonstrate why family disputes must be seen as a matter of justice. Family disputes are highly personal and usually emotionally charged, but they are also disputes about people's legal rights and they are entitled to just, legally-informed outcomes. This point was well made by Lord Phillips and Lady Hale in their joint submission to the Family Justice Review:

> The [family justice system] is, first and foremost, a justice system. . . . [I]t is looking to make arrangements for the family's future, preferably to arrange a better future than they would otherwise have. This requires services which other sectors do not require (Cafcass, mediators, contact centres, etc), specialist expertise in courts and practitioners, 'equality of arms' in a field where inequality is common, and a greater sensitivity to welfare and emotional issues.[93]

Most family disputes do not go to court, and quite right too; but this fact cannot be used as a reason to say that the law should be withdrawn from families, or to penalise those who are unable to reach acceptable agreements and who do require legal assistance. To do so would be to withdraw the very idea of justice from one of the most basic institutions of our society at some of the most vulnerable times of people's lives. If society is to lay claim to having a basis in fairness and justice, that must mean justice within families to the same full extent as justice elsewhere.

---

[93] Lord Phillips and Lady Hale, quoted in the *Family Justice Review*, [2.5].

2

Rights and Responsibilities

Key Questions

What are (family) rights? What are (family) responsibilities?

What is the relationship between rights and responsibilities?

How can a 'responsibilities' analysis be used when considering family law questions?

The importance of rights in family law is not to be underestimated, as alluded to in the opening chapter of this book. The Human Rights Act 1998 (HRA) gave added momentum to 'rights talk'[1] in the UK, but rights were a significant part of family law discourse before the HRA.[2] The practical effect of the HRA in family law is not wholly clear. The judiciary's apparent unwillingness[3] to revisit most areas of family law has been a cause of much criticism,[4] though a possible explanation might be that the HRA's main effect was to codify rights which were already protected in English law, rather than to

---

[1] M Glendon, *Rights Talk: The Impoverishment of Political Discourse* (New York, Free Press, 1991).

[2] See generally S Parker, 'Rights and Utility in Anglo-Australian Family Law' (1992) 55 *Modern Law Review* 311.

[3] A good example is *Payne v Payne* [2001] EWCA Civ 166, [2001] 1 FLR 1052.

[4] See, eg, J Herring, 'The Human Rights Act and the Welfare Principle in Family Law: Conflicting or Complementary?' [1999] *Child and Family Law Quarterly* 223; S Harris-Short, 'Family Law and the Human Rights Act 1998: Judicial Restraint or Revolution?' [2005] *Child and Family Law Quarterly* 329; J Herring and R Taylor, 'Relocating Relocation' [2006] *Child and Family Law Quarterly* 517; S Choudhry and J Herring, *European Human Rights and Family Law* (Oxford, Hart Publishing, 2010) 108 ff.

impose new rights which required accommodating.[5] Regardless of the HRA's practical impact, it has been aptly commented that '[r]ights-based arguments have found a natural home in family law disputes'.[6]

A particular focus of this debate for family lawyers has been about the compatibility of the welfare principle[7] with the requirements of the HRA.[8] The welfare principle is conventionally understood as meaning that only the child's interests are relevant to decision-making about the child's upbringing,[9] and on this view it is easy to see why the welfare principle might be seen as problematic in a post-HRA world.

Alongside the debates about rights and the welfare principle, there has been a steady rise in discourse about responsibilities in the family law context. The creation of the legal concept of *parental responsibility* may be the most obvious example of 'responsibility' appearing directly in the law.[10] Indeed, it may well be that the Law Commission's creation of parental responsibility marked the start of the current phase of 'responsibility talk'.[11]

The aim of this chapter is to introduce some of these debates, with a focus on the responsibilities discourse, and to suggest some ways in which rights and responsibilities might be seen to interact. The complexity of both sides of this discussion can make it hard to see the connections between them, and then to see how to make use of this theoretical work when thinking about practical problems in family law. The chapter will therefore start with discussion of the theories, but will also give a practical example to demonstrate how these theoretical ideas could be used in a family law analysis.

RIGHTS AND OBLIGATIONS

Offering a brief definition of what is meant by a *right* is to invite immediate controversy. John Eekelaar has cogently explained that part of the reason

---

[5] See, eg, *Re KD (A Minor) (Access: Principles)* [1988] 2 FLR 139 (HL).

[6] S Harris-Short and J Miles, *Family Law: Text, Cases and Materials*, 2nd edn (Oxford, Oxford University Press, 2011) 10.

[7] Children Act 1989, s 1(1): 'When a court determines any question with respect to the upbringing of a child . . . the child's welfare shall be the court's paramount consideration.'

[8] See, eg, S Choudhry and H Fenwick, 'Taking the Rights of Parents and Children Seriously: Confronting the Welfare Principle Under the Human Rights Act' (2005) 25 *Oxford Journal of Legal Studies* 453.

[9] This view is said to be based on *J v C* [1970] AC 668 (HL), but for critical analysis of this interpretation see ch 7 below, 'The Values of Welfare', text from n 28.

[10] Children Act 1989, s 3(1). For detailed discussion of parental responsibility, see ch 8 below, 'Parental Responsibility, Parenting and Status'.

[11] B Hale, 'Family Responsibility: Where Are We Now?' in C Lind, H Keating and J Bridgeman (eds), *Taking Responsibility, Law and the Changing Family* (Farnham, Ashgate, 2011) 25–26.

why the definition of rights is so contested is that the word can mean many things.[12] For now, a relatively broad definition will probably suffice:[13]

> A right reflects an interest which is sufficiently strong to justify imposing on another an obligation[14] which is legally enforceable,[15] usually but not necessarily by the right-holder.

The question here is about the *possibility* of enforcement. It may be, in any given case, that an individual would choose not to enforce a right, but if there is the possibility of legal enforcement then the right exists.

As implied above, an *obligation* is the correlative of a right, namely a burden imposed because of the interest of another and which is legally enforceable. As a general proposition,[16] rights and obligations can be considered to be correlative, such that a right, in the strict sense being used here, will have a corresponding obligation.[17]

It should be obvious that these summaries are immensely simplified. The reason for spending so little time on rights and obligations is that these are addressed in numerous legal and philosophical discussions, both in general and as part of family law in particular.[18] The more novel issues which this chapter addresses are in the sections which follow.

---

[12] J Eekelaar, *Family Law and Personal Life*, paperback edn (Oxford, Oxford University Press, 2007) 132.

[13] See similarly J Raz, *The Morality of Freedom* (Oxford, Clarendon Press, 1986) 166 and Eekelaar, *Family Law and Personal Life*, 135: for Eekelaar, a right is 'a claim of entitlement to an end-state necessary to protect an interest and an implication that the interest possesses sufficient weight to impose a duty to activate the means contemplated to achieve the necessary protection'.

[14] These obligations are sometimes known as duties, but 'duty' might be broad enough to include what I term responsibilities as well, which is usually not the intention of other writers.

[15] These are probably the kinds of rights to which HLA Hart refers in some of his work, since he says that the concept of rights requires a legal system to be in place in order to be meaningful: HLA Hart, *Essays in Jurisprudence and Philosophy* (Oxford, Clarendon Press, 1983) 35. It should be recognised that restricting rights to that which is legally enforceable places a limitation on the concept that many people would dispute. So-called moral or social rights which are not reflected in legal rights are not being considered here.

[16] *cf* O O'Neill, 'Children's Rights and Children's Lives' (1994) 8 *International Journal of Law and the Family* 24. O'Neill suggests that a right must have a corresponding obligation, but that not all obligations will have corresponding rights. These 'imperfect obligations' are said to arise when 'we are required to do or omit [a particular] action for *unspecified* others, but not for *all* others'.

[17] W Hohfeld, *Fundamental Legal Concepts as Applied in Judicial Reasoning* (New Haven, Yale University Press, 1928).

[18] See, eg, Choudhry and Herring, *European Human Rights and Family Law*, ch 3.

RESPONSIBILITIES AND EXPECTATIONS

Explaining the concept of *responsibility* is complex, because the word is used in many different senses. Indeed, one of the curiosities of family law is that, although the word appears quite frequently, the meaning of *responsibility* is often unclear. For example, it is not necessarily obvious whether the two questions, 'what is responsibility?' and 'what is *a* responsibility?' mean the same thing, nor whether *being* responsible and *having* responsibility are the same.[19] For example, the meaning of the words, 'Kate is responsible for *x*' depends in part on what *x* is. If *x* is a mess on the floor, probably Kate caused the mess. If *x* is another person, the implication is that Kate is in charge of them, and/or answerable (liable?) for their behaviour. If *x* is a future event, probably Kate is charged with organising that event. In a brief but insightful discussion, HLA Hart identified four main varieties of responsibility:[20]

- **Capacity responsibility:** this is a basic element of control or understanding which makes a person able to appreciate what they are doing at a fundamental level, and is the sense of responsibility seen in the idea of *diminished responsibility*.
- **Causal responsibility:** the question here is whether Kate's behaviour led to the outcome in question.
- **Liability responsibility:** this relates not to causation, but to blameworthiness; should Kate be held to blame for the outcome?
- **Role responsibility:** role responsibility arises 'whenever a person occupies a distinctive place or office in a social organisation to which specific duties are attached to provide for the welfare of others, or to advance in some specific way the aims or purposes of the organisation';[21] one example that Hart gives is of 'a man [being] morally as well as legally responsible for his wife and children'.[22]

While Hart's work has been criticised for its general focus on criminal law issues,[23] it may offer a useful tool for thinking about responsibility. For criminal lawyers and tort lawyers, capacity responsibility (is Kate a person capable of being responsible for her actions?), causal responsibility (did Kate's actions cause the outcome?) and liability responsibility (is Kate to blame for that outcome?) are probably of most interest; but for family lawyers, it seems likely that role responsibility is going to be the central issue. (The other types may

---

[19] R George, review 'Responsibility, Law and the Family, edited by Jo Bridgeman, Heather Keating and Craig Lind' (2009) 72 *Modern Law Review* 147, 147.

[20] HLA Hart, 'Varieties of Responsibility' (1967) 83 *Law Quarterly Review* 346.

[21] Ibid, 347.

[22] Ibid, 348.

[23] P Cane, *Responsibility in Law and Morality* (Oxford, Hart Publishing, 2002) 29–30.

be relevant, especially in areas like child protection or domestic violence, but role responsibility is the 'core' type for most parts of family law.)

In explaining how this type of responsibility works, Craig Lind, Heather Keating and Jo Bridgeman draw together various writings of HLA Hart, Antony Duff and John Gardner, and we can follow some of their path here.[24] Like Lind, Keating and Bridgeman, our starting point is Hart. For Hart, role responsibility involves having 'duties of a relatively complex or extensive kind, defining a "sphere of responsibility" requiring the exercise of discretion and care usually over a protracted period of time'.[25] Such a role involves a combination of retrospective and prospective responsibilities – the person is both answerable after the event for how things turn out, and has things in the present and future which are for them to take care of or attend to.[26] To put it another way, 'responsibility-laden descriptions (teacher, parent, member of a church or a team) determine the content and the direction of our responsibilities: what we are responsible for and to whom'.[27]

In his explanation of role responsibilities, Hart refers to complex or extensive 'duties'. Explaining responsibilities as duties is understandable, but may be unhelpful for our purposes. A duty is a thing that *must* be done, whereas it may be more appropriate to think of a responsibility as a thing that *should* be done. Having a responsibility is about being liable to be called to account for some act or omission, about having to explain myself and bear (some of) the consequences of that act or omission.[28] By being aware that I may be called on to explain myself, I have an incentive to act thoughtfully rather than thoughtlessly, and only for reasons which could be admitted rather than ones of which I would be ashamed.[29]

Just as it is possible to see rights and obligations as, at least to some extent, two sides of the same coin, it might be asked whether the same two-sided relationship exists in relation to responsibilities. Role responsibility involves the idea of someone (S) having capacity to call me to account for my action (X),[30] but why is that the case? Why is S given this power? It is clear that only a limited class of people can call me to account for my actions as a parent, as a member of a team, or whatever – so what is it that makes S special in this

---

[24] C Lind, H Keating and J Bridgeman, 'Taking Family Responsibility, or Having It Imposed?' in C Lind, H Keating and J Bridgeman (eds), *Taking Responsibility, Law and the Changing Family* (Farnham, Ashgate, 2011) 7–8.

[25] Hart 'Varieties of Responsibility', 347.

[26] RA Duff, *Answering for Crime* (Oxford, Hart Publishing, 2007) 30.

[27] Ibid, 24–25.

[28] For John Gardner, this is the key to what he calls 'consequential responsibility': while 'basic responsibility' is the ability to give a coherent account of your actions, 'consequential responsibility' is about owing an explanation to someone else for your actions and then having to bear at least some of the consequences of those actions: see J Gardner, 'Hart and Feinberg on Responsibility' in M Kramer, C Grant, B Colburn and A Hatzistavrou (eds), *The Legacy of HLA Hart: Legal, Political and Moral Philosophy* (Oxford, Oxford University Press, 2008).

[29] J Lucas, *Responsibility* (Oxford, Clarendon Press, 1993) 11.

[30] Lind, Keating and Bridgeman, 'Taking Family Responsibility', 8

regard? One explanation might be that S is a person who has an *expectation* in relation to me regarding X.

The word expectation is a tricky one, particularly since (like responsibility) it has a number of meanings. Two meanings which it is important to distinguish are its predictive meaning ('I expect to arrive by lunchtime') and its prescriptive meaning ('I expect you to help me clear the table'). It is only the second of these which is of interest here. An example of similar usage might be seen in Joanna Miles' description of 'responsibility in a broader sense', which she defines as 'connoting a societal expectation (possibly shared or promoted in some manner by the legal system, the wider state or its agents) of certain behaviour'.[31]

So what is an expectation in this sense? The suggestion is that an expectation is a bit like a right. Each expectation is weaker than a right, but there are probably more of them, at least in the family context. A right was defined earlier like this:

> A right reflects an interest which is sufficiently strong to justify imposing on another an obligation which is legally enforceable, usually but not necessarily by the right-holder.

Expectations are weaker versions of the same idea, and are connected to the *responsibilities* of others, rather than to the *obligations* of others. Consequently, an expectation of something will often go beyond what one has a right to have.[32] Using similar terminology, an expectation could be defined in this way:

> An expectation reflects an interest which is sufficiently strong to justify imposing on another a responsibility, but not so strong as to justify imposing on another an obligation;[33] this responsibility is not legally enforceable,[34] but enables the expectation-holder (or sometimes someone else) to call on the person owing the responsibility to account for their behaviour.

---

[31] J Miles, 'Responsibility in Family Finance and Property Law' in J Bridgeman, H Keating and C Lind (eds), *Regulating Family Responsibilities* (Farnham, Ashgate, 2011) 93.

[32] *cf* 'legitimate expectations' in administrative law, which 'are capable of including expectations which go beyond enforceable legal rights': *AG for Hong Kong v Ng Yuen Shiu* [1983] 2 AC 629 (PC), 636.

[33] If the interest were strong enough to impose an obligation then, on the definitions used here, it would be a right.

[34] *cf* M Maclean and J Eekelaar, *The Parental Obligation: A Study of Parenthood across Households* (Oxford, Hart Publishing, 1997) 1–2:

> when members of a family are living together, the law is strangely reticent in articulating and enforcing the obligations they may owe to one another. That does not mean that they do not have duties to each other. But these duties may be only indirectly recognized or enforced by the law. Indeed, they may not be legal duties at all.

Note how, as mentioned above in n 14, the word 'duty' is able to cover legal obligations and non-legal responsibilities.

If this working definition is taken, the next question would be to ask how the four concepts discussed so far – rights, obligations, expectations and responsibilities – connect to one another.

CONNECTING RIGHTS TO RESPONSIBILITIES

In reaching a definition in the previous section, we suggested that expectations and rights are on the same spectrum, but that an expectation is a weaker version of a right. It would follow from this that obligations and responsibilities are also on the same spectrum as one another, with responsibilities being weaker versions of obligations. Indeed, while this aspect is probably not that relevant to family law, the same spectrum probably carries on, to the point where what one has cannot even be called an expectation. We might term it a *hope*.[35] So, looking at the spectrum, at one end I have *rights*, then *expectations*, and finally *hopes*: as you go along this spectrum, the number of each category increases, but the strength or potency decreases. In other words:

- **hopes** cover the entire spectrum, and are very many in number, but by themselves are weak.
- **expectations** start part-way along the scale, existing alongside some hopes (but not all, because there are fewer expectations than there are hopes); expectations are of moderate power.
- **rights** enter only at the most powerful end of the spectrum and overlap with some expectations and hopes; though they are comparatively few in number, rights are the strongest elements.

The relationship between these things is illustrated in Box 2.1. The idea could equally be explained in relation to obligations and responsibilities: all the obligations are covered by the responsibilities, but there are more responsibilities than obligations, and the obligations are more powerful than the responsibilities.[36]

This view draws support from Eekelaar's book, *Family Law and Personal Life*.[37] Chapter 5 on Responsibility is worth reading in its entirety, but the section entitled 'A Fuller Concept of Responsibility' is particularly important here. Eekelaar notes that work on responsibility by some scholars has discussed the importance of people's *way of thinking* about their actions, rather than the actions themselves.[38] In other words, the contention is that a person

---

[35] Is there a word to describe the mirror image of these *hopes*?
[36] See generally Lind, Keating and Bridgeman, 'Taking Family Responsibility'.
[37] Eekelaar, *Family Law and Personal Life*.
[38] See, eg, H Reece, *Divorcing Responsibly* (Oxford, Hart Publishing, 2003).

Box 2.1: Illustration of the relationship between hopes, expectations and rights

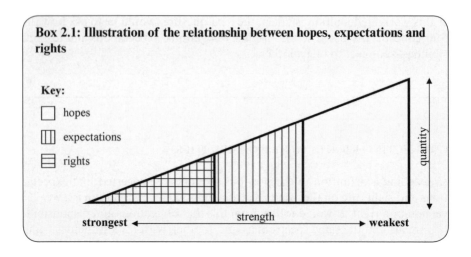

may be acting responsibly so long as they make a serious attempt to understand what they are doing. For Eekelaar, though, this view of responsibility is too detached from the lived experience of people's lives. He considers that the outcome of people's thinking is also important alongside their mode of thought. But getting the outcome right is also not enough.

Eekelaar quotes from Joseph Raz, who contends that the law's concern 'is not what the subject thinks but how he acts. I do all that the law requires of me if my actions comply with it'. [39] However, while this may be true in terms of legal entitlements and obligations, it is not enough when it comes to responsibility in its full sense. As Eekelaar says, 'to be fully responsible, people must sometimes refrain from doing what they are legally entitled to do, or do more than is necessary to comply with the law'.[40] In other words, while a responsible person does what the law requires, he or she may need to go further and do more than is technically required; and, on the other hand, 'responsible people will exercise restraint within their legal rights'.[41]

Having established this idea of responsibility, Eekelaar goes on to explain why it is important that the law itself does not attempt to *enforce* these desirable behaviours. It is okay for the law to *encourage* people to be responsible, but the law cannot go beyond informal encouragement because it is contrary to the rule of law to force people to give up their legal rights: 'what would be the value of legal rights if legal institutions themselves systematically obstructed people's exercise of them?'[42] So, 'the difference between *encouraging* such responsible behaviour and *enforcing* it is pivotal. . . . [O]nce the line

---

[39] Raz, *The Morality of Freedom*, 39.
[40] Eekelaar, *Family Law and Personal Life*, 127.
[41] Ibid, 128.
[42] Ibid, 130.

is crossed, the fuller sense of responsibility is lost, for the behaviour, while remaining a responsibility, is now a legal duty'.[43]

We saw in Box 2.1 that there is an overlap between rights and expectations (or between obligations and responsibilities), but rights are more powerful than expectations and so the latter give way to the former in the areas of overlap. That means that if an expectation becomes enforceable by law, and thereby an equivalent right is created, there is little point anymore in saying that there is an expectation. There *is* an expectation, but it is so overshadowed by the right that it goes unnoticed. There are two reasons to oppose this shift from expectations to rights, as Eekelaar shows.[44] The first is that there is the risk of a violation of the rule of law, and the second is that it removes from people the possibility to regulate their own behaviour within the bounds of responsibility. Responsibilities and expectations are less certain, less concrete, than obligations and rights, and so consequently there is a broader area of discretion which people have in deciding how to meet their responsibilities than they have in meeting their obligations. This area of discretion is perhaps especially important in family cases because of their personal nature, and so we should be careful both to preserve the line between rights and expectations, and not to undervalue those expectations.

To put the point another way, rights and obligations are the most powerful concepts that we have in our analytical arsenal, but might not always be the most important ones in family cases. In some cases, it will be both necessary and appropriate to call on rights in family law issues. The most obvious example is in public family law: when the state attempts to interfere in family life, that is an archetypal example of a time when the rights of the individual family members involved should be asserted. However, alongside rights claims it will be important to keep in mind that there are responsibilities and expectations. If we take our responsibilities and expectations seriously, we will have cause to think about *when* to assert our rights. Having *a right* to do X does not in itself constitute *a reason* to do X,[45] and 'just because one has a right to do X does not mean that it is right to do X'.[46]

Now, it might be said that while the concept of responsibilities is appropriate when thinking about family life in society in general, by the time a family dispute is before the court the main focus should be on rights. After all, rights are at the most powerful end of the spectrum, and disputes which are serious enough to go to court call for the strongest tools. There are two reasons to reject this view. First, the effects of family law as applied in the courts filter out more broadly, and so affect families far beyond the family court. This influence is especially apparent amongst families who seek legal advice, who are known to 'bargain in the shadow of the law', based on what they and

[43] Ibid, 130.
[44] Ibid, 127–31.
[45] A Marmor, 'On the Limits of Rights' (1997) 16 *Law and Philosophy* 1, 5.
[46] Choudhry and Herring, *European Human Rights and Family Law*, 121.

their legal advisors perceive the law to be;[47] but it is also true more broadly, since family law frequently appears as a topic of discussion in the media. The second reason why an analysis focused only on rights is inappropriate is that even in litigated family disputes there should be consideration of a broader range of factors. A purely rights-based analysis of family law issues 'risks focusing on too narrow a range of issues, giving inadequate attention to interests and responsibilities which go beyond rights but which are at least as important in the family context'.[48] In particular, there may be gender dimensions to family life which are masked by a focus on rights and a neglect of responsibilities.[49]

ANALYSING FAMILY LAW USING RESPONSIBILITIES AND EXPECTATIONS

In order to demonstrate the use that can be made of the idea of responsibilities and expectations, an example may be helpful. Inevitably, the illustration given here is a little simplified and abstract, but the idea is to see the value that a responsibilities/expectations discourse could offer to family lawyers. The example we take is of a relocation dispute in private child law, but think about how the same analysis might be applied in other areas of family law.

Relocation cases are disputes between separated parents where one parent seeks to move with their child to a new geographic location and the other parent objects.[50] As with all disputes about children's upbringing, the guiding principle in deciding relocation disputes is the child's welfare.[51] The courts have then developed a 'discipline' for dealing with relocation cases within the welfare principle. To summarise this approach,[52] if the application is made by a primary carer and that parent has a genuine reason for moving, then the parent's emotional and psychological well-being will usually be a very important factor in assessing the application. While there is no formal presumption in favour of reasonable and realistic relocation plans, some commentators

---

[47] R Mnookin and L Kornhauser, 'Bargaining in the Shadow of the Law: The Case of Divorce' (1979) 88 *Yale Law Journal* 950.

[48] R George, 'Regulating Responsibilities in Relocation Disputes' in J Bridgeman, H Keating and C Lind (eds), *Regulating Family Responsibilities* (Farnham, Ashgate, 2011) 163.

[49] See generally C Smart, 'The Ethic of Justice Strikes Back: Changing Narratives of Fatherhood' in A Diduck and K O'Donovan (eds), *Feminist Perspectives on Family Law* (Abingdon, Routledge-Cavendish, 2006).

[50] See, eg, A Diduck and F Kaganas, *Family Law, Gender and the State*, 3rd edn (Oxford, Hart Publishing, 2012) 472–81; J Herring, *Family Law*, 5th edn (Harlow, Longman, 2011) 527–31.

[51] Children Act 1989, s 1.

[52] The position is considerably more complex than there is space to do justice to here.

think that the overall effect is that the law is 'commonly perceived as walking and talking like a presumption'.[53]

The leading Court of Appeal decision on relocation is *Payne v Payne*,[54] which was also one of the earliest considerations by that court of the impact of the HRA on the welfare principle. That discussion has been subjected to strong academic criticism,[55] and in the relocation context Jonathan Herring and Rachel Taylor have offered an alternative rights-based analysis.[56] Herring and Taylor set out clearly the separate interests of those involved in relocation insofar as they relate to the human rights which the court ought to be taking into account in a relocation dispute.[57] Their discussion offers a useful starting point for looking at the inter-relationship between rights and expectations, and for showing how both might be important when analysing a family law problem.[58]

The first example relates to the primary carer's emotional and psychological well-being. The case law makes clear that if the parent will be psychologically devastated by being forced to remain in a location which she wishes to leave, that is a factor which weighs heavily when considering the child's welfare.[59] In considering this factor, Herring and Taylor rightly point out that this kind of impact on the applicant parent 'may be sufficient to engage her private life under Article 8 [of the European Convention on Human Rights]'.[60] The question is whether we would want to restrict consideration of the applicant's psychological well-being to cases where the impact was quite that serious. If we were to look at the applicant's *expectations* as well as at her rights, we could see that the mother's mental well-being, and her ability to discharge her care-giving responsibilities, is important in all cases (even if the Article 8 right is not engaged). Consequently, while it should carry more weight in cases where the applicant's *right* is engaged, the *expectation* will almost always be present and so the applicant's well-being should always be considered explicitly alongside the other elements of the case.

To take another example, Herring and Taylor say that 'where the child is old enough to form and express her own views, she may have a right under Article 8 for those views to be considered'.[61] This is an important

---

[53] C Geekie, 'Relocation and Shared Residence: One Route or Two?' [2008] *Family Law* 446, 451–52.

[54] *Payne v Payne* [2001] EWCA Civ 166, [2001] 1 FLR 1052.

[55] See, eg, S Harris-Short, 'Family Law and the Human Rights Act 1998: Judicial Restraint or Revolution?' [2005] *Child and Family Law Quarterly* 329, 355.

[56] J Herring and R Taylor, 'Relocating Relocation' [2006] *Child and Family Law Quarterly* 517.

[57] Ibid, 519–22 (interests of the child) and 523–26 (interests of the parents and wider family).

[58] This section draws on R George, 'Regulating Responsibilities in Relocation Disputes' in J Bridgeman, H Keating and C Lind (eds), *Regulating Family Responsibilities* (Farnham, Ashgate, 2011) 163–65.

[59] See, eg, *Payne v Payne* [2001] EWCA Civ 166, [2001] 1 FLR 1052, [41].

[60] Herring and Taylor, 'Relocating Relocation', 523.

[61] Ibid, 530.

point,[62] especially since consideration of the child's views was conspicuously absent from the court's discussion in *Payne*. However, even in those cases where the child does not have a *right* to have her views considered (probably because of her age and understanding), she may nonetheless have an *expectation* that her views, wishes and feelings will be taken into account in the decision-making process. To put it another way, while the court and the parents might not have a legal obligation to consider the child's views, they may have a responsibility to do so. By taking this analysis explicitly beyond a rights focus, issues like these may be easier to identify and articulate.

A final point with regard to the relocation example might link back to Eekelaar's 'fuller concept of responsibility'.[63] It was seen that, to be fully responsible, people must sometimes go beyond their legal duties or exercise restraint within their legal rights.[64] Something of this idea can be seen in some relocation cases. For example, in *Re C (Permission to Remove from Jurisdiction)*, Charles J noted (amongst other factors, of course) that the mother was likely to react very badly to being forced to remain in the UK, and so granted her leave to relocate with the child to Singapore, her original home country.[65] However, in granting leave, the judge also remarked tellingly that he in fact considered that the best available outcome would be for the child to remain in the UK with both parents, but thought that this solution would work only if the mother remained by her own choice, rather than because the court had forced her to do so. In other words, it could be said that the judge considered that the responsible course of action would be for the mother to remain, but thought that it was not appropriate to *require* her to do so; instead, Charles J 'invited the mother to consider carefully . . . whether she should agree to stay',[66] and thereby *encouraged* her to exercise restraint within her legal rights. This is an interesting approach for a judge to take – at the same time, granting the mother the legal right to take the child abroad and encouraging her not to exercise that right. Is this a good course of action for the court to take? Might there be any dangers to this approach?

---

[62] There may be room to debate Herring and Taylor's view of the moment at which this right crystallises enough to be enforced: *cf* N Taylor, N Tapp and M Henaghan, 'Respecting Children's Participation in Family Law Proceedings' (2007) 15 *International Journal of Children's Rights* 61.

[63] See above, text at nn 37–46.

[64] Eekelaar, *Family Law and Personal Life*, 128.

[65] *Re C (Permission to Remove from Jurisdiction)* [2003] EWHC 596 (Fam), [2003] 1 FLR 1066.

[66] Ibid, [107].

CONCLUSIONS

Thinking more generally about the use of responsibilities and expectations in the family law context in the light of what we learned earlier in this chapter, a number of questions arise:

1. Is it appropriate to bring responsibilities and expectations into the legal reasoning process? One way to put this question is to ask whether the expectations/responsibilities analysis comes too close to *enforcing* responsibilities when they should really only be *encouraged*.[67] Think about whether it is acceptable for the court to consider these issues when making a decision – is that the same thing as enforcing a right?

2. Does a responsibilities / expectations analysis add anything to the reasoning process which the court should undertake anyway? In other words, even if it is appropriate to consider the expectations and responsibilities in this way, consider whether the analysis helps to:

   a. identify factors which would otherwise be missed entirely; or
   b. articulate factors which might be identified anyway but which could otherwise be left unsaid.

3. Can the responsibilities / expectations analysis be used in all types of family law dispute? Think about:

   a. family property disputes after divorce or separation;
   b. public law cases involving a local authority seeking to intervene in a family because of concerns over a child's safety;
   c. cases about the allocation or exercise of parental responsibility.

This chapter has explored the idea of responsibilities and expectations, and illustrated how this analytical framework might be useful in family law. The focus here has been on showing how responsibilities and expectations could be connected to a rights and obligations analysis; the next step might be to think about how this discussion would fit into the *rights vs welfare* debates which were mentioned at the start of the chapter.

• If responsibilities and expectations were added to the rights analysis, would that make the arguments against the welfare principle more convincing or less?
• Look at the discussion of the welfare principle itself in chapter seven – how could the ideas from this chapter be used there?

---

[67] See above, text after n 41.

As you think about the substantive topics raised in the following chapters, take a moment to pause from time to time and ask how the issues being discussed could be fitted around the responsibilities and expectations analysis offered here. This book is not written around a responsibilities framework,[68] but many of the ideas here fit with such a perspective. Think about whether it is helpful to draw on responsibilities and expectations in family law, and ask whether there would be any significant changes which you would want to make to family law in order to take account of this analysis.

---

[68] *cf* J Bridgeman, H Keating and C Lind (eds), *Responsibility, Law and the Family* (Farnham, Ashgate, 2008); J Bridgeman, H Keating and C Lind (eds), *Regulating Family Responsibilities* (Farnham, Ashgate, 2011).

3

International Family Law

Key Questions

What is international family law?

Why is the law relating to families becoming increasingly a matter for international consideration and regulation?

If parts of family law are to be regulated at an international level, how should that be done?

Much of the international aspect of the law affecting families is so frequently ignored in mainstream family law that a Justice of the Supreme Court has described it as family law's 'forgotten international dimension'.[1] Broadly speaking, international family law can be said to incorporate two main aspects:

- the law governing families whose members are in some way international, neatly described by Nigel Lowe as 'cross-border families';[2]
- international agreements which affect domestic law, or which remove an issue from domestic law entirely and move its regulation to a supranational level.

A further issue could arise from international migration, raising questions about how minority groups are to be incorporated within, or considered alongside, a dominant culture.[3]

---

[1] B Hale, 'Families and the Law: The Forgotten International Dimension' [2009] *Child and Family Law Quarterly* 413.

[2] N Lowe, 'Where in the World Is International Family Law Going Next?' in G Douglas and N Lowe (eds), *The Continuing Evolution of Family Law* (Bristol, Family Law, 2009) 261.

[3] Thanks to John Eekelaar for this idea.

It may indeed be that migration is the central pillar of international family law,[4] and a little thought is given to that point in the opening section of this chapter. However, the main aim of this chapter is to introduce some of the ways in which family law can be seen from an international standpoint, considering three alternative approaches to 'internationalising' family law. These approaches are:

- The 'forum' approach: using international instruments to decide which country's law should resolve a particular question.
- The 'mutual recognition' approach: setting up mechanisms for the courts in one country to recognise and enforce orders made in another country.
- The 'harmonisation' approach: creating a unified family law which is applied in different countries.

To put those ideas in context, though, we start by considering why it is that family law is becoming increasingly internationalised, and with an overview of some issues which could be said to come within the remit of international family law (though there are many more).

INTERNATIONAL FAMILY LAW: WHAT IS IT, AND WHERE DID IT COME FROM?

The rise of both cross-border families and of cross-border family law is influenced by rapidly increasing amounts of international migration. The proportion of the world's population classified as international migrants has increased from 2.2 per cent in 1975 to 3.1 per cent in 2010.[5] That might not sound much, but since the total world population grew enormously in those 35 years, the increase is striking when considered numerically. Those figures translate into an increase from around 88 million people in 1975 to about 215 million in 2010 (of whom 70 million were in Europe),[6] with the number of international migrants typically increasing by more than 10 per cent every five years.[7]

For family law, increases in migration are highly significant. As examples, consider these issues:

---

[4] Hale, 'Families and the Law', 414.
[5] United Nations, 'Trends in Total Migrant Stock: The 2008 Revisions', 1, available online at www.un.org/esa/population/migration/UN_MigStock_2008.pdf.
[6] Ibid, 1–2.
[7] Ibid.

- **Intact families moving between countries:** this raises questions about the international recognition of different forms of relationship,[8] immigration and deportation of wider family members,[9] separations and divorces in countries other than the country in which the relationship was formed,[10] issues over whether a particular court has jurisdiction or not,[11] and other conflict of laws questions.[12]
- **Members of separated families moving across borders:** this could arise because of legal family relocation[13] or illegal parental child abduction,[14] with consequential issues to do with cross-border residence[15] and contact arrangements,[16] as well as post-separation property division and maintenance payments for former partners and for children.[17]
- **Families being created with members who are citizens of (and maybe resident in) different countries:** this can include cases on spousal immigration and deportation (which can also involve children moving with their parents),[18] international adoption,[19] and forced marriage.[20]

[8] See, eg, *Radwan v Radwan (No 2)* [1973] Fam 35 (HC) on the recognition of a foreign polygamous marriage, or *Wilkinson v Kitzinger* [2006] EWHC 2022 (Fam), [2007] 1 FLR 29 on the recognition of a foreign same-sex marriage.

[9] See, eg, *AS (Somalia) v Home Secretary* [2009] UKHL 32, [2009] 4 All ER 711 on whether a cousin could sponsor an orphaned child into the UK; *ZB (Pakistan) v Home Secretary* [2009] EWCA Civ 834, [2009] All ER (D) 343 (Jul) on whether an elderly parent could be a 'dependant' for immigration purposes.

[10] An EU paper in 2006 estimated that there were 170,000 'international divorces' per year within the Union, representing 16% of all divorces: Commission Staff Working Document, 'Annex to the Proposal for a Council Regulation amending Regulation (EC) No 2201/2003 as regards jurisdiction and introducing rules concerning applicable law in matrimonial matters: impact assessment' (SEC (2006) 949) 13.

[11] See D Hodson, *A Practical Guide to International Family Law* (Bristol, Family Law, 2008) ch 5.

[12] See, eg, *Radmacher v Granatino* [2009] EWCA Civ 649, [2009] 2 FLR 1181, [2]–[11], [70] and [146]–[147], aff'd [2010] UKSC 42, [2010] 2 FLR 1900, [96]–[108] and [181]–[183].

[13] See *Payne v Payne* [2001] EWCA Civ 166, [2001] 2 FLR 1052; *MK v CK (Relocation: Shared Care Arrangement)* [2011] EWCA Civ 793, [2012] 1 FLR forthcoming.

[14] See generally N Lowe, M Everall and M Nicholls, *International Movement of Children: Law, Practice and Procedure* (Bristol, Family Law, 2004).

[15] It is possible to make shared residence orders regarding children whose parents live in different countries: see, eg, *Re A (Temporary Removal from Jurisdiction)* [2004] EWCA Civ 1587, [2005] 1 FLR 639.

[16] See, eg, the revised Brussels II Regulation (Regulation (EC) 2201/2003 concerning jurisdiction and the recognition and enforcement of judgments in matrimonial matters and matters of parental responsibility).

[17] See, eg, Matrimonial and Family Proceedings Act 1984, Part III; *Agbage v Agbage* [2010] UKSC 13, [2010] 1 FLR 1813; Council Regulation (EC) No 44/2001 on jurisdiction and the recognition and enforcement of judgments in civil and commercial matters; Council Regulation (EC) No 4/2009 on jurisdiction, applicable law, recognition and enforcement of decisions and cooperation in matters relating to maintenance obligations.

[18] See, eg, *ZH (Tanzania) v Home Secretary* [2011] UKSC 4, [2011] 1 FLR 2170 on deportation of a non-British mother who was the primary carer of British children.

[19] Hague Convention on Protection of Children and Cooperation in Respect of Intercountry Adoption 1993.

[20] Forced Marriage (Civil Protection) Act 2007; see generally N Pearce, 'Forced Marriage Protection Orders: Practice and Procedure under FPR 2010' [2011] *International Family Law* 602.

> • **Influences on purely domestic family law of international agreements and discussions:** such influences can be either formal[21] or informal.[22]

The law regulating families consequently has to account for internationalisation in a number of ways. In short, families themselves are becoming increasingly internationalised and, alongside this trend, so too is the law's regulation of families. There are many factors influencing both of these trends, some of which are deliberately aimed at families or family law and others of which impact on them tangentially (though sometimes very significantly!).

Factors affecting family migration tend to be economic or political in nature. From the perspective of the UK, a major impact in recent decades has come from the provisions of EU law which allow for the free movement of workers, citizens and their families within the Union.[23] The family law consequences of this movement of people can be seen in areas like relocation law: whereas previously most relocation cases involved proposals to go to Commonwealth countries, the USA or the Far East, there is an increasing body of case law now concerning relocation to countries in Eastern Europe.[24]

For the law, influences on internationalisation include:

> • international agreements on children's rights in general[25]
> • generally applicable human rights instruments[26]
> • international agreements on the approach to specific issues, such as child abduction[27] or international adoption[28]
> • an increasing focus in EU law on issues relating to families[29]

---

[21] Key influences on English law include the European Convention on the Protection of Human Rights and Fundamental Freedoms 1950, together with decisions of the European Court of Human Rights; the United Nations Convention on the Rights of the Child 1989; and EU Law, together with decisions of the Court of Justice of the European Union.

[22] A recent example would be the debate provoked in the English courts about domestic relocation law in the wake of the Washington Declaration on International Family Relocation 2010: see below, text from n 80.

[23] Arts 20(2)(a), 21(1), 45 and 49 TFEU; see generally E Spaventa, 'Seeing the Wood Despite the Trees? On the Scope of Union Citizenship and its Constitutional Effects' (2008) 45 *Common Market Law Review* 13.

[24] See, eg, *Re B (A Child)* [2009] EWCA Civ 553 (Latvia); *Re D (Leave to Remove: Appeal)* [2010] EWCA Civ 50, [2010] 2 FLR 1605 (Slovakia).

[25] The United Nations Convention on the Rights of the Child 1989.

[26] Most especially the European Convention on the Protection of Human Rights and Fundamental Freedoms and decisions of the European Court of Human Rights.

[27] Hague Convention on the Civil Aspects of International Child Abduction 1980.

[28] Hague Convention on Protection of Children and Cooperation in Respect of Intercountry Adoption 1993.

[29] See generally C McGlynn, *Families and the European Union: Law, Politics and Pluralism* (Cambridge, Cambridge University Press, 2006).

- an increasing trend for the Court of Justice of the European Union to identify and consider family law issues in cases which are ostensibly about other things[30]
- on-going moves to consider harmonising substantive elements of the law relating to families across borders[31]
- a continuing tradition of mutual inspiration when considering family law reforms[32]
- a growing network of International Liaison Judges in family courts around the world[33]

Given these various influences, it is worth considering some of the ways in which internationalisation might be put into effect within family law. The first approach to look at focuses on a relatively straightforward question, namely *where* (ie in which country) a family law dispute should be resolved. This approach can be termed the 'forum' approach.

THE 'FORUM' APPROACH

The forum approach to international family law aims to set rules to determine which country's courts have jurisdiction in a particular case. This approach is particularly useful for cross-border cases where family members are (or could be) in more than one country. The focus is on determining which country's legal system should determine the substantive issues, but says nothing about how those substantive issues should be resolved.[34] This is often the approach adopted by the Hague Conference on Private International Law,[35] which usually concentrates on 'achieving uniformity in the principles governing jurisdiction, choice of laws and the recognition and enforcement of judgments'.[36]

---

[30] See, eg, C-60/00 *Mary Carpenter v Home Secretary* [2003] 2 FCR 711 (ECJ) on the use of provisions of EU law relating to free movement of a citizen to prevent deportation of a spouse who was not herself a citizen.

[31] See, eg, Washington Declaration on International Family Relocation 2010.

[32] See, eg, M Maclean, R Hunter, F Wasoff, L Ferguson, B Bastard and E Ryrstedt, 'Family Justice In Hard Times: Can We Learn from Other Jurisdictions?' [2011] *Journal of Social Welfare and Family Law* 319.

[33] See generally M Thorpe, 'The Work of the Head of International Family Law', online at www.familylawweek.co.uk/site.aspx?i=ed1865.

[34] See, eg, P Beaumont and P McEleavy, *The Hague Convention on International Child Abduction* (Oxford, Oxford University Press, 1999) 29–30.

[35] See www.hcch.net/index_en.php.

[36] W Duncan, 'Children's Rights, Cultural Diversity and Private International Law' in G Douglas and L Sebba (eds), *Children's Rights and Traditional Values* (Farnham, Ashgate, 1998) 42.

According to William Duncan, the forum approach gives recognition and respect to national diversity, and encourages states to ratify the Conventions; but, 'most importantly, it is a vital element in upholding certain rights and interests of the child. The balance between respect for diversity and the insistence on certain universal standards needs to be maintained'.[37] Because of these considerations, it might be thought that the 'forum' approach to international law is most likely to be successful. Indeed, that may be so, but that does not mean that it is entirely without difficulty. The best example of this approach is found in the Hague Convention on the Civil Aspects of International Child Abduction 1980 (Hague Abduction Convention),[38] which we use to illustrate some of the complexities that arise.

Put simply, as between the 82 states which have signed up to the Hague Abduction Convention, there is a common approach to cases involving children abducted from one country to another by one of their parents, and that approach is that the child should be returned to his or her country of habitual residence as swiftly as possible so that the substantive dispute can be addressed by the courts of that country. In other words, when a child is taken from Country A to Country B without proper consent,[39] the court in Country B should not make detailed enquiries into the question of where it would be best for the child to live, but should presumptively make an order returning the child to Country A for the courts of that country to resolve the issue. The Convention does not decide which country the child should live in, but simply determines which court will decide that question – and, other than in exceptional circumstances, the answer is that the court in Country A will be the one to decide the substantive questions about the child's upbringing. The role of the court in Country B is primarily to determine whether the case falls within the remit of the Hague Abduction Convention and, if it does, to order the child returned to Country A.

The Hague Abduction Convention is 'widely and rightly regarded as being a most successful international instrument for the protection of children',[40] and has clear objectives based on shared aims. The objectives are two-fold:[41]

- to secure the prompt return of children wrongfully removed to or retained in any Contracting State; and
- to ensure that rights of custody and of access under the law of one Contracting State are respected in other Contracting States.

---

[37] Ibid, 43.
[38] See generally A-M Hutchinson, R Roberts and H Setright, *International Parental Child Abduction* (Bristol, Family Law, 1998); Beaumont and McEleavy, *The Hague Convention on International Child Abduction*; Lowe, Everall and Nicholls, *International Movement of Children*, chs 12–18.
[39] Either by everyone with the equivalent of parental responsibility for the child or by a court.
[40] Lowe, Everall and Nicholls, *International Movement of Children*, p vii.
[41] Hague Abduction Convention, Art 1.

These objectives are based on the conviction 'that the interests of children are of paramount importance in matters relating to their custody'; in the context of international abduction, this focus on children's best interests leads to a desire 'to protect children internationally from the harmful effects of their wrongful removal or retention and to establish procedures to ensure their prompt return to the State of their habitual residence'.[42] In other words, because the wrongful removal of a child from her country of residence is generally agreed to be harmful to the child, it is reasonable to assume that the best way to respond to international abduction is to return the child to her original place of residence as quickly as possible.

However, while the theory of the Hague Abduction Convention is straightforward, in practice a number of difficulties arise. Even though the Convention is concerned only with the 'forum' question (where the dispute will be heard), and even though all the signatories to the Convention agree that these disputes should be heard in the country in which the child is habitually resident (not the country to which she has been abducted), when it comes to putting the rules into practice different countries take different approaches.

In determining whether a case is a Hague case or not, a number of key questions need to be answered. These questions include:

- in which country is the child 'habitually resident'?[43]
- does the applicant parent (the one who alleges the abduction) have 'rights of custody' as understood in the Convention,[44] and was that parent 'actually exercising the custody rights' at the time of the removal?[45]
- has the child become 'settled in its new environment'?[46]
- is there a 'grave risk' that returning the child would 'expose the child to physical or psychological harm or otherwise place the child in an intolerable situation'?[47]
- did the applicant parent consent to the removal, or subsequently acquiesce in it?[48]

On some of these questions, the contracting states have reached 'a remarkable unanimity of interpretation',[49] but in other areas there has been considerable variation. Rhona Schuz has noted important lack of international conformity with regard to the definitions of 'habitual residence',[50] whether a

---

[42] Ibid, preamble; see Lowe, Everall and Nicholls, *International Movement of Children*, 198.
[43] Hague Abduction Convention, Arts 3 and 4.
[44] Ibid, Arts 5 and 15.
[45] Ibid, Arts 3(b) and 13(a).
[46] Ibid, Art 12.
[47] Ibid, Art 13(b).
[48] Ibid, Art 13(a).
[49] Lowe, Everall and Nicholls, *International Movement of Children*, 247.
[50] R Schuz, 'Habitual Residence of Children Under the Hague Abduction Convention: Theory and Practice' [2001] *Child and Family Law Quarterly* 1.

child has become 'settled' in the new environment,[51] and as to what kinds of 'rights of custody' will qualify.[52]

The last of these is, perhaps, the most surprising, since the Hague Abduction Convention provides a mechanism for a court in Country B to enquire of a court in Country A about the nature of the applicant's rights with regard to the child.[53] However, even the interpretation of this enquiry mechanism has been given different interpretations in different countries! The prevailing view of the English courts before 2006 was that the enquiry was purely about the domestic law of Country A – the purpose was, effectively, to ask the court in Country A to explain more about what the applicant parent was entitled to under the law of Country A.[54] It was then for the court of Country B to determine how that answer affected the application of the Hague Abduction Convention. The English courts altered this approach in 2006 when, in *Re D (Abduction: Rights of Custody)*,[55] the House of Lords ruled that the enquiry could relate not only to the nature of the applicant's rights under domestic law in Country A, but also to whether those rights qualified to bring an application under the Hague Abduction Convention. In other words, the court in Country B can ask the court in Country A to decide whether the rights that the applicant has in Country A make the case a Hague Abduction Convention case or not, even though the case is being decided in Country B.

While that approach has merit,[56] the difficulty is in departing from what seemed to be a settled interpretation of the provision and, importantly, from an interpretation adopted in other countries. A majority of the New Zealand Court of Appeal in *Fairfax v Ireton*, for example, refused to adopt *Re D*.[57] In his dissenting judgment in *Fairfax*, Baragwanath J commented tellingly that '[i]t is a misfortune that the courts of England and New Zealand, which have so much in common, should be unable to agree on this fundamental aspect of an international Convention that should receive a single interpretation'.[58]

Similarly, when it comes to putting the agreed-upon principles of the Hague Abduction Convention into practice, there is considerable variation

---

[51] R Schuz, 'In Search of a Settled Interpretation of Article 12(2) of the Hague Child Abduction Convention' [2008] *Child and Family Law Quarterly* 64; see also Lowe, Everall and Nicholls, *International Movement of Children*, 297–300.

[52] R Schuz, 'The Influence of the UN Convention on the Rights of the Child on the Implementation of the 1980 Hague Child Abduction Convention' (paper presented at the *International Child Abduction, Forced Marriage and Relocation Conference*, London Metropolitan University, July 2010).

[53] Hague Abduction Convention, Art 15.

[54] See, eg, *C v S (A Minor) (Abduction)* [1990] 2 FLR 442 (CA), 446, aff'd on other grounds [1990] 2 FLR 450 (HL); *Hunter v Murrow* [2005] EWCA Civ 976, [2005] 2 FLR 1119, [46]–[47].

[55] *Re D (Abduction: Rights of Custody)* [2006] UKHL 51, [2007] 1 FLR 961.

[56] The court in Country A is more likely to know whether parenting arrangements which are particular to that country should 'qualify' under the Hague Convention than is the court in Country B, where different parenting arrangements are used.

[57] *Fairfax v Ireton* [2009] NZCA 100, [2009] NZFLR 433, [28]–[30].

[58] Ibid, [149].

between countries, with Marilyn Freeman describing the global position as being 'in a haphazard state'.[59] For example, there are very limited circumstances under the Convention when it is appropriate for the court to conduct a full enquiry into the child's welfare,[60] but different countries interpret the meaning of these provisions differently. Freeman calls for greater consistency 'so that the valid, and valuable, opportunities to safeguard the welfare of individual children are not lost in the lottery of abduction that now pervades the operation of the Convention within the signatory states'.[61]

Given the variation found under the forum approach, there is reason to ask whether there might be a more effective way to regulate international family law issues. The next system we can consider is the 'mutual recognition' approach.

THE 'MUTUAL RECOGNITION' APPROACH

Whereas the aim of the 'forum' approach to international law is primarily to determine which country should have jurisdiction to decide an issue, the 'mutual recognition' approach is intended to enable courts in Country A to give effect to decisions taken in Country B. In some ways, this approach is simply an application of general principles of the conflict of laws. As the leading text in that field explains,[62] conflict of laws cases can raise three main questions:

- does the English court have jurisdiction to decide the case?
- if the English court does have jurisdiction, should it apply English law or the law of another jurisdiction?
- will the English court recognise and enforce a foreign judgment which purports to determine the issue?

While this is the general approach, there are a couple of ways in which family law is different.[63] One way is that English courts sometimes answer these questions – especially the second – differently when the case is about family law. For example, if the court decides that it has jurisdiction to hear a

---

[59] M Freeman, 'In the Best Interests of Internationally Abducted Children? Plural, Singular, Neither or Both?' [2002] *International Family Law* 77, 79.

[60] One example arises if the Art 13(2) defence is raised by the respondent, namely that 'there is a grave risk that his or her return would expose the child to physical or psychological harm or otherwise place the child in an intolerable situation'.

[61] Freeman, 'In the Best Interests of Internationally Abducted Children?', 81.

[62] L Collins, C Morse, D McClean, A Briggs, J Harris and C McLachlan (eds), *Dicey, Morris and Collins on the Conflict of Laws*, 14th edn (London, Thompson Reuters, 2010) [1.003].

[63] Try to contain your surprise . . .

divorce application, it will apply the English law on divorce and post-divorce financial settlements no matter what.[64]

Another specifically family law aspect of the conflicts question, which is the focus of this section, relates to the third question. There are a number of international agreements which attempt to standardise the answers to the question of whether foreign orders will be recognised and enforced in domestic courts.[65] Recently, this approach has been favoured in the EU's work on family issues, and we can take the revised Brussels II Regulation (Brussels IIR) as an example.[66]

One of the key issues addressed by Brussels IIR is the recognition and enforcement of orders relating to children's upbringing and other issues governed by parental responsibility. Brussels IIR provides that orders which fall within its scope shall be automatically recognised and enforced across the Union – all that needs to be done is for the order to be registered in the new state.[67] Or at least, that is the theory.

In practice, the matter may be more complex. The English High Court decision of *Re ML and AL (Children) (Contact Order: Brussels II Regulation)* is an interesting case study, and is discussed in Box 3.1.[68]

Box 3.1: Illustration of issues arising with the Brussels IIR Regulation, drawing on *Re ML and AL (Children) (Contact Order: Brussels II Regulation)* [2006] EWHC 2285 (Fam), [2007] 2 FLR 475

In *Re ML and AL*, the mother had been given permission to relocate from the UK to Austria with the children. The relocation order expressly reserved jurisdiction over the case to the English courts,[69] and supervised contact was later ordered, which was to take place in England.[70] Two days before contact was due to take place, the mother applied to the Austrian court for an emergency order suspending contact.[71] The Austrian court granted the application, but then returned the case to the London court, since that was where primary jurisdiction lay.

---

[64] See, eg, *Radmacher v Granatino* [2010] UKSC 42, [2010] 2 FLR 1900, [103].

[65] See, eg, the Hague Convention on the Recognition of Divorces and Legal Separations 1970; Family Law Act 1986, Part II.

[66] Regulation (EC) 2201/2003 concerning jurisdiction and the recognition and enforcement of judgments in matrimonial matters and matters of parental responsibility. Discussion of the Regulation is conspicuously absent from family law textbooks.

[67] Brussels IIR, Art 21.

[68] *Re ML and AL (Children) (Contact Order: Brussels II Regulation)* [2006] EWHC 2285 (Fam), [2007] 2 FLR 475. Thanks to Charles Hale for drawing this case to my attention.

[69] Brussels IIR, Art 12. This order overrides the normal rule, whereby jurisdiction passes three months after the child's habitual residence changes.

[70] The mother had expressly agreed to return the children to the UK if required.

[71] Brussels IIR, Art 20. This provision allows the local court to make orders despite not having jurisdiction if the issue is urgent.

Giving judgment, Deputy Judge Nicholas Mostyn QC considered that the Austrian order was an abuse of the Regulation's provisions and should not have been made. There was no urgency about the case which could not have been addressed adequately in London. Indeed, the Deputy Judge thought that the only legitimate purpose of making orders under the 'urgent case' provision was to reinforce the original order; as an example of an appropriate use of the emergency powers, the Deputy Judge suggested a case where the local court intervened to prevent the children being removed to a third country, thereby safeguarding the contact ordered by the original court.[72] Conversely, the effect of the Austrian court's intervention in *Re ML and AL* was 'entirely to overthrow the [original] order'.[73] Given that the Austrian court seemed to have undermined the point of the Regulation's scheme, the Deputy Judge thought that the case called into question 'whether the high principles of the regulation devised by the Commission are to be conscientiously and faithfully applied by the member states, or whether, if I might quote St Paul, its words merely speak into the empty air'.[74]

In the previous section of this chapter it was suggested that international provisions focused on forum could be open to varying interpretations in different countries. Does the example of *Re ML and AL* suggest that similar concerns might apply to provisions focused on mutual recognition? If so, might the answer be simply to create a single system of family law which is applied around the world? In short, that is the idea of the final approach considered in this chapter, called the harmonisation approach.

THE 'HARMONISATION' APPROACH

The aim of the harmonisation approach to family law is 'to resolve the conflict of laws between different systems by establishing uniform domestic laws'.[75] It is fair to say that creating a single body of family law to be applied in different countries is a significantly more ambitious idea than the other approaches considered in this chapter (though they are themselves quite ambitious!). Indeed, in countries where family law is regulated at a subnational level (the United States, Canada and Australia are good examples,

---

[72] Ibid, [35].
[73] Ibid, [40].
[74] Ibid, [1].
[75] Duncan, 'Children's Rights, Cultural Diversity and Private International Law', 42.

though the UK falls within this category as well) there is often considerable variation in family law *within* countries; even attempts to unify national family law tend to meet with limited success.[76] The task of finding specific areas where rules and principles can be agreed internationally may therefore be rightly seen as rather daunting.

In some areas of family law, it seems obvious that international agreement will not be forthcoming soon. An easy example would be same-sex marriage. Around the world, there are ten countries which allow same-sex marriages,[77] and another 21 allow same-sex couples to enter civil unions or registered partnerships. Conversely, homosexuality is a criminal offence (attracting serious penalties, including the death penalty in some cases) in many countries, most of them in Africa, the Middle East and the Caribbean. Even within countries, there is much debate, as the position in the USA illustrates. In 2011, New York joined the list of US States which allow same-sex marriage, bringing the total to six;[78] but against that, 41 States specifically ban same-sex marriage, and at least two candidates seeking to be the Republican Party's Presidential nominee in the 2012 election pledged to seek a Constitutional amendment limiting marriage to heterosexual unions.[79] It is consequently unsurprising that no one is presently seeking a uniform law on same-sex marriage.

By contrast, one area of family law where thought is being given to the possibility of unifying international approaches is international relocation (cases where one parent applies to court for permission to take their child to live permanently in another jurisdiction). While the law in most western countries bases relocation law on the welfare of the child, there is considerable variation in how welfare is interpreted in the relocation context,[80] with consequent variation in case outcomes.[81] In response to this variation, an international conference of judges and other experts was convened in Washington DC in March 2010, with representatives of 14 countries in attendance. The purpose of this meeting, according to Thorpe LJ who attended on behalf of the United Kingdom, was 'to explore the development of common principles to guide the exercise of [judicial] discretion in granting or refusing a relocation'.[82]

---

[76] See, eg, the USA's Uniform Marriage and Divorce Act 1970, which was enacted by only eight States, and then only in part: see S Katz, *Family Law in America* (Oxford, Oxford University Press, 2003) 3.

[77] Argentina, Belgium, Canada, Iceland, the Netherlands, Norway, Portugal, Spain, South Africa and Sweden.

[78] The others are Connecticut, Iowa, Massachusetts, New Hampshire and Vermont, along with the District of Columbia; Maryland recognises same-sex marriages performed elsewhere, but does not allow its own ceremonies.

[79] Mitt Romney and Michele Bachmann; for comment, see C Warriner, 'Do We Need to Worry About an Anti-Gay Marriage Amendment?', online at www.sosogay.org/2011/opinion-do-we-need-to-worry-about-an-anti-gay-marriage-amendment.

[80] A Worwood, 'International Relocation: The Debate' [2005] *Family Law* 621.

[81] R George, 'Practitioners' Views on Children's Welfare in Relocation Disputes: Comparing Approaches in England and New Zealand' [2011] *Child and Family Law Quarterly* 178; see also ch 7 below, 'The Values of Welfare', text from n 51.

[82] M Thorpe, 'Relocation Development' [2010] *Family Law* 565, 565.

From this conference came a 13-point Declaration. For our purposes, the crucial aspects, under the heading 'Factors Relevant to Decisions on International Relocation', are points 3 to 6, set out in Box 3.2.

Box 3.2: sections from The Washington Declaration on International Family Relocation 2010

3   In all applications concerning international relocation the best interests of the child should be the paramount (primary) consideration. Therefore, determinations should be made without any presumptions for or against relocation.

4   In order to identify more clearly cases in which relocation should be granted or refused, and to promote a more uniform approach internationally, the exercise of judicial discretion should be guided in particular, but not exclusively, by the following factors listed in no order of priority. The weight to be given to any one factor will vary from case to case:

   i)   the right of the child separated from one parent to maintain personal relations and direct contact with both parents on a regular basis in a manner consistent with the child's development, except if the contact is contrary to the child's best interest;

   ii)   the views of the child having regard to the child's age and maturity;

   iii) the parties' proposals for the practical arrangements for relocation, including accommodation, schooling and employment;

   iv)   where relevant to the determination of the outcome, the reasons for seeking or opposing the relocation;

   v)   any history of family violence or abuse, whether physical or psychological;

   vi)   the history of the family and particularly the continuity and quality of past and current care and contact arrangements;

   vii) pre-existing custody and access determinations;

   viii) the impact of grant or refusal on the child, in the context of his or her extended family, education and social life, and on the parties;

   ix)   the nature of the inter-parental relationship and the commitment of the applicant to support and facilitate the relationship between the child and the respondent after the relocation;

   x)   whether the parties' proposals for contact after relocation are realistic, having particular regard to the cost to the family and the burden to the child;

> xi)   the enforceability of contact provisions ordered as a condition of relocation in the State of destination;
> xii) issues of mobility for family members; and
> xiii) any other circumstances deemed to be relevant by the judge.
>
> 5 While these factors may have application to domestic relocation they are primarily directed to international relocation and thus generally involve considerations of international family law.
> 6 The factors reflect research findings concerning children's needs and development in the context of relocation.

It should not be thought that the Washington Declaration could, as it stands, be incorporated into the domestic law of any country:[83] it is a working document, 'certainly not intended . . . to be conclusive',[84] and should be seen as the start of a conversation rather than the conclusion of one. However, even within the English courts the Declaration has provoked a wide variety of responses. Compare, for example, the remarks of Wilson LJ and of Mostyn J set out in Boxes 3.3 and 3.4.

Box 3.3: extract from *Re H (Leave to Remove)* [2010] EWCA Civ 915, [2010] 2 FLR 1875, [27] (Wilson LJ)

With some hesitation I make the following aside. In that the principal charge against our guidance, as it stands, is that it ascribes too great a significance to the effect on the child of the negative impact upon the applicant of refusal of the application, one is interested to discern the way in which, in [4] of the Declaration, that factor is addressed. One finds (does one not?) that it is not squarely addressed at all. The closest to any address of it is to be found in (viii), namely 'the impact of grant or refusal on the child, in the context of his or her extended family, education and social life, and on the parties.' Some may share my initial perplexity even at the terminology of (viii) in that it appears to train the consideration of the court upon impact not only 'on the child' but also, and by way of contradistinction, 'on the parties', apparently irrespective of impact on the child. It is axiomatic that our notion of paramountcy excludes from consideration all factors which have no bearing on the child. But, that possible curiosity apart, there is no square address in (viii) of the impact upon the child likely to flow from negative impact

---

[83] Some apparently took the view that it could be; but, as the Court of Appeal pointed out, that idea 'lacked elementary legal discipline': *Re H (Leave to Remove)* [2010] EWCA Civ 915, [2010] 2 FLR 1875, [26].

[84] Thorpe, 'Relocation Development', 565.

upon the applicant of refusal of the application. Indeed the reference to the child's extended family, education and social life, seems almost to draw attention away from such a factor. I wonder whether consideration might need to be given as to whether, if the present law of England and Wales does indeed place excessive weight upon that factor, paragraph [4] of the Declaration, as presently drawn, by contrast places insufficient weight upon it.

Box 3.4: extract from *Re AR (A Child: Relocation)* [2010] EWHC 1346 (Fam), [2010] 2 FLR 1577, [11]–[12] (Mostyn J)

The Declaration supplies a more balanced and neutral approach to a relocation application, as is the norm in many other jurisdictions. It specifically ordains a non-presumptive approach. It requires the court in a real rather than synthetic way to take into account the impact on both the child and the left behind parent of the disruption of the periodicity and quantum of the prevailing contact arrangement. The hitherto decisive factor for us – the psychological impact on the thwarted primary carer – is relegated to a seemingly minor position at the back end of para 4(viii).

[Mostyn J then quoted the section of Wilson LJ's judgment in *Re H (Leave to Remove)* seen in Box 3.3, and continued:] I agree with this, up to a point. Certainly the factor of the impact on the thwarted primary carer deserves its own berth and as such deserves its due weight, no more, no less. The problem with the attribution of great weight to this particular factor is that, paradoxically, it appears to penalise selflessness and virtue, while rewarding selfishness and uncontrolled emotions. The core question of the putative relocator is always 'how would you react if leave were refused?' The parent who stoically accepts that she would accept the decision, make the most of it, move on and work to promote contact with the other parent is far more likely to be refused leave than the parent who states that she will collapse emotionally and psychologically. This is the reverse of the Judgment of Solomon, where of course selflessness and sacrifice received their due reward.

• If judges within a single jurisdiction take such divergent views about one possible framework for an international agreement, is it likely that many countries would in fact ascribe to any agreement?
• If there were countries which signed up to some kind of agreement, would you be confident that they would interpret the details of the agreement in the same way?

- If an international framework about child law were based on the welfare principle (as would seem likely), would that help or hinder the harmonisation of the law when answering substantive questions of law?[85]

CONCLUSIONS

The internationalisation of families and of family law remains a curiously underexplored issue for family lawyers. The aim of this chapter has not been to address the detail of the many areas of international family law which are worthy of further consideration,[86] but it should have introduced some key questions and illustrated some of the complexities which lie ahead. These issues are not going to go away – indeed, it would be a safe bet that they are going to grow, both in number and in prominence, in the years to come. Insofar as the international elements of family law have previously been forgotten,[87] it is time we started remembering them.

---

[85] See further ch 7 below, 'The Values of Welfare'.
[86] On some of the issues relating to children, see T Buck, *International Child Law*, 2nd edn (Abingdon, Routledge-Cavendish, 2010).
[87] Hale, 'Families and the Law'.

4

Regulating Adult Relationships

Key Questions

- How does the law regulate different forms of intimate adult relationship?
- Why are some adult relationships not regulated by law at all, while others are regulated to different extents depending on their form?
- Why do people enter into particular types of relationship, and does the form of relationship affect people's perceptions of their obligations within that relationship?

Intimate relationships between adults come in many forms, and there is considerable variation between individual relationships even when they are of the same type.[1] In the UK context, three main forms of relationship tend to dominate family law thinking:[2] marriage, civil partnership,[3] and non-marital cohabitation.[4] The three chapters which follow are all broadly about the law's regulation of these intimate adult relationships. Lady Hale once pointed out that '[s]ociety wants its intimate relationships . . . to be stable, responsible and

---

[1] A Diduck, 'Relationship Fairness' in A Bottomley and S Wong (eds), *Changing Contours of Domestic Life, Family and Law: Caring and Sharing* (Oxford, Hart Publishing, 2009) 73.

[2] A further category, namely people who are 'living apart together' (LAT), is starting to gain recognition in some textbooks. Put shortly, LATs are in committed relationships but have separate households for one reason or another: see J Haskey and J Lewis, 'Living Apart Together in Britain: Context and Meaning' (2006) 2 *International Journal of Law in Context* 37.

[3] Although marriage and civil partnership are treated synonymously in this book, the factual differences between them (primarily in terms of who may enter a marriage or a civil partnership) requires them to be distinguished at this point.

[4] In the UK, people in these relationships are usually termed 'cohabitants', but other terms are used elsewhere, such as New Zealand's 'de facto couples'.

secure'[5] – but is that desire in itself a sufficient justification for the state adopting this role in people's personal lives?

This chapter addresses the different ways in which intimate relationships are regulated by the law in general. As an introduction to those issues, it may be helpful to think about some of the measures by which different types of relationship might be distinguished. Consider the following issues and the extent to which they can be used to divide up relationship types:

- **Who can enter such a relationship** – how many people could be in the relationship, what sex those people can be, and so on.
- **How the relationship is started and terminated** – whether formally or informally, under what circumstances, and so on.
- **How the law treats the relationship while it is in existence** – the rights, privileges and duties which attach to the relationship, if any; or, conversely, the positive disincentives which the law offers against the relationship.
- **How the law treats the former members of the relationship if it ends** – the rights, privileges and duties which exist as the relationship is ending and then once it has fully terminated.

Family law textbooks usually include useful information about changing demographic trends in relationship types, demonstrating that over the last decades the marriage rate has been declining while the divorce rate has been rising.[6] At the same time, non-marital cohabitation has been increasing,[7] with research suggesting that such relationships are becoming more stable and long-lasting.[8] Despite these changes, it seems clear that the institution, or idea, or marriage remains of great importance to many people, to the extent that many of those who are excluded from it consider that their fundamental rights have been violated.[9]

Shifts in the demographics of intimate partnership arrangements have led to a number of debates for family lawyers. One of those debates looks at the nature of marriage itself, and aspects of that topic are addressed in the next chapter. Two other issues which tend to feature in textbooks are:

- whether the traditional definition of marriage should be retained or expanded, with particular reference in recent years to the question of whether marriage should be available to same-sex couples[10] (rather than offering

---

[5] *Ghaidan v Godin-Mendoza* [2004] UKHL 30, [2004] 2 FLR 600, [143].

[6] See, eg, J Herring, *Family Law*, 5th edn (Harlow, Longman, 2011) 40 and 102. The divorce rate in the UK actually fell between 2003 and 2009, but rose by 4.9% in 2010: Office for National Statistics, *Statistics Bulletin: Divorces in England and Wales 2010* (Newport, ONS, 2011) 8.

[7] Herring, *Family Law*, 82.

[8] See, eg, A Barlow, S Duncan, G James and A Park, *Cohabitation, Marriage and the Law: Social Change and Legal Reform in the 21st Century* (Oxford, Hart Publishing, 2005).

[9] A Diduck and F Kaganas, *Family Law, Gender and the State: Text, Cases and Materials*, 3rd edn (Oxford, Hart Publishing, 2012) 36.

[10] This is the position in Argentina, Belgium, Canada, Iceland, the Netherlands, Norway, Portugal, Spain, South Africa and Sweden, as well as six States of the USA.

same-sex couples an alternative legally recognised union with the same rights as marriage;[11] a legally recognised union with different (fewer) rights;[12] or no legal recognition at all);[13]
- whether non-marital cohabitation relationships should attract some or all of the same legal rights, duties and privileges as marriage; three complications here are i) how to decide which relationships would qualify for this legal recognition, ii) whether couples could choose to 'opt out' of being recognised by the law, and iii) precisely which rights, etc would be given to such couples.

These are the debates on which this chapter builds, looking at the ways in which the law does and could regulate intimate adult relationships. We also ask about how people respond to these different forms of regulation when organising their personal lives. The chapter starts with two short sections, one on the ways in which all interpersonal relationships are regulated by law, the other on how we decide which relationships count as 'intimate adult relationships' and so are regulated by family law in some way. We then ask about different ways in which the law could decide which of these relationships to regulate, and finally about how people organise and evaluate their intimate relationships.

REGULATING RELATIONSHIPS

Relationships of all kinds are regulated by law. Consider these relationships and the different ways in which they are, or might sometimes be, legally regulated:

- two parties to a commercial contract
- two people involved in a road traffic accident
- a doctor and her patient
- a doctor and an attending nurse
- a teacher and the parent of a pupil
- a teacher and the grandparent of a pupil
- a parent and their child
- the two parents of a child

---

[11] Such as under the UK's Civil Partnership Act 2004, which offers same-sex couples access to a union which is legally all but identical to marriage.
[12] Such as the French *Pacte Civil de Solidarité* (PACS), which offers limited legal rights and is open to same-sex and opposite-sex couples: Loi 99/944 of 15 November 1999.
[13] On the international elements of this debate, see ch 3 above, 'International Family Law', text at nn 77–79.

- a union member and his employer
- two members of the same club
- two patrons of the same pub

In (almost?) every type of relationship, the law sets limits on what we are able to do, whether by *prohibiting* actions, by *refusing to recognise* actions, by *facilitating* actions, or by *requiring* actions. Even the relationships which are least regulated – two strangers passing in the street, perhaps – are regulated: one may not intentionally hit the other,[14] for example, and even where there is no intention to come into contact with one another the law imposes a requirement that reasonable care be taken to avoid accidental injury to the other.[15] Equally obvious is the fact that some relationships are regulated to a greater extent than others, and that the manner of the regulation varies considerably from case to case.

This chapter is focused on the legal regulation of people's personal lives, and in particular on what we might call 'intimate adult relationships' or 'intimate partnerships'. We ask about the forms of relationship which the law recognises, and the variety of ways in which it appears to regulate the different forms. We also ask about the ways in which people 'choose' to enter different relationship types – why they enter them at all, and why one type rather than another – and discuss why the word *choose* in this sentence needs to be in inverted commas.

First, though, it may be worth thinking about the basic divisions which can be observed in the law as it stands. It is possible to see these divisions as a form of hierarchy of relationship types, each layer attracting different legal consequences. The hierarchy in English law seems to have four basic categories, as set out in Box 4.1.[16] Think about which relationships fall into which category, and about why that might be the case.

Even looking at this list, though, it is possible to ask whether all the many types of intimate adult relationship which people might choose to enter have been accounted for. For example, where does the relationship between two parents who are no longer together – or who were never together – fit into this hierarchy? More generally, what kinds of intimate adult relationship should the law regulate, and who gets to make that decision?

---

[14] That would be the crime of battery and the tort of trespass to the person.

[15] Absence of due care would engage the tort of negligence.

[16] Different countries draw this hierarchy in different ways. By contrast with the position in English law set out in the text, New Zealand law draws very little distinction between married couples and people in what are called '*de facto* relationships'. A de facto relationship is two people living together in a relationship which is of the nature of a marriage: Interpretation Act 1999 (New Zealand) s 29A(1). Despite being started and terminated entirely without formalities, the de facto relationship is a legally recognised relationship status, bringing with it most of the rights and benefits of marriage. At the same time, though, it seems to be envisaged (though there are no known cases on this point) that 'it is possible for a person to be in two or more *de facto* relationships at the one time': D Inglis, *New Zealand Family Law in the 21st Century* (Wellington, Thompson Brookers, 2007) 53.

Box 4.1: A hierarchy of intimate adult relationships

- **Forbidden relationships** – some relationships are specifically not allowed under the law. A good example is an incestuous relationship, which is criminalised if it involves a sexual element.[17] Here, the law imposes sanctions for behaviour considered positively harmful or 'wrong'.

- **Non-recognised relationships** – some relationships, while not actually forbidden, are not accepted by the law as a valid form of relationship. An example might be a polygamous relationship. People are free to form a multi-party relationship if they want to (so long as it is not forbidden for some other reason), but it has to be done privately – it could not, for example, be registered with the state as a marriage or a civil partnership,[18] and would not be seen as deserving of state protections and benefits.[19]

- **Accepted relationships** – these are relationships which the law is prepared to admit, and consequently to endow with limited legal consequences. In English law, the best example is the unmarried cohabiting relationship, though it might be that the key feature for the law is dependency.[20] Relationships in this category obtain some legal protections and benefits, and so are, to a limited extent, promoted and 'incentivised' by the state as desirable forms of relationships.

- **Privileged relationships** – in English law, it is clear that marriage and civil partnership are top of the hierarchy of relationships, receiving special protections and benefits from the law, and thus privileging people in this category over those in any other category.[21] As the category receiving the most protections and benefits, the relationships here are the most incentivised, the ones that the state would most like its citizens to form.

---

[17] Sexual Offences Act 2003, ss 64 and 65.

[18] *Hyde v Hyde* (1866) LR 1 P&D 130 (HL).

[19] If there was a child involved in such a relationship, that aspect might be treated differently. For example, there seems to be no reason in principle why several adults in a polygamous relationship should not all obtain parental responsibility for the child; *cf*, by analogy, *Re G (Shared Residence Order: Parental Responsibility)* [2005] EWCA Civ 462, [2005] 2 FLR 957, on the allocation of parental responsibility to a step-parent who was no longer in a relationship with the child's biological parent.

[20] Hence a person who is a dependant may seek the law's assistance under statutes like the Fatal Accidents Act 1976 and the Inheritance (Provision for Family and Dependants) Act 1975.

[21] Whether marriage and civil partnership are different in this regard is a matter for debate; for brief discussion, see ch 5 below, 'The Meanings of Marriage', n 2.

WHAT COUNTS AS AN INTIMATE ADULT RELATIONSHIP?

As we saw at the start of this chapter, marriage, civil partnership and non-marital cohabitation are the three forms of intimate adult relationship which most readily spring to mind for the family lawyer. These relationships have much in common with one another: they are 'forms of living arrangement which can broadly be considered "familial"',[22] and they probably share a similar understanding of the word 'intimate'. In particular, the archetypal example of each of these three relationships would probably be a monogamous sexual relationship, though these elements are not essential.[23] But why should these forms of domestic relationship be recognised by the law and others not?[24] Is a sexual, two-person intimacy all that differentiates these from other adult relationships and, if so, why is that important? If we adopted a broader understanding of the word 'intimate', would we reach different answers? Consider these types of relationships – why does the law presently treat them so differently from one another?

- spouses (meaning those married or in a civil partnership)
- non-marital cohabitants (and how broadly can we define that category?)
- those 'living apart together'[25]
- those sharing the same household
- adult siblings[26]
- friends (or what about 'best friends'?)[27]
- neighbours

What about the relationship between a child's parents where the pregnancy was the unplanned result of a one-night stand?[28] Or the relationship between a gay man who is the biological father of a child born to a lesbian couple?[29]

---

[22] J Eekelaar, *Family Law and Social Policy*, 2nd edn (London, Weidenfeld and Nicolson: 1984) 3.

[23] See, eg, *Ghaidan v Godin-Mendoza* [2004] UKHL 30, [2004] 2 FLR 600, [141]; *X City Council v MB, NB and MAB* [2006] EWHC 168 (Fam), [2006] 2 FLR 968, [62].

[24] See generally A Bottomley and S Wong, 'Changing Contours of Domestic Life, Family and Law: Caring and Sharing' in A Bottomley and S Wong (eds), *Changing Contours of Domestic Life, Family and Law* (Oxford, Hart Publishing, 2009).

[25] Haskey and Lewis, 'Living Apart Together in Britain'.

[26] *Burden v United Kingdom* (Application 13378/05) [2008] 2 FLR 787 (ECtHR, Grand Chamber).

[27] J Eekelaar, *Family Law and Personal Life*, paperback edn (Oxford, Oxford University Press, 2007) ch 2.

[28] See, eg, *Re G (Parental Responsibility Order)* [2006] EWCA Civ 745, [2006] 2 FLR 1092.

[29] See, eg, *Re D (Contact and Parental Responsibility: Lesbian Mothers and Known Father)* [2006] EWHC 2 (Fam), [2006] 1 FCR 556.

What about the relationship with a long-term lodger living in one's home?[30]

- Why are some of these adult relationships considered part of the law's remit for 'family law' regulation and others not?
- How should we decide which relationships 'count' in legal terms, and therefore come within a particular part of family law's regulatory framework?

If we leave family law aside for a moment and think about the law of obligations,[31] there are two main ways in which legally recognised relationships are created. One is for the parties to make a decision together to create a legal relationship, the archetypal example being the two parties to a contract. The other is for a legal relationship to be created by the conduct of one or both of the parties in relation to the other, such as a tortious relationship. The law of obligations is traditionally divided into categories based on this distinction, but other areas of the law include both types of relationship within the same area. Consider the law of trusts: some trusts are created intentionally (express trusts), while others are created based on the behaviour of one or both parties (constructive trusts, for example).

Because 'family law' includes elements of many other areas of law,[32] it is perhaps unsurprising that the regulation of family relationships is also governed by a combination of both tests. Some adult relationships attract legal regulation because the parties have expressly chosen to enter into a legally recognised relationship type with one another (marriage or civil partnership), whereas other relationships attract legal regulation because of the behaviour of one or both people in relation to one another (such as a couple living together 'as husband and wife' and thereby creating a relationship of interdependency). In English law, the two 'routes' to legal regulation produce different legal consequences: although in some instances the consequences will be the same, overall the two types of relationship are at different points on the hierarchy of relationships. Married couples have more legal rights and obligations than unmarried couples, even if a particular cohabiting couple is materially identical to a married couple apart from the form of their relationship.

Thinking about the legal consequences of being married, a significant overarching legal obligation of marriage, from which many of the particular consequences flow, is the mutual obligation of support between spouses.[33] While it

---

[30] Eekelaar, *Family Law and Personal Life*, 32.

[31] Might some or all of family law be thought of as part of the law of obligations? *cf* J Eekelaar, 'Personal Obligations' in M Maclean (ed), *Family Law and Family Values* (Oxford, Hart Publishing, 2005).

[32] Such as contract, tort, property, crime, administrative law, EU law, private international law and so on.

[33] As Lady Hale has noted, the obligation of support was originally a common law obligation owed by the husband to the wife (and their legitimate children); 'the obligations of husband and wife only became fully mutual with the major reforms which came into force in 1971 and are now largely contained in the Matrimonial Causes Act 1973': *Radmacher v Granatino* [2010] UKSC 42, [2010] 2 FLR 1900, [141]. Any remaining thought that a husband has a duty to maintain his wife will be removed by s 198 of the Equality Act 2010 (which is not in force at time of writing). In the

might be said that the single most important manifestation of this mutual obligation of support is that it grants the parties access to the court's powers over finances in the event of divorce,[34] there are many consequences during the marriage as well.[35] Nigel Lowe and Gillian Douglas see the legal effects of marriage as falling into two broad categories, namely *personal consequences* and *property consequences*.[36] As to the personal consequences, they identify eight particular issues (see Box 4.2),[37] though, as they point out, although these aspects typically arise with marriage, they are not necessarily all consequences of it.

Box 4.2: Some of the personal consequences of marriage

1. **Use of surname:** while spouses usually use the same surname, there is no requirement that they do so; nor, indeed, is there anything to prevent an unmarried couple from using the same surname, so long as doing so is not intended to perpetrate a fraud.
2. **Sexual intercourse:** while marital rape is a crime,[38] there may be 'a mutual right to, or perhaps legitimate expectation of, sexual intercourse after the marriage has been consummated, and that a refusal to have intercourse, or perhaps an unreasonable rationing of its frequency, might ground a petition for divorce based upon behaviour such that one spouse could not reasonably be expected to live with the other'.
3. **Marital confidences:** there are three requirements for a claim of breach of confidence: i) confidential information; ii) communication in circumstances of confidence or where the recipient knows that the information is private; and iii) unauthorised use of that information to the detriment of the person communicating it. There is some suggestion that a spouse will receive greater protection.[39]
4. **Evidence in legal proceedings:** while the protections given to spouses in legal proceedings have been narrowed considerably, some remain. In particular, in only limited circumstances can a spouse be compelled to give evidence *against* his/her partner.[40]

US, it was held unconstitutional to say that marital obligations fell on the husband alone: *Orr v Orr* (1979) 440 US 268 (US Supreme Court).

[34] J Herring, P Harris and R George, 'Ante-Nuptial Agreements: Fairness, Equality and Presumptions' (2011) 127 *Law Quarterly Review* 335.

[35] This includes a power for the court to make financial orders during a marriage if one partner is failing to maintain the other (or their child): Matrimonial Causes Act 1973, s 27.

[36] N Lowe and G Douglas, *Bromley's Family Law*, 10th edn (Oxford, Oxford University Press, 2007) chs 3 and 4.

[37] Ibid, 111–27.

[38] *R v R* [1992] 1 FLR 217 (HL).

[39] *A v B Plc* [2002] EWCA Civ 337, [2002] 1 FLR 1021; *cf Tchenguiz v Imerman* [2010] EWCA Civ 980, [2010] 2 FLR 814.

[40] Police and Criminal Evidence Act 1984, s 80.

5. **Contracts:** spouses are presumed not to intend to enter into legal contracts with one another (though this presumption is rebutted with relative ease).

6. **Torts:** as against one another, spouses are able to bring tort claims in the same way as if they were unmarried.[41] Nonetheless, marriage has some significance in tort law. For example, a claim for psychiatric injury as a 'secondary victim' (ie where the claimant suffers no physical injury herself) requires that the claimant have a close tie of love and affection with the primary victim (ie the person who was physically injured); such a tie is presumed for only three categories of people, namely spouses, fiancé(e)s, and parents/children, and rebutting the presumption in either direction is difficult.[42]

7. **Criminal law:** spouses cannot be guilty of conspiracy with one another, and prosecution for theft or property damage against one spouse in respect of the other's property requires the Director of Public Prosecutions' consent. Wives continue to have a special defence in respect of criminal offences committed in the presence of, and coerced by, their husbands.[43]

8. **Citizenship and the right to live in the UK:** spouses of British citizens are given certain advantages in obtaining British citizenship as compared with other applicants; marriage may also be a significant factor for a person seeking to resist deportation.

Turning to the property consequences, it is sometimes thought that, because of the court's wide discretion over finances after divorce, property law has little relevance to spouses. Lowe and Douglas explain why such a view is mistaken: 'Strict property rights are still of the greatest importance on the death or insolvency of one spouse, because they alone will have to be applied to resolve any dispute between the other spouse and the personal representatives or creditors'.[44] It is not easy to summarise the law in this area; Box 4.3 offers a brief overview,[45] though note again that some of these points apply to unmarried couples as well.

---

[41] But *cf* Law Reform (Husband and Wife) Act 1962, s 1.

[42] *Alcock v Chief Constable of South Yorkshire* [1992] 1 AC 310 (HL).

[43] Criminal Justice Act 1925, s 47. This defence is not gender neutral and does not apply as between civil partners; it is one of the few provisions of this kind not amended by the Equality Act 2010.

[44] Lowe and Douglas, *Bromley's Family Law*, 131.

[45] Ibid, 132–38.

Box 4.3: Some of the property consequences of marriage

1. **Property owned by the partners on entering the relationship:** absent express agreement, marriage does not alter the ownership of property which either spouse has at the time of marriage, even if that property is then used by both partners.

2. **Gifts between engaged couples:** the question is whether the gift was subject to a condition (express or implied) that it be returned if the marriage does not take place.[46] The question is whether it was a gift to the person (such as a birthday present) or a gift to them *as future spouse* – the latter should be returned, the former not.

3. **Income and investments:** income prima facie belongs to the individual who receives it, but money which is paid into a shared account normally becomes joint property. Property bought with money from a joint account will be jointly owned if the thing is for shared use (like a family car), but solely owned if not (like clothes).

4. **Allowances for housekeeping and maintenance:** any excess from an allowance paid by husband to wife is owned jointly unless the parties agreed otherwise.[47] The Equality Act 2010 includes provisions to make this rule gender neutral and applicable to civil partners as well.[48]

5. **Personal property:** property purchased by A with A's money presumptively belongs to A alone, as does property which A buys for him/herself from the shared account (see 3); this presumption is rebuttable by evidence of intention to make a gift. Property bought by one spouse but intended for both may be subject to an express trust.[49]

6. **Gifts to partners from third parties:** in general, the donor's intention is the key issue here; for wedding gifts, there is a presumption that the gift is to the partners jointly.

7. **The family home:** there is a distinction between properties registered in just one partner's name and those registered in both names: the former are presumptively owned entirely by that partner, the latter shared equally. These presumptions can be rebutted using a constructive trust or proprietary estoppel, if applicable.[50]

---

[46] Law Reform (Miscellaneous Provisions) Act 1970, s 3(1).

[47] Married Women's Property Act 1964, s 1.

[48] Equality Act 2010, ss 200–201 (which are not in force at time of writing).

[49] Because this is personal property, not land, there are no formality requirements, and so an oral declaration of trust will be effective.

[50] See ch 6 below, 'Fairness in Family Finances', text from n 87.

There are also less direct consequences of marriage. These range considerably, from things like inheritance tax and pension rights to emigration and hospital visitation rights. So why do all these rights and obligations flow from marriage? What does it say about marriage that all these consequences come with it?

The 'reason' that marriage is treated so differently from other relationship types is primarily historical – marriage was legally recognised and gave rise to specific legal consequences, and other forms of relationship did not.[51] That position has changed in the relatively recent past, but the law's present bifurcated approach raises questions:

- is it sensible to have two different routes to regulate relationships which are, in many ways, the same?
- would it be *possible* to find a single method of deciding which adult relationships to regulate?
- would it be *desirable* to do so?

In other words, is it a good idea to adopt a purely 'functional approach' to the regulation of adult relationships? As Sonia Harris-Short and Joanna Miles say, the question is whether 'the law should adopt an entirely functionalist or "de facto" model, providing rights, duties and remedies for parties to those relationships which in fact need them for practical reasons, given their stability, duration, economic interdependence, and so on'.[52] This functional approach can be linked to feminist scholarship, focusing on people's lives as they are actually lived (rather than as the law categorises them), and 'positing law's role as reflecting and assisting actual families' experiences and needs, rather than as encouraging or mandating a particular family form'.[53]

There are many ways in which this could be done, but one idea would be to borrow from another area of the law which imposes legal obligations on people based on their relationship with one another guided by a single broad principle, namely the tort of negligence and its 'neighbour principle', as discussed in Box 4.4.

---

[51] See, eg, R Probert, *Marriage Law and Practice in the Long Eighteenth Century: A Reassessment* (Cambridge, Cambridge University Press, 2009).

[52] S Harris-Short and J Miles, *Family Law: Text, Cases and Materials*, 2nd edn (Oxford, Oxford University Press, 2011) 100.

[53] J Millbank, 'The Role of the "Functional Family" in Same-Sex Family Recognition Trends' [2008] *Child and Family Law Quarterly* 155, 156.

Box 4.4: A 'neighbour principle' for family law?

In the tort of negligence, one of the key tests for determining whether A owes a duty of care to B involves asking whether there is sufficient 'proximity' between the two.[54] The proximity test is a reflection of a general legal principle in negligence which stems from Lord Atkin's judgment in *Donoghue v Stevenson*:

> The rule that you are to love your neighbour becomes in law, you must not injure your neighbour; and the lawyer's question, Who is my neighbour? receives a restricted reply. You must take reasonable care to avoid acts or omissions which you can reasonably foresee would be likely to injure your neighbour. Who, then, in law is my neighbour? The answer seems to be: persons who are so closely and directly affected by my act that I ought reasonably to have them in contemplation as being so affected when I am directing my mind to the acts or omissions which are called in question.[55]

This dictum has become established as a legal principle of general application in the law of negligence, known simply as 'the neighbour principle'.

Clearly the application of the neighbour principle requires consideration of many elements – A's position, A's acts (or omissions), B's position relative to A, the likely effect of A's acts (or omissions) on B, and so on. Since these questions are inevitably fact-specific, the principle being applied has be to stated in a very abstract way: if it were made more specific, it could not be applied to the full range of cases. Despite the vagueness and generality of the neighbour principle, it is undoubtedly one of the cornerstones of the tort of negligence, and so of the legal regulation of certain forms of behaviour. Could we adopt a similar approach to the legal regulation of intimate adult relationships? In other words, could the law regulate adult relationships by asking about the 'proximity' or 'neighbourhood' between the people involved, asking the extent to which they should have one another in mind when deciding what to do?

It might be that the 'neighbour' approach – albeit not with this name! – already exists in some writing about family law. One example could be the proposal of American law professor and reform campaigner Nancy Polikoff to 'value all families under the law'.[56] For Polikoff, writing in the American context, a large part of the problem is that the law attaches many consequences to marriage only,[57] meaning that many people are excluded from the law's protections. The gist of Polikoff's answer to this

---

[54] See generally *Caparo Industries v Dickman* [1990] 2 AC 605 (HL).

[55] *Donoghue v Stevenson* [1932] AC 562 (HL), 580.

[56] N Polikoff, *Beyond (Straight and Gay) Marriage: Valuing All Families Under the Law* (Boston, Beacon Press, 2008).

[57] Ibid, 123.

problem is that the legal consequences of relationships, especially those that do or might involve caring for someone, should be given to any relationship which can be seen to be fulfilling the purpose for which that legal consequence exists. There are three stages to this process:[58]

1. Identify the *purpose* of any law which currently grants legal consequences only to marriage.
2. Identify all relationships which do, or could, further that purpose.
3. Allocate the legal consequences which are currently allocated to marriage to all relationships which further the purpose for which those consequences exist.

This approach can be best illustrated with some of Polikoff's examples.

Example 1: Karen and Edward lived together in Michigan. They were not married, but had been in a relationship for several years, and Karen was expecting their baby. When they went to the hospital after Karen entered labour, Edward was not allowed to be present for the birth, because only spouses or members of the mother's immediate family were allowed in the delivery room.[59] The *purpose* of this law was to limit the number of people in the delivery room, while also allowing the mother's closest loved ones to be there with her for the birth. The relationship between Karen and Edward was such that his presence would have fulfilled the second of these purposes, while the question of whether he was a spouse or not had no bearing on the first purpose. Consequently, the law should allow Edward to attend, regardless of his marital status.[60]

Example 2: Mary was in a long-term same-sex relationship. When her partner Liz was sick, Mary requested three days off work under a Colorado law which allowed people unpaid time off work to care for members of their 'immediate family' who were unwell. Mary's employer refused her request because the list of 'immediate family' did not include unmarried partners. However, thinking about the *purpose* of this rule, the aim must be to identify the most suitable person to provide care for a sick relative, and then to free that person from work obligations for a limited time in order to provide that care. An unmarried couple, whether same-sex or opposite-sex, is (for this purpose) in an analogous position to a married couple. Consequently, the law should allow Mary time off work to care for her partner, regardless of marital status.[61]

---

[58] Ibid, 5.
[59] Ibid, 160.
[60] The Michigan appeal court held that the rule violated Michigan's civil rights law: *Whitman v Mercy-Memorial Hospital* (1983) 128 Mich App 155.
[61] Polikoff, *Beyond (Straight and Gay) Marriage*, 169, drawing on *Ross v Denver Department of Health and Hospitals* (1994) 883 P 2d 516 (Colorado Court of Appeal).

These examples show different ways in which legal consequences which are intended to help 'families' in general can sometimes be allocated in a way which some see as being too restrictive. Under Polikiff's proposal, the aim is to allocate them to anyone who is providing society with the benefit which the rule is designed to promote. Might it be possible to use a version of the neighbour principle to help with this process? Would that be desirable? Are there any significant differences between a tortious relationship and a family relationship which should make us cautious about this idea? Consider:

- the interests of the *state* in adult relationships
- the interests of *third parties* (such as children, or mortgage lenders) in adult relationships

Could the 'neighbour' approach to family law adequately protect these interests? What other complications might there be in adopting this approach?

On the other hand, maybe we should be less concerned with allocating legal protections to couples who do not enter a marriage or civil partnership. After all, people may be making an active choice not to enter these state-regulated relationships, in which case imposing legal consequences may be seen as inappropriate.[62] If the state thinks that committed couples who want to be given legal protections should enter a marriage or a civil partnership, it might make sense for the legal consequences of unmarried relationships to be limited.[63]

One version of this view might be seen in a decision of the House of Lords on appeal from the Northern Ireland Court of Appeal. Northern Irish law said that only people who were married (or who were single) could apply to adopt a child. This law was challenged by an unmarried cohabiting couple, who had fostered a child for several years but had been denied permission to apply to adopt him because of their marital status. By a majority, the House of Lords allowed their appeal, holding that the law violated the applicant couple's rights under the Human Rights Act 1998. However, consider the obiter comments from Lady Hale's concurring opinion set out in the extract in Box 4.5.

---

[62] See R Deech, 'The Case Against Legal Recognition of Cohabitation' (1980) 29 *International and Comparative Law Quarterly* 480.

[63] This argument is less powerful insofar as legal consequences relating to children are concerned: children should not be in a different legal position because of decisions of their parents over which they have no control.

Box 4.5: extract from *Re P (Adoption: Unmarried Couple)* [2008] UKHL 38, [2008] 2 FLR 1084 (Lady Hale)

[108] Some unmarried relationships are much more stable than some marriages, and vice versa. The law cannot force any couple, married or unmarried, to stay together. But being married does at least indicate an initial intention to stay together for life. More important, it makes a great legal difference to their relationship. . . . People who want to adopt a child may find it hard to contemplate the ending of their relationship, whether by death, divorce or separation. But . . . the possibility is by no means remote. It is not at all unknown for the advent of children and family responsibilities, which bring such a radical change to the finances and everyday lives of the couple, to lead to a breakdown in their relationship. If the relationship does break down, the parent who is the primary carer of the child will be much less financially secure if the parents are unmarried. And if the primary carer is less secure then so will the child be.

[109] It is therefore appropriate to look with deep suspicion at the reasons why a couple who wish to adopt are unwilling to marry one another. These are not the olden days when the husband and wife were one person in law and that person was the husband. A desire to reject legal patriarchy is no longer a rational reason to reject marriage. It is not expensive to get married. Marriage should not be confused with the wedding. The only rational reason to reject the legal consequences of marriage is the desire to avoid the financial responsibilities towards one another which it imposes on both husband and wife. Why should any couple who wish to take advantage of the law in order to become the legal parents of a child be anxious to avoid those responsibilities which could become so important to the child's welfare if things went wrong in the future?

In this passage, Lady Hale refers to people's reasons for rejecting the *legal consequences* of marriage.

- Do you think that avoidance of legal consequences is the motivation of many unmarried couples?
- Is it right that, legal consequences aside, the only inherent difference between married and unmarried cohabiting couples is that those who have married have indicated publicly their intention to stay together for life?

The state might also prefer to allocate legal rights to marriage because it sees marriage as offering objective *goods* to society. It is possible to demonstrate that people who are married and who remain married perform better on numerous measures of personal well-being than non-married people;[64] and that marriage is, on average, the most stable form of intimate adult relationship.[65] The *correlation* of these facts with marriage seems reasonably clear – but the *causation* is much more contested. In particular, it is difficult to isolate the effects of the marriage itself from the effects of other factors which are usually associated with marriage.[66] For example, a recent study by the Institute for Fiscal Studies shows that, when research controls for background factors,[67] there is no statistically significant difference in children's achievement at ages 3, 5 or 7 between those whose parents are married and those whose parents cohabit.[68] Similarly, when those background factors are taken into account, there is only a small difference in the overall stability of marriage compared with cohabitation, and the IFS conclusion is that 'the majority of the difference in the likelihood of separation between cohabiting and married couples is driven by the types of people who choose to get married, rather than that marriage plays a large role in promoting relationship stability'.[69]

Consequently, as John Eekelaar and Mavis Maclean have said, there is reason to exercise considerable caution 'over claims that marriage is *uniquely* capable of producing certain "goods". The picture is more complex'.[70] In order to explore that complexity, it may be helpful to move away from the law itself and to think about people's lived experiences. Why do people marry or not marry? How do people in different types of intimate adult relationship view themselves and their personal obligations?

WHY MARRY? WHY NOT?

It is fair to say that the legal consequences of a particular behaviour may be one factor influencing people's decisions, but in most instances motivation is

---

[64] See, eg, L Waite and M Gallagher, *The Case for Marriage* (New York, Broadway Books, 2000).

[65] See, eg, C Crawford, A Goodman, E Greaves and R Joyce, *Cohabitation, Marriage, Relationship Stability and Child Outcomes: An Update*, IFS Commentary C114 (London, Institute for Fiscal Studies, 2011) 29–30.

[66] See, eg, J Eekelaar, 'Why People Marry: The Many Faces of an Institution' (2007) 41 *Family Law Quarterly* 413.

[67] These include ethnicity, immigration status, religion, history of care proceeding, whether one's parents were separated, educational qualifications, occupational status and household income.

[68] Crawford, Goodman, Greaves and Joyce, *Cohabitation, Marriage, Relationship Stability and Child Outcomes*.

[69] Ibid, 33.

[70] J Eekelaar and M Maclean, 'Marriage and the Moral Bases of Personal Relationships' (2004) 31 *Journal of Law and Society* 510, 537.

more complex than that. There are two aspects to that complexity which are of especial significance here:

- the general population may have only a vague, partial or inaccurate understanding of the legal consequences of being in different types of adult relationship;
- the legal consequences of a particular form of relationship will usually be only one of several guiding reasons which apply when people are deciding what to do in their personal lives.

The first of these points is readily illustrated by looking at the idea of 'common law marriage', discussed in Box 4.6.

Box 4.6: The myth of the 'common law marriage'

According to consistent findings from nationally representative surveys,[71] more than half of people believe that if two people live together for a certain period of time (2 years is the usual view), then the law will treat them for all purposes as if they were formally married. Despite there being no historical justification for this view,[72] people seem to rely on advice given by friends and family, and rarely consult a lawyer.[73] In one study, even amongst couples who were shortly going to marry, more than 40% thought that their legal position would be unchanged by virtue of being married.[74] A government information campaign seemed to have relatively modest effects on people's understanding of the issues or, more importantly, their behaviour.[75]

People's understanding of the legal consequences of being in any particular form of intimate adult relationship is consequently a rather complex factor when thinking about their motivations for their behaviour. The accuracy of people's perceptions of the law varies hugely and, seemingly regardless of this fact, 'in most cases people's perceptions of the legal consequences had no impact on their decision to cohabit or marry'.[76]

So what factors are relevant when people are organising their personal lives? In a qualitative study of married and unmarried couples, John Eekelaar

---

[71] See, eg, A Barlow, C Burgoyne, E Clery and J Smithson 'Cohabitation and the Law: Myths, Money and the Media' in A Park, J Curtice, K Thomson, M Phillips, M Johnson and E Clery (eds), *British Social Attitudes: The 24th Report* (London, Sage Publishing, 2008).

[72] See Probert, *Marriage Law and Practice in the Long Eighteenth Century*.

[73] A Barlow, 'Regulation of Cohabitation, Changing Family Policies and Social Attitudes: A Discussion of Britain Within Europe' (2004) 26 *Law and Policy* 57, 72–73.

[74] M Hibbs, C Barton and J Beswick, 'Why Marry? Perspectives of the Affianced' [2001] *Family Law* 197.

[75] A Barlow, C Burgoyne and J Smithson, *The Living Together Campaign: An Investigation of its Impact on Legally Aware Cohabitants* (London, HMSO, 2007).

[76] A Barlow, 'Regulation of Cohabitation', 73.

and Mavis Maclean explored various aspects of these questions.[77] Looking first at people who are married, their study revealed three broad categories of 'reason' why people had decided to marry:[78]

- **Pragmatic reasons:** the decision to marry was designed to fulfil an entirely separate objective, such as to make emigration easier or to minimise inheritance tax liability.
- **Conventional reasons:** marriage was seen as part of a social tradition of some kind, whether religious or cultural, and people's decision to marry was designed to conform to that convention.
- **Internal reasons:** here, the aim of marriage was to satisfy some internal goal, such as to mark the 'completion' of the relationship in its mature form, or as a way of strengthening the bond between the partners.

These reasons are not, of course, mutually exclusive, and many people in the study expressed several different reasons for choosing to marry. A range of views was also apparent amongst those who had not married.[79] Some people were motivated by 'strong negative views about marriage', a view which may be associated with a previous bad experience of marriage. As one female participant explained when asked by the researchers why she and her current partner were not married: 'I would never marry again . . . it's like bungee jumping . . . once is enough, it was not a nice time; we're fine now and we don't want to change it'.[80]

By contrast, others simply thought that being married would make no difference to them, either legally or otherwise.[81] The expense of a wedding seemed to be a significant factor for some people,[82] who appeared to equate the wedding day and the marriage. The role of inertia should not be discounted for unmarried couples, who can 'drift' into a long-term relationship with little thought given to the matter.[83] It may also be worth bearing in mind that one partner may have wished to marry but the other did not.

There is consequently a wide range of relevant considerations when trying to explain why people end up in the types of intimate relationships that they do. In their study, Eekelaar and Maclean went on to ask people about their

[77] See Eekelaar and Maclean, 'Marriage and the Moral Bases of Personal Relationships'; M Maclean and J Eekelaar, 'The Obligations and Expectations of Couples Within Families: Three Modes of Interaction' [2004] *Journal of Social Welfare and Family Law* 117; J Eekelaar and M Maclean, 'The Significance of Marriage: Contrasts between White British and Ethnic Minority Groups in England' (2005) 27 *Law and Policy* 379.

[78] Eekelaar and Maclean, 'Marriage and the Moral Bases of Personal Relationships', 518–23.

[79] Ibid, 523–24.

[80] Ibid, 523.

[81] *cf* Box 4.6 on the myth of common law marriage.

[82] A civil marriage ceremony or civil partnership ceremony costs £77 if performed in a registry office. Newspaper reports in 2008 noted that the average price of a wedding had passed £20,000, though research conducted for the website www.compareweddinginsurance.org.uk reported a drop in 2011 (to £15,500), which the site attributed to the effects of the economic downturn.

[83] J Lewis, *The End of Marriage? Individualism and Intimate Relations* (Cheltenham, Edward Elgar Publishing, 2001).

sense of 'obligation' within their relationships.[84] Their purpose was to explore the view that marriage was an example or reinforcement of people accepting the existence of 'obligation' to another, which in turn served the 'goods' of steadfastness and stability.[85] Looking at their data, Eekelaar and Maclean say that they 'are led to wonder whether the sense of obligation can come only from an external source [such as marriage] and therefore to doubt whether marriage is either a necessary or sufficient context for the acceptance of personal obligation'.[86] Indeed, in their study the researchers see little difference between married and unmarried cohabitants, with both groups expressing a range of views, and both groups tending to draw on the same set of sources for their sense of obligation within the relationship.

Maclean and Eekelaar looked at the feelings of obligation in married and unmarried partnerships. Another way to compare the two groups would be to ask about more practical aspects, such as day-to-day financial arrangements within the relationships.[87] As Carolyn Vogler explains:

[T]he different ways in which couples manage money can be seen as a tangible expression of how they resolve the tensions . . . between, on the one hand, individual autonomy versus commitment to the welfare of the couple as a collective unit, and, on the other, equality versus inequalities in power and living standards between individuals within the same relationship.[88]

Any two people can be said to have some 'system' for managing their money. Two strangers usually have a system of keeping their money entirely separate. Friends usually do the same, but they might, for example, have a system of alternating who pays for coffee, or a system of sharing the cost of a holiday. Because financial matters tend to become more intertwined in intimate adult relationships than in other personal interactions (with joint household bills, joint savings, shared childcare costs, and so on), the systems adopted by couples often reflect that interconnection. While every relationship has its own idiosyncrasies, Jan Pahl has suggested that there are five main 'types' of money management system,[89] which Vogler summarises in this way:[90]

1. the *female whole wage* system in which women manage all the money except the man's personal spending money

---

[84] Eekelaar and Maclean, 'Marriage and the Moral Bases of Personal Relationships', 524 ff. See also Maclean and Eekelaar, 'The Obligations and Expectations of Couples Within Families'.
[85] Eekelaar and Maclean, 'Marriage and the Moral Bases of Personal Relationships', 533–34.
[86] Ibid, 534.
[87] For discussion of financial arrangements on relationship breakdown, see ch 6 below, 'Fairness in Family Finances'.
[88] C Vogler, 'Managing Money in Intimate Relationships: Similarities and Differences Between Cohabiting and Married Couples' in J Miles and R Probert (eds), *Sharing Lives, Dividing Assets: An Interdisciplinary Study* (Oxford, Hart Publishing, 2009) 61.
[89] J Pahl, *Money and Marriage* (Basingstoke, Macmillan, 1989).
[90] Vogler, 'Managing Money in Intimate Relationships', 64–65.

2. the *male whole wage/housekeeping allowance* system in which men either manage all the money or men manage most of the money except for the woman's housekeeping allowance
3. the *joint pooling* system in which couples pool all the money, usually in a joint bank account and in theory manage it jointly, each taking money out as needed
4. the *partial pool* in which couples pool some of their income to pay for collective expenditure and keep the rest to spend as they choose, without having to discuss it with the other partner
5. the *independent management* system in which both partners have their own independent incomes which they keep completely separate, and each partner has responsibility for different items of household expenditure.

It can be seen that the first three systems involve the couple behaving as a single economic unit, while the last two involve separate financial arrangements.

In order to investigate the use of these different systems, heterosexual couples were interviewed about their financial arrangements. In the youngest category of participants – those under 35 – Vogler finds interesting results, especially when comparing married and unmarried couples who do not have children.[91] For example, 70 per cent of married respondents reported using one of the first three systems, compared with 39 per cent of unmarried respondents. By contrast, 40 per cent of childless cohabitants use system 4 (partial pooling) and 21 per cent use system 5 (independent management) compared with 20 per cent and 10 per cent respectively for married couples without children.[92]

However, if the couple has children, these differences become far less pronounced. Indeed, in Vogler's study the differences between married and unmarried couples if they had children were not statistically significant,[93] meaning that they might have been random rather than indicating any pattern. The presence of children as being a key factor affecting how couples manage their money receives support from work by Carole Burgoyne and Stefanie Sonnenberg.[94] As they note:

> [R]ecent studies of newly married couples suggest that individualised ways of dealing with money are not necessarily confined to cohabitation. Many married couples also start off with an independent management or partial pooling system, although some of these move towards a more collective view of their finances during the first year of marriage.[95] (references omitted)

---

[91] Ibid, 74.

[92] Ibid, 74.

[93] Ibid, 74; see similarly V Elizabeth, 'Managing Money, Managing Coupledom: A Critical Examination of Cohabitants' Money Management Practices' (2001) 49 *Sociological Review* 389, 390.

[94] C Burgoyne and S Sonnenberg, 'Financial Practices in Cohabiting Heterosexual Couples' in J Miles and R Probert (eds), *Sharing Lives, Dividing Assets: An Interdisciplinary Study* (Oxford, Hart Publishing, 2009).

[95] Ibid, 93. See similarly J Pahl, 'Individualisation in Couple Finances: Who Pays for the Children?' (2005) 4 *Social Policy and Society* 381, 384.

However, Burgoyne and Sonnenberg's work allows us to move beyond the 'technical' financial arrangements adopted by a couple and, linking back to our earlier work on couples' feelings of obligation, to think instead about how couples *feel* about their money. As the authors explain, the name on the bank account is not necessarily the key issue: more important may be the way in which the money is viewed or, in other words, the 'psychological – or *perceived* – ownership of money'.[96] One consequence of focusing on how people perceive their money is being able to see that 'a joint account may not always mean equal sharing in practice, and that individual accounts may not signify separate financial entities or a lack of commitment'.[97]

CONCLUSIONS

It may be hard to know what conclusions to draw from these studies. Unmarried cohabitants tend to keep their financial affairs more separate – at least on paper – than married couples; but if there are children involved then these differences often disappear. Moreover, although there are differences, it is also true that a significant number of married couples keep their finances at least partially separate, especially in the early years of marriage.

One possibility is that the differences being seen here are not about married versus unmarried couples at all, but in fact reflect a generational change in attitude: the prevailing views of one generation about how to manage money in intimate relationships is giving way to a new, more individualised approach of a new cohort.[98] In this new model, money is kept quite separate in the early years of the relationship and becomes more shared over time, especially if the couple has children – and a similar pattern is seen whether the partners have married or not (though, because marriage is associated with longer and more stable relationships,[99] spouses may be more likely than cohabitants to develop a sharing system).

Such a finding might lend strength to the caution expressed by Eekelaar and Maclean about the claim that the mere fact of marriage, without taking into account the surrounding factors, is uniquely good for society.[100] It might be suggested that relationships which are *like* marriages, whether they in fact include a marriage ceremony or not, tend to produce similar goods and

---

[96] Burgoyne and Sonnenberg, 'Financial Practices in Cohabiting Heterosexual Couples', 100.
[97] Ibid, 103.
[98] Ibid, 105.
[99] Crawford, Goodman, Greaves and Joyce, *Cohabitation, Marriage, Relationship Stability and Child Outcomes*.
[100] Eekelaar and Maclean, 'Marriage and the Moral Bases of Personal Relationships', 537.

benefits to society, and to develop and be seen by the people in them in similar ways. If this is true, what might be the consequences for family law and social policy? In particular, what place should marriage be given in our law and culture? The next chapter focuses around the idea of marriage, and asks fundamental questions about what marriage is and how the law constructs different aspects of marriage.

5

The Meanings of Marriage

Key Questions

- What is a marriage/civil partnership?
- Is marriage/civil partnership a state-regulated status or a private contract between the two parties?
- If marriage/civil partnership is seen as a contract, to what extent are the parties able to change the terms of that contract?

In the last chapter, we looked at the law's regulation of intimate adult relationships, and observed that marriage continues to hold a special place despite the increasingly varied ways in which people live their lives.[1] One of the complexities of this view is simply that the 'idea of marriage' may be somewhat elusive – is my idea the same as yours? Whose version of marriage should we choose? Is the idea of 'same-sex marriage' a contradiction in terms or, conversely, is it so obvious that 'marriage' could be either a heterosexual or a homosexual partnership that it is otiose to add the adjective 'same-sex'?

In order to understand these questions a little further, this chapter explores some possible ideas about marriage itself. As throughout this book, references to marriage include civil partnership unless otherwise indicated, though whether they are truly the same or not is a debate for another day![2] To help

---

[1] See ch 4 above, 'Regulating Adult Relationships'.

[2] It might be said that the existence of a separate legal regime for same-sex couples implies that one of two things is happening. One possibility is that there is a *legal difference* between marriage and civil partnership, in which case one group (almost undoubtedly same-sex couples, rather than opposite-sex couples) is being discriminated against in law. While there are small legal differences, they may be sufficiently small to dismiss this option. The more likely possibility is that the only difference is in the name, and that two *different but equal* systems are in operation. But this too is discrimination: *cf* the US Supreme Court's reasoning in *Brown v Board of*

with this discussion, the Supreme Court decision in *Radmacher v Granatino* will be used.[3] *Radmacher* was primarily about the weight which a judge should give to an ante-nuptial agreement (commonly referred to as a pre-nup) when making orders about the parties' financial arrangements on or after divorce.[4] Much could be said about that decision. The most obvious questions, about the policy considerations involved in making financial orders after spouses separate, will be discussed in detail in the next chapter.[5] A less direct question coming from *Radmacher* asks what the Supreme Court's decision tells us about the nature and scope of marriage itself, and that is the focus of this chapter. As a starting point, it may be helpful to think a little about the idea of marriage.

THE IDEA OF MARRIAGE

The classic understanding of marriage is taken to come from Lord Penzance's speech in *Hyde v Hyde*: 'marriage, as understood in Christendom, may . . . be defined as the voluntary union for life of one man and one woman to the exclusion of others'.[6] Rebecca Probert has cogently argued that there are reasons to think that Lord Penzance was not intending to provide a conclusive definition of marriage, and that any definition from case law needs to be read in its social, historical and factual context.[7] So, while *Hyde* may still offer a useful starting point, more is needed. The next step is to distinguish, on the one hand, the requirements for entering a legally valid marriage or for terminating a marriage (which are not our focus here) from, on the other hand, the legal consequences of being in a marriage.

In terms of entering and leaving a marriage, there are numerous legal rules. For example, there are restrictions on who is able to marry,[8] as well as on when, where, how, and by whom a marriage ceremony may be performed.[9]

Education of Topeka, 347 US 483 (1954), saying clearly that two institutions which perform the same function but which are separate from one another cannot, by definition, be equal and are, consequently, discriminatory.

  [3] *Radmacher v Granatino* [2010] UKSC 42, [2010] 2 FLR 1900 [hereafter, *Radmacher v Granatino*].
  [4] Matrimonial Causes Act 1973 [hereafter, MCA 1973], ss 23–25.
  [5] See ch 6 below, 'Fairness in Family Finances', text from n 70.
  [6] *Hyde v Hyde* (1866) LR 1 P & D 130 (HL), 133.
  [7] R Probert, '*Hyde v Hyde*: Defining or Defending Marriage?' [2007] *Child and Family Law Quarterly* 322.
  [8] See, eg, Marriage Act 1949, ss 1, 2 and 3; MCA 1973, s 12(c); Civil Partnership Act 2004 [hereafter, CPA 2004] ss 3(1), 4 and 50(1).
  [9] Marriage Act 1949, ss 4 *et seq*; CPA 2004, ss 2 and 5 *et seq*.

Moreover, marriages remain voidable under certain circumstances,[10] and can be terminated by the parties under other circumstances.[11]

Leaving that aside, though, what does it mean to be married? In some ways, the answer is a matter for the individual couple. Whether a marriage carries a religious significance or not, for example, depends on the people involved, and cannot even necessarily be determined according to whether the marriage ceremony was religious or civil.[12] As Martha Fineman explains, marriage can mean

> a legal tie, a symbol of commitment, a privileged sexual affiliation, a relationship of hierarchy and subordination, a means of self-fulfilment, a social construct, a cultural phenomenon, a religious mandate, an economic relationship, the preferred unit for reproduction, a way to ensure against poverty and dependence on the state, a way out of the birth family, the realization of a romantic ideal, a natural or divine connection, a commitment to traditional notions of morality, a desired status that communicates one's sexual desirability to the world, or a purely contractual relationship in which each term is based on bargaining.[13]

As we discussed in more detail in the previous chapter, people have many reasons for marrying or not marrying;[14] but in addition to the parties' internal views of their relationship, there are social consequences of marriage – how a couple is viewed by other people, or treated by other people, in purely social ways – which are hard to gauge. This aspect is particularly tricky to assess, since cohabiting couples (particularly those with children) are often *assumed* to be married whether they in fact are or not. We also saw in the previous chapter that a large number of legal consequences attach to the decision to marry.[15] Our next question might be: why do all these rights and obligations flow from marriage? What does it say about marriage that all these consequences come with it?

THE CONTRACT OF MARRIAGE?

One way to think about this issue is to ask whether marriage is best viewed as being a status, or as a contract between the parties. If marriage is a status,

[10] MCA 1973, s 12; CPA 2004, s 50.
[11] MCA 1973, s 1; CPA 2004, s 44.
[12] Civil partners cannot have any religious service as part of their ceremony: CPA 2004, s 2(5). This prohibition is not affected by s 202 of the Equality Act 2010, which permits civil partnership ceremonies to be conducted on religious premises. It is hard to see why, if a civil partnership is to be celebrated on religious premises, it should not include a religious service as well.
[13] M Fineman, *The Autonomy Myth* (New York, New Press, 2004) 99.
[14] See ch 4 above, 'Regulating Adult Relationships', text from n 79.
[15] See ch 4 above, 'Regulating Adult Relationships', Boxes 4.2 and 4.3.

what does that mean? A status can be described as 'the condition of belonging to a particular class of persons to whom the law assigns certain peculiar legal capacities or incapacities'.[16] In the context of marriage, the status view has a number of consequences:[17]

- unlike commercial contracts (where the terms of that contract are entirely for them to decide, unless there is a statutory restriction or the terms fall foul of public policy), when people marry, their rights and duties are primarily controlled by the law, and cannot be determined by the spouses themselves;
- unlike commercial contracts (which affect only on the parties to the contract[18]), marriage can affect the rights and duties of third parties (such as children, mortgage lenders and pension providers in the event of divorce or a spouse's death) as well as the relationship between each spouse and the state.

However, alongside this view, we can also see that marriage has a contractual aspect. In some jurisdictions, a degree of individual choice has been introduced into marriages. This trend has been particularly evident in some American States, where couples are able to choose between several 'models' of marriage. The differences are particularly evident when looking at how the marriage can be ended, with a range from 'divorce on demand' to so-called 'covenant marriage' under which divorce is available only in the event of adultery or, in some cases, not at all.[19] As Jonathan Herring puts it, '[t]he main argument in favour of this approach is that is provides freedom of choice, that parties should be able to choose to limit their freedom to divorce in order to give deeper commitment to the marriage'.[20]

While English law has not reached this position, it could be suggested that recent developments have started to place greater emphasis on the contractual nature of marriage. Would this be a fair reading of the majority judgment in *Radmacher v Granatino*, for example? Certainly in her dissenting judgment, Lady Hale was concerned about this danger, and explained why she opposed a contractual approach, as seen in the extract in Box 5.1.

---

[16] C Allen, 'Status and Capacity' (1930) 46 *Law Quarterly Review* 277, 288.

[17] See further N Lowe and G Douglas, *Bromley's Family Law*, 10th edn (Oxford, Oxford University Press, 2007) 40.

[18] In limited circumstances, a third party can gain *rights* under the contract, but cannot have *duties* imposed on them by the contract: Contracts (Rights of the Third Parties) Act 1999.

[19] See J Herring *Family Law*, 5th edn (Harlow, Longman, 2011) 127.

[20] Ibid.

Box 5.1: extract from *Radmacher v Granatino* [2010] UKSC 42, [2010] 2 FLR 1900 (Lady Hale)

[132] The issue in this case is simple: what weight should the court hearing a claim for ancillary relief under the Matrimonial Causes Act 1973 give to an agreement entered into between the parties before they got married which purported to determine the result? . . .

[133] The issue may be simple, but underlying it are some profound questions about the nature of marriage in the modern law and the role of the courts in determining it. Marriage is, of course, a contract, in the sense that each party must agree to enter into it and once entered both are bound by its legal consequences. But it is also a status. This means two things. First, the parties are not entirely free to determine all its legal consequences for themselves. They contract into the package which the law of the land lays down. Secondly, their marriage also has legal consequences for other people and for the state. Nowadays there is considerable freedom and flexibility within the marital package but there is an irreducible minimum. This includes a couple's mutual duty to support one another and their children. We have now arrived at a position where the differing roles which either may adopt within the relationship are entitled to equal esteem. The question for us is how far individual couples should be free to re-write that essential feature of the marital relationship as they choose.

While the majority judges were not proposing to see marriage purely as a contract between the two parties, they were concerned to have 'respect for individual autonomy' and so to give effect to the parties' agreement about their financial affairs.[21] While this reasoning has an inherent attraction, it raises concerns from a gender and equality perspective. Drawing on work by David McLellan,[22] Alison Diduck and Felicity Kaganas summarise the argument in the extract given in Box 5.2.

Box 5.2: extract from A Diduck and F Kaganas, *Family Law, Gender and the State*, 3rd edn (Oxford, Hart Publishing, 2012) 328, quoting from D McLellan, 'Contract Marriage: The Way Forward or Dead End?' (1996) 23 *Journal of Law and Society* 234, 241–43

McLellan then goes on to present the argument against contract marriage. Most importantly, he reminds us that it is premised upon a particular view

---

[21] *Radmacher v Granatino*, [78].
[22] D McLellan, 'Contract Marriage: The Way Forward or Dead End?' (1996) 23 *Journal of Law and Society* 234.

of the individual and that individual's relationship with others and with the state: '[I]t is closely connected with the political doctrine of minimal government and the Adam Smithian optimism that some hidden hand will promote universal well-being through the pursuit by each of economic self-interest.' It depoliticises the family by removing it into the private sphere of individual bargains where the stronger still rule, but in a non-regulated way. And finally, it presupposes that the individual bargainers are operating from the proverbial 'level playing field', a presupposition that is belied by the fact that the only women who would be able to negotiate a mutually advantageous relationship with men are those (relatively) few who are economically independent. McLellan, therefore, concludes by cautioning against the contractualisation of marriage.

In addition to these points, there may be some far-reaching practical consequences of seeing marriage as a contract, as Peter Graham Harris, Jonathan Herring and I have pointed out.[23] If the argument of the majority judges in *Radmacher* is convincing,[24] the question is whether the same logic might take us further, and into territory which neither the Supreme Court, nor most people, would want to go.

As we saw, one of the characteristics of marriage is that it is a status, and so consequently many of its legal consequences are determined by the state. As Thorpe J once explained in the High Court:

> The rights and responsibilities of those whose financial affairs are regulated by statute cannot be much influenced by contractual terms which were devised for the control and limitation of standards that are intended to be of universal application throughout our society.[25]

Consequently, spouses are not able to modify most of the statute-based elements of marriage. For example, the MCA 1973 sets out conclusively the circumstances under which divorce is permitted, which means two things:

- people cannot specify before they marry (or afterwards, for that matter) that, for their marriage, adultery will not qualify as evidence of the irretrievable breakdown of the relationship;[26]
- people cannot add to the list of facts which can be proved to found a claim for irretrievable breakdown, such as that if a spouse were to wear a yellow hat, that would be sufficient to initiate divorce proceedings.[27]

---

[23] P Harris, R George and J Herring, 'With This Ring I Thee Wed (Terms and Conditions Apply)' [2011] *Family Law* 367.

[24] See Harris, George and Herring, 'With this Ring I Thee Wed (Terms and Conditions Apply)'; J Herring, P Harris and R George, 'Ante-Nuptial Agreements: Fairness, Equality and Presumptions' (2011) 127 *Law Quarterly Review* 335.

[25] *F v F (Ancillary Relief: Substantial Assets)* [1995] 2 FLR 45 (HC), 66.

[26] In other words, they cannot 'contract out' of MCA 1973, s 1(2)(a).

[27] In other words, they cannot add to the list of facts in MCA 1973, s 1(2).

These restrictions on the availability of divorce are a reflection of the fact that marriage is a state-regulated relationship status, but it seems unlikely that the majority judges in *Radmacher* would say that they show inadequate 'respect for individual autonomy', nor that they are 'patronising and paternalistic' (as the Justices said about restrictions on pre-nups).[28]

While the yellow hat example may seem silly, it illustrates a broader point. The Supreme Court in *Radmacher* concluded that 'autonomy' was a sufficiently important consideration to justify changing the law's approach to pre-nups, which is to say the law's approach to the division of financial resources in the event of divorce. However, unless there is some significant difference between the court's powers over financial arrangements after divorce and its powers to grant a divorce in the first place, it is hard to see where the difference lies between a pre-nup and the yellow hat case. Anyone who would claim that pre-nups are somehow 'special' needs to be able to explain why that is the case, and why it should be. (This seems especially important since both the relevant powers are found under the same statute: why can the parties modify ss 23–25 but not s 1 of the MCA 1973?) If marriage is to be seen in an increasingly contractual light where the parties' autonomy is a powerful consideration,[29] what might this tell us about marriage, and how far can the ideas be pushed? In order to explore these questions, the yellow hat example can be left behind in favour of what might be called *the sunset clause marriage*.

THE SUNSET CLAUSE MARRIAGE

The term 'sunset clause' is usually found in relation to Acts of Parliament, and refers to legislation which, unusually, has a built in termination date – the Act specifies that it will cease to have effect on a given date unless it is specifically renewed by Parliament. The sunset clause marriage works in a similar way: the marriage terminates automatically on a given date (or perhaps when a specified event occurs, such as 'when the youngest child of the marriage turns 18') unless the parties specifically renew it. Since the entire basis of this marriage is in contract, the parties are free to give it whatever length they wish, so long as it is sufficiently clear so as to meet general requirements of contractual certainty. One example would be the annual marriage, which terminates at midnight on December 31st each year unless renewed.[30] Others might prefer a longer term

---

[28] *Radmacher v Granatino*, [78].

[29] For discussion of the rise of individualistic and autonomy-based reasoning in this context, see ch 6 below, 'Fairness in Family Finances', text from n 66.

[30] See C Irvine, 'John Cleese: Marriage Should be Renewed "Like Dog Licence"', *The Telegraph* (31 October 2008).

– five years? The method of renewal ought, logically, also to be a matter for the parties to determine in their contract.[31] For evidential reasons, the renewal might need to be done (or evidenced) in writing – perhaps even with witnesses? – but otherwise the matter is surely one for the parties.

Is it right to say that the sunset clause marriage is essentially the same as the pre-nup case? It seems reasonably clear that many proponents of pre-nups would not support this suggestion, but the question is whether there is a material difference which justifies the court in giving effect to pre-nups but rejecting sunset clauses. A number of arguments could be advanced to explain this distinction, two of which we address here.

A. The 'Apples and Oranges' Argument

Perhaps the most fundamental (and compelling) argument against comparing the sunset clause marriage with a pre-nuptial agreement is that it compares apples and oranges. In other words, using the pre-nups case to justify the sunset clause conflates two essentially different aspects of marriage law. According to this argument, the legal aspects of a marriage should be divided into two categories of rules: the primary rules, which govern the formation and termination of a marriage; and the secondary rules, which govern the substance of a marriage. With this distinction in place, we can readily see that a pre-nup is a contractual alteration of the secondary rules of marriage (ie the post-marriage financial obligations), whereas the sunset clause is a contractual alteration of primary rules (ie the ways in which a marriage can terminate). So, although (limited) alterations to the secondary rules are permitted,[32] alterations to the primary rules are not, and that is why pre-nups are allowed but sunset clauses are not.

The question, then, is whether this argument is conclusive or not. The basic premise, that there is some conceptual difference between rules governing formation/termination and rules governing substance, seems to be right – but does it follow from that point that primary rules are universal and unalterable whereas secondary rules are not? To answer that, there are two angles that might be considered. First, we can look at the nature of the two types of rule to see whether there ought to be any difference between then in this way. Second, we can look at other marriage rules, primary and secondary, because if it turns out *either* that there are alterable primary rules *or* that there are unalterable secondary rules, then the basis of the distinction between pre-nups and sunset clauses falls away.

---

[31] One might see each renewal as a new marriage which must comply with the statutory requirements for entering a marriage. On the other hand, it is not clear that those requirements themselves would not be open to challenge by the parties choosing to contract out of them!

[32] There are limitations on the terms which are permitted under a pre-nup: *Radmacher v Granatino*, [76]–[84].

Starting with the nature of the rules, then, it could be said that the primary rules are more 'fundamental' than the secondary rules, because they govern the limitations of marriage. Just as contract law does not allow the parties to say that a total failure of consideration by A will not give rise to a remedy for B,[33] or to write a contract under which duress is permitted,[34] so family law does not allow parties to contract out of its primary rules for marriages. By contrast, just as the substantive terms of a contract are for the parties to determine (the court will not, for example, enquire as to the adequacy of consideration[35]), so the secondary, substantive rules of marriage may be altered, even though there is a standard set of rules which the parties are taken to accept unless they indicate otherwise.

For this argument to be compelling, its contractual comparisons have to be sound. Marriage is obviously a contract in the sense that it is entered into in much the same way as a contract, and is subject to many of the same basic limitations (such as that the parties must be of sound mind, not be acting under duress, and so on). However, in other, crucial ways, a marriage is not like the standard two-party contract, because the state and/or society has an interest in the contract as well. Entering a marriage is, in some ways, more like joining a club. If you meet the entry requirements, you may become a member, but that does not entitle you to alter the club's rules unilaterally. You can join the club or not, and you can campaign to change the rules of the club whether you are a member or not; but you cannot both be a member of the club and refuse to abide by its current rules. The 'club' of marriage has rules which are set by society, based on society's interests in marriage.[36] The 'club' provides significant benefits to its members;[37] but access to those benefits comes at a cost, and part of that cost is that members must take on the burdens imposed by the club's rules as well. The most significant of those burdens is the obligation of mutual support between spouses and, since post-separation financial regulation is conventionally seen as part of that obligation,[38] it seems odd to allow pre-nups which society (through the court) considers to be unfair,[39] but to say that other aspects of marriage are fundamental and unalterable.

Next, other marriage rules could be considered. The question is whether it is correct to say that primary and secondary rules are inherently different in some way, so as to justify a difference between a pre-nup (valid) and a sunset clause (invalid). The question can be asked either way:

---

[33] *Whincup v Hughes* (1871) LR 6 CP 78 (Court of Common Pleas).

[34] *Universe Tankships Inc of Monrovia v International Transport Workers Federation* [1983] 1 AC 366 (HL); duress makes a contract voidable, rather than void, but the point remains.

[35] *Bolton v Madden* (1873) LR 9 QB 55 (Court of Queen's Bench).

[36] See, eg, J Herring, 'Why Financial Orders on Divorce Should Be Unfair' (2005) 19 *International Journal of Law, Policy and the Family* 218

[37] See ch 4 above, 'Regulating Adult Relationship', Boxes 4.2 and 4.3.

[38] *cf* below, text from n 45.

[39] *Radmacher v Granatino*, [75].

- are all primary rules inherent and unalterable by the parties?
- are all secondary rules flexible and open to modification by the parties?

It is necessary for the answer to both these questions to be 'yes' in order for the primary/secondary distinction to be a satisfactory answer to why pre-nups are valid but sunset clauses not.

However, neither question is very easy to answer. The second question, in particular, is hard to analyse because the situations in which it would be tested rarely arise publicly. The special aspect of post-divorce financial arrangements is, precisely, that they apply once the marriage is over, whereas most marital obligations end on divorce. What happens within marriages is not normally of concern to the law.[40] How might this question be tested? Think about some other secondary rules/obligations of marriage (Boxes 4.2 and 4.3 might help) – can spouses enter into valid agreements to change them? Consider these examples:

- an agreement that the spouses will not live together
- an agreement that all property obtained by either party during the marriage will be owned by A alone during the marriage (but not excluding MCA 1973 ss 23–25)
- an agreement that A alone will be responsible for child-raising, cooking and housework, that both A and B will be employed, and that all other marital rights and duties will be shared equally

A similar problem arises regarding primary rules as well, though there may be ways to think about it. If the primary rules of marriage are about the formation and termination of marriage, questions about *who* is able to marry must be primary rules. It is clear that these rules are not presently open to negotiation or change by couples who do not, for whatever reason, meet the requirements: if A is 12 years old, or if A and B are within the prohibited degrees of relation, or if A and B are not of the appropriate sexes, they are not able to marry, no matter what agreement they reach amongst themselves. However, that is not to say that these primary rules are unchanging and therefore in some way inherent. Until 1967,[41] many States of the USA had legal prohibitions on two people of different races marrying one another.[42] More recently, a Californian law[43] prohibiting marriage between two people of the same sex was held to be unconstitutional by a state court.[44] These examples do not 'prove' anything in relation to couples being able to 'contract out' of

---

[40] *cf* MCA 1973, s 27.

[41] *Loving v Virginia* (1967) 388 US 1, 87 S Ct 1817 (US Supreme Court).

[42] See, eg, Racial Integrity Act 1924 (Virginia). Britain never had race restrictions on marriage, though of course we had – and have – many other restrictions.

[43] Marriage Protection Act 2008 (California, USA).

[44] *Perry v Schwarzenegger* (2010) Civil Case No 09-CV-2292 VRWA (US District Court). A case challenging civil partnership as discriminatory as compared with marriage was rejected by the English High Court: *Wilkinson v Kitzinger* [2006] EWHC 2022 (Fam), [2007] 1 FLR 295.

these primary rules of marriage, and nor are they designed to. However, they might show that the primary rules are not as clear or as firm as they at first appear. Can you think of better ways to test this question?

B. The 'Financial Provisions are Different' Argument:

An alternative explanation[45] of why pre-nups are different from sunset clauses suggests that, rather than *all* secondary rules being different from primary rules, it is in particular the courts' powers over post-divorce finances that are special. This argument claims that, unlike most legal provisions relating to marriage, the basis of the court's powers over a couple's finances is that, by marrying, the parties implicitly agree to make themselves subject to those powers in the event of divorce. On that basis, if the parties enter into an otherwise valid agreement about their financial affairs which indicates that they do not agree to the court having the usual discretion in their case, the moral basis for making a discretionary award disappears.

There are three difficulties with this argument. First, it seems doubtful whether we should accept the idea that divorcing couples are subject to the court's powers over their finances simply because they agreed to be. There are gender and equality questions to consider here,[46] and we might ask whether it is acceptable to see the basis of these powers as mere consent. This issue is explored more fully in the next chapter,[47] but the implications for the delivery of justice in the family context of allowing people to opt out of the public norms attached to fair, non-discriminatory financial arrangements after divorce are significant.[48] The family is not exempt from general principles of justice, and those principles include non-discrimination and the positive promotion of equal chances in life.[49] In particular, justice requires that the burdens of family caring responsibilities be shared fully, and that divorce law protect both adults and children from undue vulnerability.[50]

Secondly, *Radmacher* is clear that the courts retain their discretion when it comes to post-divorce financial arrangements, and therefore that it is the court which sets the limits on what pre-nup terms are acceptable. If the parties were opting out of court power over their finances, why would this residual control remain? In other words, if financial provisions truly are different and exist only because the parties consent to them, why are there any limitations at all?

[45] Thanks to Lucinda Ferguson for this idea, though she made the argument more convincingly than I have managed, and in any case I am not sure whether it is a position that she holds herself.
[46] *Radmacher v Granatino*, [137].
[47] See ch 6 below, 'Fairness in Family Finances', text from n 61.
[48] See also ch 1 above, 'Family Law and Family Justice', text from n 51.
[49] See, eg, J Rawls, *Justice as Fairness: A Restatement* (Cambridge MA, Harvard University Press, 2001).
[50] Ibid, § 4.2 and § 50.3.

Thirdly, it is hard to see why the moral or legal basis of the court's financial powers would be different from all the other legal provisions relating to marriage. It could, perhaps, be suggested that there are public policy reasons for the other provisions of marriage, but not for the financial arrangements. However, insofar as there are compelling public interests at stake in marriage law, it is hard to see why they do not apply to the parties' finances. Financial arrangements reflect broader considerations about equality of contribution to relationships, as Lady Hale explained in *Radmacher*: 'We have now arrived at a position where the differing roles which either [spouse] may adopt within the relationship are entitled to equal esteem. The question for us is how far individual couples should be free to re-write that essential feature of the marital relationship as they choose.'[51]

CONCLUSIONS

There are a number of other arguments which can be made against the sunset clause marriage. Consider, for example, the importance of *the sanctity of marriage*. What does that mean? Does it mean the same to everyone? Can you think of arguments about why a sunset clause marriage might actually promote the sanctity of marriage? Think, for example, about the potential power of a regular renewal of vows. What other arguments might there be for or against marriages of this kind?

More to the point, all of this is not to say that the law should embrace sunset clause marriages. Far from it. I do not accept most of these arguments. The point is only this: the sunset clause marriage may not be as many steps removed from the Supreme Court majority's decision in *Radmacher* as it may at first appear, and there are some hard questions which arise from that decision about the nature of marriage. If one does not agree with the Supreme Court's view that pre-nups should be presumptively 'given effect to' by the courts,[52] then there is no need to answer these challenges, because marriage can be seen as a status and a pre-nup as one of many factors – albeit potentially a powerful factor – which the court would consider when making a fair order for post-divorce financial arrangements.[53] It is only those who seek to give pre-nups some kind of prominent status in the law who need to explain what it is that makes financial arrangements different from other aspects of

---

[51] *Radmacher v Granatino*, [133]; see further ch 6 below, 'Fairness in Family Finances'.
[52] *Radmacher v Granatino*, [75].
[53] See *White v White* [2000] 2 FLR 981 (HL); *Miller v Miller, McFarlane v McFarlane* [2006] UKHL 24, [2006] 2 FLR 1186; this issue is discussed further in ch 6 below, 'Fairness in Family Finances'.

marriage, and this chapter has sought to lay out some of the difficulties with finding a convincing explanation.

The focus of this chapter has been on the boundaries of what we mean by marriage. The idea of marriage, in both its legal and its social contexts, is complicated – its boundaries are hard to see, and it is not certain whether those that can be seen are fixed or not. Understanding the legal rights and duties which are actually *consequences* of marriage, rather than one which arise *alongside* marriage (but could arise in other circumstances) is not easy, and the increasingly contractualised understanding of marriage does not help to clarify matters. It is clear that '[m]arriage still counts for something in the law of this country',[54] but less clear what that 'something' is.[55] Similarly unclear is the extent to which the parties can, and should be able to, decide that 'something' for themselves.

Since the key issue which some people seem to want to take control over at the moment is the financial consequences of relationship breakdown, that is the topic of the next chapter. When reading it, the ideas from this chapter should be kept in mind: the way in which the law should approach post-separation financial arrangements depends in large part on what 'vision' of marriage society has. At the same time, after you have read that work you will be in a position to come back and think about the issues in this chapter again. But ask yourself which is cause and which is effect – is there a danger that trying to learn about marriage based on the financial consequences of divorce (rather than deciding on post-divorce financial obligations based on an understanding of the nature of marriage) might allow the tail to wag the dog?

---

[54] *Radmacher v Granatino*, [195].
[55] N Mostyn, 'What Is Marriage? What Should It Be?', online at www.familylawweek.co.uk/site.aspx?i=ed70850.

6

Fairness in Family Finances

Key Questions

- What does 'fairness' mean in the context of post-separation family financial arrangements?
- Are there differences in the meaning of fairness when used to guide the financial arrangements of divorcing spouses compared with separating cohabitants?
- Is the standard of fairness helpful, and if so in what way is it helpful?

When financial issues are being determined after an intimate adult relationship comes to an end, the distinction between married and unmarried couples is of huge significance.[1] Before we look at the differences, though, there are two areas governing financial issues which are common to both married and unmarried couples. These are the financial provisions relating to children, and are summarised in Box 6.1.

For financial issues not related to children, on the other hand, the law provides very different rules for formerly married partners compared with their unmarried counterparts, primarily though the Matrimonial Causes Act 1973.[2] The Act provides the court with a number of important powers, collectively termed financial remedies,[3] which include broad discretionary powers to redistribute property ownership,[4] to reallocate pension payments,[5] and

---

[1] References to 'marriage' and 'divorce' in this chapter should be taken to include civil partnership and dissolution.

[2] For civil partners, see Civil Partnership Act 2004, Schedule 5.

[3] These powers were formally known as 'ancillary relief', the primary relief being the grant of divorce itself.

[4] MCA 1973, s 24.

[5] MCA 1973, s 24B.

Box 6.1: Financial arrangements which can be made regardless of the parents' previous marital status:

1. **Child support payments through the Child Maintenance and Enforcement Commission:**[6] while this system is far from perfect, it benefits huge numbers of children,[7] and – perhaps as importantly – made the idea that parents have an obligation to support their children financially even when the parents are not living together a normal part of society's expectations.[8]

2. **Court orders under Schedule 1 of the Children Act 1989 to benefit children through periodic payments, lump sum money transfers or the transfer of property from one parent to the other:**[9] although the courts have power to make these very significant orders for the benefit of children regardless of the parents' previous marital status, in practice they are rarely called upon to do so.[10] Divorcing spouses rarely have need of the powers under the Children Act 1989, because it is easier to make such provision as part of the general divorce settlement.[11] Separating cohabitants, by contrast, seem not to use these powers because they do not know that they exist.[12]

to order one former partner to pay lump sums or make periodic payments to the other.[13] By contrast, for those who did not marry, any claims have to be brought within the law of property.[14]

However, despite these potentially stark differences between the situations of divorcing spouses and separating cohabitants, there may yet be some threads of

---

[6] Child Maintenance and Other Payments Act 2008; Child Support Acts 1991, 1995 and 2000.

[7] For a useful summary, see J Herring, *Family Law*, 5th edn (Harlow, Longman, 2011) 196–97.

[8] B Fehlberg and M Maclean, 'Child Support Policy in Australia and the United Kingdom' [2009] *International Journal of Law, Policy and the Family* 1, 9.

[9] Children Act 1989, Sch 1.

[10] See, eg, Law Commission, *Cohabitation: The Financial Consequences of Relationship Breakdown*, Consultation Paper No 179 (London, HMSO, 2006) [4.34].

[11] Matrimonial Causes Act 1973 (MCA 1973), s 25(1).

[12] M Maclean, J Eekelaar, J Lewis, S Arthur, S Finch, R Fitzgerald and P Pearson, 'When Cohabiting Parents Separate: Law and Expectations' [2001] *Family Law* 373.

[13] MCA 1973, s 23.

[14] The Family Law (Scotland) Act 2006 introduced a scheme which allows limited financial orders to be made between separated cohabitants; see, eg, F McCarthy, 'Cohabitation: Lessons from North of the Border?' [2011] *Child and Family Law Quarterly* 277. The Law Commission proposed a similar scheme for England and Wales (*Cohabitation: The Financial Consequences of Relationship Breakdown*, Report No 307 (London, HMSO, 2007)), but the government does not intend to pursue those proposals. In both Australia and New Zealand, unmarried cohabitants who fulfil statutory criteria fall within the same financial schemes as married couples: in New Zealand, see the Property (Relationships) Act 1976 and the Family Proceedings Act 1980; much of the Australian legislation is at State level, but see, eg, New South Wales's Property (Relationships) Act 1984 or South Australia's Domestic Partners Property Act 1996.

..iality – or, at least, of apparent commonality. The thread which we will
,iore in this chapter is _fairness_, which has risen in prominence in much of the
judicial rhetoric in cases involving married and unmarried couples alike. We
start by exploring some possible meanings of fairness and then assess the ways
in which the courts have drawn on this idea in recent case law, looking first at
the divorce context and then at cohabitation cases. Finally, the chapter closes
by asking whether the standard of fairness is helpful.

THE MEANINGS OF FAIRNESS

The use of _fairness_ as a central component in family finance disputes came to
the fore in 2000 with the momentous House of Lords decision in _White v
White_.[15] According to Lord Nicholls' judgment, the very purpose of the
court's powers over finances after divorce is 'to enable the court to make fair
financial arrangements'.[16]

Before looking at the applications of fairness in practice, though, it is
worth pausing to ask whether we are able to say anything about the idea of
fairness in general. Is it possible to give any substantive meaning to fairness,
or is Rebecca Bailey-Harris right to say that 'fairness is a concept of such
self-evident generality that its content in the individual case must be largely
dependent on judicial subjectivity'?[17]

One way to think about this question is to return to the discussion of _justice_
introduced in the opening chapter of this book.[18] That analysis drew on work
by John Rawls, for whom fairness is the very core of justice.[19] More particularly, Rawls sees justice as being about a fair system of social cooperation,
where an established social structure regulates 'bargaining advantages' and pre-
vents undue amounts of power accumulating with one person at the expense of
another.[20] The overall aim of this approach is to 'put all citizens in a position to
manage their own affairs on a footing of a suitable degree of social and economic equality'.[21] Discrimination on the basis of gender is specifically prohibited on Rawls' account,[22] and he is clear that the law must take action to ensure

---

[15] _White v White_ [2000] 2 FLR 981 (HL) [hereafter, _White v White_].
[16] _White v White_, 989.
[17] R Bailey-Harris, 'The Paradoxes of Principle and Pragmatism: Ancillary Relief in England
and Wales' [2005] _International Journal of Law, Policy and the Family_ 229, 232.
[18] See ch 1 above, 'Family Law and Family Justice', text from n 51.
[19] J Rawls, _Justice as Fairness: A Restatement_ (Cambridge MA, Harvard University Press,
2001).
[20] Ibid.
[21] Ibid, § 42.3.
[22] Ibid, § 50.4.

that the burdens of raising children (and, one might add, of other caring responsibilities) are divided between the sexes reasonably equally.[23]

Another way to analyse the idea of fairness, used effectively by Alison Diduck, is to draw on a feminist approach and focus on *ways of thinking* about fairness, rather than concentrating solely on looking at the substance of fairness.[24] Diduck's first point is to reject the idea that fairness can be seen as a purely private matter – that is, fairness (only) between the separating partners and their immediate dependants. Instead, fairness should be seen to 'include "public" norms such as equality or non-discrimination, or might locate the parties' claims and circumstances in their social and economic context'.[25] That context includes issues such as:[26]

- the general reduction in the incomes of women and children after separation compared with the general increase in the incomes of men;[27]
- the disproportionately high poverty rate of older women, especially if divorced;[28]
- the disproportionately high poverty rate of lone parents, 90% of whom are women.[29]

Consequently, Diduck argues that it is important to see that 'having a private life' does not mean that there is some isolated 'private sphere' in which private lives are lived, separate from the wider public context.[30] Diduck draws on Nancy Fraser's model of social justice, with involves three domains of justice: the economic, the cultural/symbolic, and the political.[31] A key element is to recognise the social and political aspects of so-called 'individual decisions' about intimate relationships. As Diduck explains, this feminist approach to thinking about fairness 'reinforces the ideas, first, that the source of familial obligations is both social and personal, and second, that obligation arises not only from private individual choices but also from the moral and social conditions within which those choices are expressed' (references omitted).[32]

[23] Ibid, § 4.2.

[24] A Diduck, 'Relationship Fairness' in A Bottomley and S Wong (eds), *Changing Contours of Domestic Life, Family and Law: Caring and Sharing* (Oxford, Hart Publishing, 2009).

[25] Diduck, 'Relationship Fairness', 71. See similarly J Herring, 'Why Financial Orders on Divorce Should Be Unfair' [2005] *International Journal of Law, Policy and the Family* 218.

[26] Diduck, 'Relationship Fairness', 72.

[27] G Douglas and A Perry, 'How Parents Cope Financially on Separation and Divorce: Implications for the Future of Ancillary Relief' [2001] *Child and Family Law Quarterly* 67.

[28] See A Diduck and F Kaganas, *Family Law, Gender and the State*, 3rd edn (Oxford, Hart Publishing, 2012) 237–46; D Price 'Pension Accumulation and Gendered Household Structures' in J Miles and R Probert (eds), *Sharing Lives, Dividing Assets: An Interdisciplinary Study* (Oxford, Hart Publishing, 2009).

[29] *ESRC Society Today: Welfare and Single Parenthood in the UK*, Fact Sheet, 2005.

[30] Diduck, 'Relationship Fairness', 74; *cf* Rawls, *Justice as Fairness*, § 50.4: 'If the so-called private sphere is a place alleged to be exempt from justice, then there is no such thing'.

[31] Diduck, 'Relationship Fairness', 75–78, citing N Fraser, 'Reframing Justice in a Globalising World' (2005) 36 *New Left Review* 69 and N Fraser, 'Mapping the Feminist Imagination: From Redistribution to Recognition to Representation' (2005) 12 *Constellation* 295.

[32] Diduck, 'Relationship Fairness', 74.

ᴸo summarise, then, the key elements of fairness might be:

- non-discrimination;[33]
- a degree of real autonomy for all individuals, which relies upon reasonable social and economic equality;
- regulation of 'bargaining advantages' to protect the weak against undue use of power by the strong.

Moreover, context is crucial. People do not make entirely private, personal choices about the organisation of their intimate lives: they are affected by their circumstances, resources, available options and so on.

With these thoughts in mind, we can now turn to see how the courts use the language of fairness in their analysis of financial orders when spouses divorce and cohabitants separate.

THE APPLICATION OF FAIRNESS TO DIVORCING SPOUSES

Starting, then, with financial orders in the case of divorce, the fairness rhetoric has to be applied within a statutory context. The MCA 1973 provides the relevant powers,[34] and gives the court some guidance about how to use those powers. The court is instructed to 'have regard to all the circumstances of the case', with first consideration being to the welfare of any minor child of the family.[35] There then follows a list of eight further factors to which 'the court shall in particular have regard', which are set out in Box 6.2.

Box 6.2: The factors listed in the Matrimonial Causes Act 1973, s 25(2):

(a) the income, earning capacity, property and other financial resources which each of the parties to the marriage has or is likely to have in the foreseeable future, including in the case of earning capacity any increase in that capacity which it would in the opinion of the court be reasonable to expect a party to the marriage to take steps to acquire;

(b) the financial needs, obligations and responsibilities which each of the parties to the marriage has or is likely to have in the foreseeable future;

---

[33] By 'non-discrimination', we mean 'an absence of impermissible discrimination': on the difference between permissible and impermissible discrimination, see J Gardner, 'On the Ground of Her Sex(uality)' (1998) 18 *Oxford Journal of Legal Studies* 167.

[34] MCA 1973, ss 23, 24, 24A and 24B.

[35] MCA 1973, s 25(1).

(c) the standard of living enjoyed by the family before the breakdown of the marriage;

(d) the age of each party to the marriage and the duration of the marriage;

(e) any physical or mental disability of either of the parties to the marriage;

(f) the contributions which each of the parties has made or is likely in the foreseeable future to make to the welfare of the family, including any contribution by looking after the home or caring for the family;

(g) the conduct of each of the parties, if that conduct is such that it would in the opinion of the court be inequitable to disregard it;

(h) in the case of proceedings for divorce or nullity of marriage, the value to each of the parties to the marriage of any benefit which, by reason to the dissolution or annulment of the marriage, that party will lose the chance of acquiring.

Peter Graham Harris has described this list of considerations as 'little more than a rag-bag of Parliamentary anxieties and statements of the obvious'.[36] Moreover, it is to be noted that s 25(2) is merely a list of highlighted factors, and in no way fetters consideration of other, unlisted, considerations. In part, this broad approach is probably inevitable, given the diversity of views on what marriage should be and the diversity of ways in which marriages are lived in fact.[37]

However, while there is clearly need for care when attempting to apply any general principles to particular cases, it is still possible to look at some overall trends and at those general principles themselves. Diduck has provided an insightful analysis of changing judicial language in ancillary relief cases from 1994 to 2009.[38] This work is useful for our analysis, and a brief summary of the pre-2000 case law, given in Box 6.3, will help to contextualise the discussion which follows.

Box 6.3: Judicial approaches to ancillary relief in the 1990s, summarised from A Diduck, 'What Is Family Law For?' [2011] *Current Legal Problems* 1.

• **The mid 1990s:** court judgments were typically in paternalistic/ welfarist language, which 'reinforced the values and obligations of the traditional patriarchal family'.[39] Courts assumed that one spouse (usually the husband) was the main wage-earner, while the other spouse

---

[36] P Harris, 'The Miller Paradoxes' [2008] *Family Law* 1096, 1097.
[37] See generally ch 4 above, 'Regulating Adult Relationships'.
[38] A Diduck, 'What is Family Law For?' (2011) 64 *Current Legal Problems* 1.
[39] Diduck, 'What is Family Law For?', 6.

(usually the wife) focused on caring for the house and raising children. The husband's marital obligation to support his dependants was, in effect, continued after the divorce with periodic payments alongside any initial property transfer.

- **The late 1990s:** judicial language started to shift towards an equality and rights focus, with wage-earners required 'to "share" what became re-conceived as the "fruits of the marital partnership"'.[40] The key ideas here were non-discrimination, mutuality, right/entitlement and equality, informed by substantively feminist thinking.

It is against this background that the House of Lords came to hear *White v White* in the autumn of 2000. *White* had the effect of 'dramatically shifting the discourse' of ancillary relief cases:[41] equality, sharing and non-discrimination were now given centre stage, and the entire discourse was couched in the language of fairness.

Giving the leading judgment in *White*, Lord Nicholls recognised that while the aim might be for a fair outcome, the meaning of a fair order would vary depending on the circumstances of the particular case:

> Features which are important when assessing fairness differ in each case. And, sometimes, different minds can reach different conclusions on what fairness requires. Then fairness, like beauty, lies in the eye of the beholder.[42]

However, despite fairness being a flexible concept, Lord Nicholls attempted to give some guidance about what it means to say that all the circumstances of a case need to be considered when judging a fair outcome:

> [T]here is one principle of universal application which can be stated with confidence. In seeking to achieve a fair outcome, there is no place for discrimination between husband and wife and their respective roles. . . . [W]hatever the division of labour chosen by the husband and wife, or forced upon them by circumstances, fairness requires that this should not prejudice or advantage either party when considering . . . the parties' contributions.[43]

This non-discrimination principle was seen by many commentators as the truly significant part of *White*,[44] and can be seen to conform with the first aspect of fairness identified in the previous section of this chapter.[45] In particular, it was suggested that Lord Nicholls' explanation of non-discrimination might move the law of financial remedies towards a substantive version of

---

[40] Diduck, 'What is Family Law For?', 7.

[41] Diduck, 'What is Family Law For?', 14.

[42] *White v White*, 983–84.

[43] *White v White*, 989.

[44] See, eg, Bailey-Harris, 'The Paradoxes of Principle and Pragmatism', 232–33; A Diduck, 'Fairness and Justice for All? The House of Lords in White v White' (2001) 9 *Feminist Legal Studies* 173.

[45] Above, text at n 33.

equality 'which recognises the advantages and disadvantages that arise from adopting particular marital roles'.[46]

However, this vision of equality was met with somewhat mixed reactions, and there followed a period which Diduck describes as involving 'discursive uncertainty' and a number of conflicting ideas 'jostling for dominance'.[47] Perhaps in part for this reason, the House of Lords returned to the issue of financial remedies in May 2006 in *Miller; McFarlane*,[48] with two main judgments given by Lord Nicholls and Lady Hale.

Lord Nicholls started by reiterating his core theme from *White*:

> Discrimination is the antithesis of fairness. In assessing the parties' contributions to the family there should be no bias in favour of the money-earner and against the home-maker and the childcarer. This is a principle of universal application. It is applicable to all marriages.[49]

In similar vein, Lady Hale suggested that '[t]he ultimate objective is to give each party an equal start on the road to independent living'.[50] Both judgments then outline three 'strands' which are relevant to an assessment of fairness:

- need (generously interpreted)
- compensation
- equal sharing

Two issues about these strands will be discussed here. The first is the possibility of 'double-counting' in areas where the different strands might overlap. Joanna Miles has suggested that there may sometimes be no difference between need and compensation, since the two 'will often be coterminous: the applicant's need is a symptom of the fact that he or (more usually) she forewent earning capacity in order to contribute to the welfare of the family through caring for home and children'.[51] However, while there may be *overlap* between these two elements, there is reason to be cautious about saying that they are likely to be 'coterminous'. Miles herself points out that some needs are not caused by anything which would give rise to a claim for compensation;[52] but more significant may be those cases where a claim for compensation would go far beyond any claim for needs.

---

[46] Diduck, 'Fairness and Justice for All?', 177.

[47] Diduck, 'What is Family Law For?', 15.

[48] *Miller v Miller; McFarlane v McFarlane* [2006] UKHL 24, [2006] 2 FLR 1186 [hereafter, *Miller; McFarlane*].

[49] *Miller; McFarlane*, [1].

[50] *Miller; McFarlane*, [144]. Given that Lady Hale sees periodic payments as forming part of this 'road' in many cases, it is clear that former spouses will not always be fully independent of one another even once they are living separately – but independence is the aim at the end of the road.

[51] J Miles, 'Charman v Charman (No 4): Making Sense of Need, Compensation and Equal Sharing After Miller/McFarlane' [2008] *Child and Family Law Quarterly* 378, 389.

[52] J Miles, 'Responsibility in Family Finance and Property Law' in J Bridgeman, H Keating and C Lind (eds), *Regulating Family Responsibilities* (Farnham, Ashgate, 2011) 106.

In law, compensation is generally understood as 'a method of making good a "loss", of replacing something of which a person has been deprived'.[53] While these 'losses' (particularly wages lost as a result of giving up paid employment to care for a home and family) may indeed create needs, there is no reason to think that meeting those needs will be adequate compensation for the losses incurred. The relationship between need and compensation is illustrated in Box 6.4.

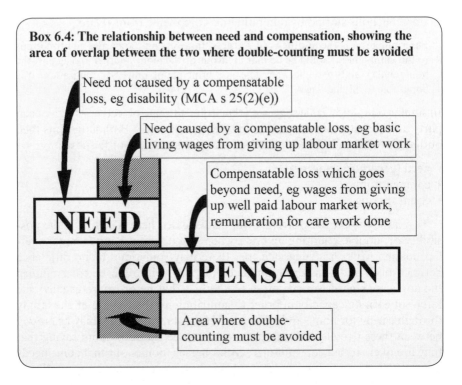

Box 6.4: The relationship between need and compensation, showing the area of overlap between the two where double-counting must be avoided

Need not caused by a compensatable loss, eg disability (MCA s 25(2)(e))

Need caused by a compensatable loss, eg basic living wages from giving up labour market work

Compensatable loss which goes beyond need, eg wages from giving up well paid labour market work, remuneration for care work done

NEED

COMPENSATION

Area where double-counting must be avoided

So, while it is important not to count the same aspect more than once, it is equally important to see that:

• needs may be unconnected to a compensatable loss; and
• compensation may be due for losses which go far beyond needs.

Consequently, it seems right to retain these as separate strands.

The second potential difficulty in having separate strands of fairness is in knowing how the process works when applying the three principles to a particular case.[54] In *Miller; McFarlane*, the House of Lords considered that there

---

[53] P Cane, *Atiyah's Accidents, Compensation and the Law*, 7th edn (Cambridge, Cambridge University Press, 2006) 4.

[54] See, eg, E Cooke, 'Miller/McFarlane: Law in Search of Discrimination' [2007] *Child and Family Law Quarterly* 98; Miles, 'Charman v Charman (No 4)'.

would be no universal rule 'about whether one starts with equal sharing the departs if need or compensation supply a reason to do so, or whether one starts with need and compensation and shares the balance'.[55] However, the approach adopted may significantly affect the outcome reached, as Miles explains with a simplified example using need and equal sharing, as summarised in Box 6.5.[56]

Box 6.5: Simplified model showing the difference between i) meeting needs and then sharing surplus equally and ii) sharing equally unless needs requires otherwise

Total asset pool: 200 units

Needs of party A: 30 units   Needs of party B: 70 units

Approach 1: Meet needs and then share surplus equally

From the 200-unit pot, deduct 30 for A's needs and 70 for B's needs. That leaves 100 units which are split equally, giving an additional 50 to each. Consequently:

A receives 80 units   B receives 120 units

Approach 2: Share equally and then modify if need requires a different outcome

The 200-unit pot is split equally, giving 100 each. If either party has needs of more than 100 units, the split should be changed – but clearly that is not the case here, since both parties' needs are less than 100 units. Consequently:

A receives 100 units   B receives 100 units

These two approaches produce quite different outcomes, and there is judicial support for both. The idea of sharing any surplus only after compensation and need have been met receives some support from *Miller; McFarlane*. Lord Nicholls pointed out that in many everyday cases the process will never go beyond an assessment of needs.[57] While recognising that, in some cases, an assessment of compensation and then sharing will subsume any requirement to look at need separately, his Lordship said clearly that '[i]n some cases provision for the financial needs may be more fairly assessed first along with compensation and the sharing entitlement applied only to the residue of the assets'.[58] By

---

[55] *Miller; McFarlane*, [144] and similarly [29].
[56] Miles, 'Charman v Charman (No 4)', 389.
[57] *Miller; McFarlane*, [12].
[58] *Miller; McFarlane*, [29]; see similarly Lady Hale at [144].

contrast, an approach of sharing equally unless need or compensation requires a different outcome was preferred by the Court of Appeal in *Charman v Charman*.[59] Sir Mark Potter P noted that, at least in big money cases, 'it is probable that the sharing, whether equal or occasionally unequal, will cater automatically for needs';[60] consequently, everything would be shared equally unless there was good reason otherwise.

Returning to fairness, though, there are reasons to prefer the first approach to the second. Favouring equal division of assets sounds instinctively 'fair', but it removes the contextual reality from cases and assumes that formal equality satisfies the demand for a fair outcome. In Box 6.6, we adapt the model which Miles suggests,[61] but now adding a compensation element and some context to show why this matters.

Box 6.6: Simplified model showing the difference between i) meeting needs, compensating losses and then sharing surplus equally and ii) sharing equally unless needs or compensation require otherwise

Total asset pool: 200 units

Needs of party A: 30 units   Needs of party B: 70 units

Compensation owed to party A: Compensation owed to party B:
0 units   30 units

Context:

B has greater needs than A. One reason why this might be so is because B is providing most of the day-to-day care for their children, and so consequently needs more housing and more resources to pay for food, clothes, and so on. A is owed no compensation whereas B requires compensation of 30 units. This might reflect B's lost employment prospects (separate from her needs), as well as a degree of remuneration for her care work of the home and children, both past and future.

Approach 1: Meet needs, compensate losses and then share surplus equally

A gets 30 units for his needs and 0 as compensation (total 30), while B gets 70 units for her needs and 30 as compensation (total 100). That leaves 70 units in the pot to be divided equally, giving each a further 35 units. Consequently:

A receives 65 units   B receives 135 units

---

[59] *Charman v Charman (No 4)* [2007] EWCA Civ 503, [2007] 1 FLR 1246.
[60] Ibid, [77(c)].
[61] Miles, 'Charman v Charman (No 4)', 389.

Approach 2: Share equally and then modify if need or compensation require a different outcome

The 200-unit pot is divided equally giving 100 units each. A's needs of 30 units are clearly met, and no compensation is due. B's needs of 70 units plus compensation due of 30 units total 100 units, which is what she is gets under the equal division. Consequently, there is no need to modify the equal division outcome, so:

A receives 100 units   B receives 100 units

On approach 2 (*Charman*), both parties end up with 100 units. On approach 1 (*Miller; McFarlane*), A gets 65 units whereas B get 135 units. It is important to see past the superficial attraction of 'equality' to understand why the unequal split is the fair result. The reason is simple: equal division removes all context from the case. There are at least two ways in which this is important.

First, looking at the reason why B should be compensated and why her needs are greater, it is likely that her on-going earning capacity from labour market work has been decreased – perhaps very significantly – over a number of years. The different future earning capacities of A and B will massively affect their living standards and vulnerability to poverty.[62] Secondly, if all assets are divided equally, then once B's needs have been met (much of which relate to the parties' children, remember) and once she has been compensated for the losses which she accepted for the family's overall wellbeing, she is receiving nothing extra at all; the entirety of the surplus assets would go to A, leaving him with 70 extra units after his needs have been met. What possible justification could there be for this outcome? The only answer would be that financial contributions count for more than caring contributions, and we know (both from general principles[63] and from *White* and *Miller; McFarlane*) that this kind of discrimination between different types of contribution to the family's wellbeing should be considered illegitimate.

The key difference between these approaches is their awareness of social and economic context. As Diduck explains, former spouses' choices need to be considered in context, and not taken in the abstract.[64] This approach allows a truly non-discriminatory fair outcome to be reached, while also allowing power dynamics to be considered. One party (usually the man in a heterosexual relationship) will often have greater control over financial assets;[65] fairness demands that these power dynamics be acknowledged and

---

[62] See above, nn 26–29.

[63] See, eg, Rawls, *Justice as Fairness*, discussed above at nn 18–23 and ch 1 above, 'Family Law and Family Justice', text from n 51.

[64] Diduck, 'What is Family Law For?', 20.

[65] See generally J Eekelaar, 'Family Justice: Ideal or Illusion?' (1995) 48(2) *Current Legal Problems* 191, 210.

regulated by the law,[66] and the *Miller; McFarlane* analysis allows this to be done.

However, cases since *Miller; McFarlane* suggest that this discourse is no longer dominating judicial thinking about ancillary relief cases. Diduck shows in her work that, although the terms *fairness, equality* and *non-discrimination* remain in common use, the discourse has become 'infused also with the language of individualism, autonomy and choice'.[67] In particular, 'choices' are now being constructed as entirely personal (individual) decisions and as expressions of autonomy which therefore automatically deserve judicial support without being subjected to the tempering effect of social (or even family) context, public equality or justice.[68]

Many examples could be given of this trend,[69] but the most blatant and potentially far-reaching is the judgment of the majority of the Supreme Court in *Radmacher v Granatino*,[70] which was about the appropriate weight to be given to an ante-nuptial agreement (commonly called a pre-nup). We now consider in detail some of the implications of *Radmacher* for understanding what the courts mean by fair financial outcomes after divorce.

Before *Radmacher*, English law allowed a judge to give consideration to the existence of a pre-nup, but that agreement was 'but one factor in the process'.[71] Now, however, courts are to give greater weight to the terms of the pre-nup, as shown by the summary given by the majority judges in the Supreme Court:

> The court should give effect to a nuptial agreement that is freely entered into by each party with a full appreciation of its implications unless in the circumstances prevailing it would not be fair to hold the parties to their agreement.[72]

It can be seen from this summary that fairness remains a key issue. However, when a pre-nup is present, the judge's task is not to set out to find the fair solution by herself and then modify it because of the pre-nup;[73] rather, the judge's job is to give effect to the pre-nup unless it is unfair. The difference between a judge seeking a fair result, and a litigant seeking to persuade a judge that the presumed result is unfair, is potentially stark. This is particularly so since a pre-nup may legitimately include 'provisions that conflict with what the court would otherwise consider to be the requirements of fairness'.[74]

---

[66] See further ch 1 above, 'Family Law and Family Justice', text from n 66.

[67] Diduck, 'What is Family Law For?', 6.

[68] Diduck, 'What is Family Law For?', 27–28.

[69] See, eg, *S v S (Non-Matrimonial Property: Conduct)* [2006] EWHC 2793 (Fam), [2007] 1 FLR 1496 (Burton J); *H v H* [2007] EWHC 459 (Fam), [2007] 2 FLR 548 (Charles J); *RP v RP* [2006] EWHC 3409 (Fam), [2007] 1 FLR 2105 (Coleridge J); *Charman v Charman (No 4)* [2007] EWCA Civ 503, [2007] 1 FLR 1246 (Potter P, Thorpe and Wilson LJJ). Note that all these judges are men: is that relevant?

[70] *Radmacher v Granatino* [2010] UKSC 42, [2010] 2 FLR 1900 [hereafter, *Radmacher v Granatino*].

[71] See, eg, *K v K (Ancillary Relief: Prenuptial Agreement)* [2003] 1 FLR 120 (HC).

[72] *Radmacher v Granatino*, [75].

[73] cf Lady Hale's dissent in *Radmacher v Granatino*.

[74] *Radmacher v Granatino*, [75].

Moreover, the mere fact that there is a pre-nup 'is capable of altering what is fair'.[75] If that means that two cases, identical apart from the presence or absence of a pre-nup, would be decided differently, then there is no real problem: no one suggests that the court should pretend that there was no agreement at all. However, it might be thought that *Radmacher* goes rather further than that, because pre-nups are to be 'given effect to' unless they are positively unfair. The Justices are 'assuming that the agreement itself is, presumptively, reflective of what is fair. . . . There is a slip, from the agreement *affecting* what is fair, to the agreement *being* what is fair'.[76]

The relationship between a pre-nup and the three strands of fairness – need, compensation and sharing – is a key part of this discourse. Need was given a broad meaning in *Miller; McFarlane*, summarised as 'need (generously interpreted)'.[77] By contrast, need has a strict interpretation under *Radmacher*, since only if the agreement would leave a former spouse in 'a predicament of real need' will it make the outcome unfair.[78]

As to compensation, *Radmacher* was clear that if one partner had looked after home and family while the other built up financial assets, then 'it is likely to be unfair to hold the parties to an agreement that entitles the latter to retain all that he or she has earned'.[79] However, this test is notably not a demand to ensure that a spouse be compensated for losses which she has incurred as a result of these family decisions. Indeed, the majority adopted the individualistic rhetoric seen earlier[80] when discussing compensation on the facts of the case:

> There is no compensation factor in this case. The husband's decision to abandon his lucrative career in the city for the fields of academia was not motivated by the demands of his family, but reflected his own preference.[81]

Compare Lady Hale's analysis of the husband's change of career:

> Most spouses want their partners to be happy – partly, of course, because they love them and partly because it is not much fun living with a miserable person. So, choices are often made for the sake of the overall happiness of the family. The couple may move from the city to the country; they may move to another country; they may adopt a completely different life-style; one of them may give up a well-paid job that she hates for the sake of a less lucrative job that she loves; one may give up a dead-end job to embark upon a new course of study. These sorts of things happen all the time in a relationship. The couple will support one another while they are

---

[75] *Radmacher v Granatino*, [75].
[76] P Harris, R George and J Herring, 'With this Ring I Thee Wed (Terms and Conditions Apply)' [2011] *Family Law* 367, 371.
[77] *Miller; McFarlane*, [144].
[78] *Radmacher v Granatino*, [81].
[79] *Radmacher v Granatino*, [81]. Note that it is only *likely*, rather than *inevitable*, that such an agreement will be unfair.
[80] Above, text at n 69.
[81] *Radmacher v Granatino*, [121].

together. And it may generate a continued need for support once they are apart. Whether this is seen as needs or compensation may not matter very much.[82]

As Diduck notes, Lady Hale's approach 'framed Mr Granatino's choice to leave his job in a contextualized, situated autonomy discourse', rather than the majority's 'discourse of formal equality, gender neutrality and acontextual autonomy'.[83]

Finally, when it comes to the sharing of (surplus) assets, *Radmacher* holds that a pre-nup can entirely remove the obligation to share. So long as minimal needs and compensation are met, the judge should make an order reflecting the terms of the agreement, regardless of what (if any) sharing is proposed.[84] Of course, in small- and medium-money cases, that will not matter much – but then, how many of those cases are going to involve a pre-nup in the first place? The immediate practical consequences are for big-money cases, but more significant may be the messages which *Radmacher* sends out about financial orders after divorce in general.

The position seems to be this: needs, at a basic level, must be met; and losses must be compensated, at least to some extent; but if there are surplus assets once that has been done, it is acceptable for one person to take them all. In other words, it is okay for one former partner to say to the other: 'I will make sure that you are not left in a predicament of real need; and I will give you minimal compensation for the losses you are bearing as a result of our family decisions; but when we come to the leftovers which we built up together over all these years, I am unwilling to share them with you.' *Radmacher* is an explicit judicial endorsement of gender discrimination,[85] undermining the genuinely fair, non-discriminatory approach of *White* and *Miller; McFarlane*. By allowing people to opt out of sharing the fruits of their marriage, *Radmacher* raises serious questions about whether we believe in equality within marriage,[86] and about the meaning of fairness in the context of finances after divorce.

THE APPLICATION OF FAIRNESS TO SEPARATING COHABITANTS

For all the complexity of 'fairness' in the ancillary relief cases, it is at least broadly accepted that fairness is an appropriate standard to use when explain-

---

[82] *Radmacher v Granatino*, [188].

[83] A Diduck, 'Family Law', 27–28.

[84] *Radmacher v Granatino*, [82].

[85] J Herring, P Harris and R George, 'Ante-Nuptial Agreements: Fairness, Equality, and Presumptions' (2011) 127 *Law Quarterly Review* 335, 338.

[86] B Hale, 'Equality and Autonomy in Family Law' [2011] *Journal of Social Welfare and Family Law* 3, 12.

ing legal principles and applying them to individual cases. For unmarried cohabitants,[87] by contrast, the governing principles come from the law of trusts and, in that context, the relevance of 'fairness' is disputed. Some brief legal background is required before moving onto discussion of fairness.

There are two basic ways in which a couple may own property in law – either in joint names (with both partners' names on the legal title) or in the sole name of just one partner. We will call these 'joint-names cases' and 'sole-name cases'. The difference between these cases is important because it is presumed, as a starting point, that the equitable (or beneficial) ownership of the property is the same as the legal title.[88] So, if the property is registered in the joint names of A and B, the presumption is that the parties have a beneficial joint tenancy.[89] If the property is in A's name alone, by contrast, the presumption is that A owns the entirety of the beneficial interest and B owns nothing. These are presumptive starting points and can be rebutted by evidence.

The easiest way for parties to rebut the presumption is with express agreement. Assuming that it complies with the relevant formalities,[90] an express declaration of beneficial interests will be conclusive evidence of how the property is owned.[91] The more complicated question is how the presumption is to be rebutted if there is no express agreement. Two key questions arise:

1. The establishment question: how, if at all, can the parties establish that they intended to own the property differently from the presumptive starting point? In a sole-name case, this is about B showing that she has any beneficial interest in the house at all; in a joint-names case, it is about B showing that she owns more than half the property.
2. The quantification question: if the parties satisfy (1), how does the court quantify the parties' beneficial interests in the property? In other words, how do we decide how much each person owns?

The quantification question is our focus, because that is where the debate about fairness is seen. Unlike the divorce context, there continues to be significant controversy over the use of fairness as a guiding principle at all in these cases. For example, the Court of Appeal in *Stack v Dowden* had focused its attention on finding a fair outcome,[92] but, in the House of Lords, Lady

---

[87] These principles also apply to married couples if there is a property dispute outside the divorce context, such as if there is a default on mortgage payments and the lender seeks to repossess the property.

[88] *Stack v Dowden* [2007] UKHL 17, [2007] 1 FLR 1858, [54]; *Jones v Kernott* [2011] UKSC 53, [2012] 1 FLR 45, [17].

[89] *Stack v Dowden*, n 88 above, [66]; *Jones v Kernott*, n 88 above, [51(1)]. *Beneficial joint tenancy* means that A and B co-own the entirety of the property with no shares or division. If the parties have separate shares in the property, even if the shares are equal, then there is a *beneficial tenancy in common*.

[90] Law of Property Act 1925, s 53.

[91] *Goodman v Gallant* [1986] 1 FLR 513 (CA); *Savill v Goodall* [1993] 1 FLR 755 (CA).

[92] *Stack v Dowden* [2005] EWCA Civ 857, [2005] 2 FLR 739; see also *Oxley v Hiscock* [2004] EWCA Civ 546, [2004] 2 FLR 669.

Hale explained why she considered that the approach should be expressed as a search for the parties intentions:

> First, it emphasises that the search is still for the result which reflects what the parties must, in the light of their conduct, be taken to have intended. Second, therefore, it does not enable the court to abandon that search in favour of the result which the court itself considers fair.[93]

However, at the same time, Lady Hale said that the aim was 'to ascertain the parties' intentions, actual, inferred *or imputed*'(emphasis added).[94] While the meaning given to the word 'impute' is not always consistent, the conventional understanding is that it means an intention 'which is attributed to the parties, even though no such actual intention can be deduced from their actions and statements, and even though they had no such intention'.[95] If the court is allowed to impute intentions to parties then '[i]t is difficult to see how this process can work without the court supplying . . . [an intention which] the court considers to be fair'.[96]

The Supreme Court in *Jones v Kernott* clarified the position: an outcome based on 'fairness' can be imposed as 'a fallback position' if more conventional property law analysis proves fruitless.[97] Consequently, the approach to resolving cohabitants' property disputes can be seen to involve a number of stages, with 'fairness' coming into play explicitly in only a small number of cases which reach the final stage. Box 6.7 contains a summary of the relevant stages.[98]

Box 6.7: Summary of the approach taken to quantifying former cohabitants' beneficial interests in their family home

1. **Presume that beneficial ownership mirrors legal ownership.** So, if the property is in A's name alone, then A has the entire beneficial ownership. If A and B own the property as legal joint tenants, then they are beneficial joint tenants as well.
2. **Search for evidence of a common intention that the beneficial ownership is different from (1).** The easiest evidence will be an express written declaration of the parties' beneficial interests,[99] but many other factors may add up to show that the parties had some intention different from (1).[100]

---

[93] *Stack v Dowden*, n 88 above, [61].
[94] *Stack v Dowden*, n 88 above, [60].
[95] *Stack v Dowden*, n 88 above, [126].
[96] *Jones v Kernott* [2009] EWHC 1713 (Ch), [2010] 1 FLR 38, [31].
[97] *Jones v Kernott*, n 88 above, [47]; the Supreme Court accepted that this was an approach 'which some courts may not welcome'.
[98] This summary is an expanded version of that found in R George, 'Cohabitants' Property Rights: When Is Fair Fair?' [2012] *Cambridge Law Journal* 39.
[99] *Goodman v Gallant*, n 91 above; *Savill v Goodall*, n 91 above.
[100] This evidence must be either expressed or implied, not imputed: *Jones v Kernott*, n 88 above, [51(2)]; *cf* Lord Wilson at [84], suggesting that imputed intentions might suffice at this stage.

(Note that stage (2) seems to require only a negative intention – ie the intention need only be '*not* what was presumed in (1)' – whereas at stage (4) a positive intention will be required, showing was *is* intended. Of course, a positive intention would suffice at stage (2) as well, but only a negative intention is *required*.) If there is no evidence of such an intention, the answer is as (1); if there is such evidence, go to (3).

3. **Ask whether the evidence in (2) is sufficient to justify departing from the starting point in (1).** The key question here is what the word 'sufficient' means. An express agreement is 'sufficient' in all cases, but if there is no such agreement then the answer seems to vary depending on whether it is a sole-name or a joint-names case.

   (a) Sole-name cases: If B can be said to have made any direct financial contribution, no matter how small, to the purchase of the property (either to the initial purchase price or to mortgage payments) then that is definitely sufficient to get through stage (3).[101] Significant building work by B will also be sufficient if it affects the value of the property. It is arguable that indirect financial contributions (such as paying household bills) could suffice as well,[102] though courts have been reluctant to adopt this view. So, to be 'sufficient' in a sole-name case, the evidence needs to show an express agreement or a financial contribution, but – crucially – any financial contribution at all to the purchase price (initially or to the mortgage) will do.

   (b) Joint-names cases: Unlike in sole-name cases, in joint-names cases the parties' financial contributions are not that important: even if B pays all of the money to buy the house and pays the bills, this will not necessarily be sufficient to justify departing from the presumption of a beneficial joint tenancy.[103] Indeed, only 'very unusual' cases will succeed in this task: in joint-names cases, stage (3) involves 'a heavy burden',[104] and trying to convince the court to depart from the presumption in (1) 'is not a task to be lightly embarked upon'.[105] While this point is not entirely clear, it seems that only if the parties do not have a 'materially communal relationship' (in other words, if they do not pool their collective resources for their common good) will a joint-names case succeed at stage (3).[106]

---

[101] *Lloyd's Bank v Rosset* [1990] 2 FLR 155 (HL).
[102] *Stack v Dowden*, n 88 above, [63].
[103] *Fowler v Barron* [2008] EWCA Civ 377, [2008] 2 FLR 831.
[104] *Stack v Dowden*, n 88 above, [33]
[105] *Stack v Dowden*, n 88 above, [68].
[106] *Jones v Kernott*, n 88 above, [21], citing S Gardner, *An Introduction to Land Law*, 2nd edn (Oxford, Hart Publishing, 2009) and S Gardner and K Davidson, 'The Future of Stack v Dowden' (2011) 127 *Law Quarterly Review* 13.

So, applying whichever of these tests is relevant, if the evidence is not 'sufficient' then the answer remains as per the starting point in stage (1); if it is 'sufficient', then the enquiry moves to stage (4).

4. **Ask whether there is evidence, expressed or implied from the parties' whole course of dealing as regards the property, of a common intention as to the proportions in which the property is owned.** At this stage, common intentions are assessed objectively from the parties' conduct, the question being what a reasonable bystander would have understood them to mean.[107] The list of factors which may be relevant here is long: in fact, anything which might shed any light at all on what the parties intended about the property can be considered.[108] If this assessment reveals a common intention as to what the parties' shares in the house should be, then the court will give effect to that intention. (Note that, unlike at stage (2), the evidence now must show a positive intention to share in particular proportions.[109]) However, if 'it is not possible to ascertain by direct evidence or by inference what their actual intention was as to the shares in which they would own the property',[110] then go to stage (5).

5. **Look at the whole course of dealing between the parties as regards the property and decide what proportions are fair in the light of that conduct.** While this stage explicitly involves imposing on the parties an outcome which there is no evidence that they ever actually intended, the process is still built on the facts of the particular case and the same factors as are used at stage (4) are relevant here.[111] The court's job is to decide 'what the parties, as reasonable people, would have thought at the relevant time, [having] regard . . . to their whole course of dealing in relation to the property'.[112] In other words, looking at how the parties behaved in relation to the property, 'each is entitled to that share which the court considers fair'.[113]

As can be seen, then, 'fairness' comes into play in the cohabitation context only rarely, as 'a fallback position' where the presumption in stage (1) is rebutted but the quantification method in stage (4) fails to provide an answer.

---

[107] *Jones v Kernott,* n 88 above, [51(3)].

[108] *Stack v Dowden,* n 88 above, [69].

[109] This is clear from the minority's analysis in *Jones v Kernott*: Lords Kerr and Wilson considered there to be clear evidence that the parties had an intention not to be beneficial joint tenants – a negative intention at stage (2) – but could see no evidence of what the parties actually intended the shares to be – so, no positive intention at stage (4). Consequently, the minority proceeded in their analysis to the 'fairness' approach in stage (5).

[110] *Jones v Kernott,* n 88 above, [51(4)].

[111] *Jones v Kernott,* n 88 above, [51(4)]

[112] *Jones v Kernott,* n 88 above, [33].

[113] *Jones v Kernott,* n 88 above, [68(iv)].

However, it is worth asking how the idea of fairness is being used by the courts in this context. Consider these questions as a starting point:

- Is fairness being used in the cohabitation context in the same way as it is used in the divorce context?
- How does the idea of fairness for cohabitants compare with the general discussion of fairness in the first part of this chapter?

Another way to think about these issues is to compare the explicit use of fairness in stage (5) with the overall effect of the process for quantifying cohabitants' property rights, as summarised in Box 6.6. Most cases will not reach stage (5), remember, so it is worth asking about the overall effect of the law on cohabitants' property. One way of looking at the law, particularly in the light of the apparent differences between sole-name and joint-names cases at stage (3), would be to characterise it as having 'a bias towards finding (partial) shared ownership as the final outcome'.[114] In other words, the suggestion is that the law pushes cohabitants towards shared ownership of their home, by making it relatively easy to rebut the presumption of sole ownership in a sole-name case, but relatively hard to rebut the presumption of equal shared ownership in a joint-names case. Do you think that is right? Consider the example given in Box 6.8.

Box 6.8: Illustration of the push towards shared ownership in the law on cohabitants' property rights

The facts: A and B are in a monogamous relationship and have not married. Two years into their relationship, they have a child and buy a house worth £200,000. They agree that A will continue to work full-time, while B will give up paid work to care for their child. To buy the house, they pay a £20,000 deposit from money which they saved together (90% from A's salary, 10% from B's), and A then funds all the mortgage payments and household bills from his salary. They have no discussions about how the house should be owned. They keep generally separate finances, but their relationship is otherwise 'materially communal'.[115] The relationship breaks down after some years, and the question is how the property is owned.

Case 1 – The house was registered in A's name alone: At stage (1), the starting point would be that A owned the entire beneficial interest in the house. However, at stage (2), B would show that she contributed to the initial purchase price (10% of the deposit), and that this is sufficient evidence at stage (3) to justify departing from the presumed starting point.[116] There is

---

[114] George, 'Cohabitants' Property Rights', 41.
[115] Gardner, *An Introduction to Land Law*, [8.3.7].
[116] *Lloyd's Bank v Rosset* [1990] 2 FLR 155 (HL).

no doubt that B will be held to own a significant part of the beneficial title – she could expect at least 40%, and there seems no reason in principle why she could not get 50%.[117]

Case 2 – The house was registered in the joint names of A and B: At stage (1), the starting point would be that the parties had a beneficial joint tenancy. A's claim at stage (2) to own more than half of the property would be based on his greater financial contribution but, given the other facts of the case and the joint-names registration, it seems unlikely that the court at stage (3) would consider this a sufficient ground for departing from the presumed starting point.[118] The outcome would therefore be that both parties had a 50% share once the property was sold.

If there is a push towards shared ownership for cohabitants, why is the law pursuing that aim? Do you think it is right for the law to do this?

- How does the overall aim of ending up with cohabitants sharing their property relate to the explicit fairness criterion which is used in stage (5) of the analysis?
- How would a push towards sharing in this way in cohabitation cases compare with the use of 'sharing' in divorce cases (where equal sharing is one of the three strands of fairness identified in *Miller; McFarlane*)?

IS FAIRNESS A HELPFUL STANDARD?

Few would contend that a court should set out to find an *unfair* solution to a case. However, without a fuller rationale and explanation of fairness, it is difficult to know how fairness should be applied, what to do when fairness conflicts with some other value, or how to assess the usefulness of fairness for the law. For the most part, these are questions to think about, but the final section of this chapter will introduce one perspective on the final issue, namely whether fairness is a useful tool for the law to draw upon in family finance cases.

We saw in chapter one that there is a view that private family law is a matter of 'personal choices' which the law should leave for individuals to resolve by themselves.[119] The reason why this view should be rejected is the need to

---

[117] See, eg, *Oxley v Hiscock*, n 92 above.
[118] *Fowler v Barron*, n 103 above.
[119] See ch 1 above, 'Family Law and Family Justice', text from n 31.

ensure that justice is done within families.[120] Power dynamics – especially during and after separation – are such that the law needs to regulate people's behaviour so as to ensure (gender) equality and that all citizens are able to manage their affairs on the basis of a reasonable degree of social and economic equality.[121] In other words, in order to ensure that everyone is in a position to make genuinely free choices about their lives, the wrongful exercise of power by one person over another must be constrained by the law.[122] This is why the law is concerned with the financial arrangements of separating couples at all.

However, against that background it is also recognised that enabling people to make their own arrangements is beneficial in many cases.[123] The law therefore has a general stance of encouraging negotiation and settlement, so long as that settlement is within the acceptable framework set out by the law itself.[124] However, given this general aim of promoting settlement, some might say that it is unhelpful for the law to put so much emphasis on a vague and shifting idea like fairness. It might be said that, since the outcome of litigation depends so much on the individual judge's view of what is fair, there is insufficient predictability for the parties (and their advisers) to negotiate towards the 'right' outcome.

This approach has an initial attraction, but there is an alternative view put forward by Peter Graham Harris.[125] According to Harris's argument, the inherent uncertainty of 'fairness' is in itself an incentive for parties to reach negotiated settlements. As he puts it, because the judge is instructed only to find 'a fair outcome', lawyers advise their clients that 'whatever the facts and arguments, the "court may do anything" [and that warning] is a strong incentive for the parties to try and get some control over the risks . . . through negotiating rather than litigating'.[126] This point can be illustrated with two simplified examples, set out in Box 6.9. Keep in mind that these examples ignore many of the incentives involved, such as lawyers' fees and the costs regime; the purpose is to illustrate only the potential difference between fixed and flexible disposal rules.

[120] See ch 1 above, 'Family Law and Family Justice', text from n 51.
[121] Rawls, *Justice as Fairness*, § 40.3.
[122] M Henaghan, 'The Normal Order of Family Law' (2008) 28 *Oxford Journal of Legal Studies* 165, 180.
[123] See, eg, *White v White*, 984.
[124] J Eekelaar, M Maclean and S Beinart, *Family Lawyers: The Divorce Work of Solicitors* (Oxford, Hart Publishing, 2000) 185.
[125] Harris, 'The Miller Paradoxes'.
[126] Ibid, 1100. This point is supported by empirical evidence: see ch 1 above, 'Family Law and Family Justice', text at nn 24–31.

Box 6.9: Illustration of the effects of fixed and flexible rules on case settlement in the family law context

Example 1 – a fixed rule: in the first case, a strict rule about post-separation family finances says that A must pay B £100,000 for each of facts X, Y or Z that are proved, so that if all three are proved then £300,000 is owed. If there was no real doubt about whether X, Y and Z were true, this approach might promote settlement: after all, why pay a lawyer to litigate when the outcome is so clearly fixed? However, in family law matters the facts are rarely clear or undisputed. So, if A has a chance (even a small chance) of showing that X, Y or Z is not true, the strict rule might now encourage litigation, because the potential benefit to A of litigating is greater than the risk. In other words, because each fact offers only a binary choice of outcomes (liable for £100,000 / not liable at all), parties may be incentivised to litigate in the hope of winning these battles. The line of reasonable returns will be different for everyone, but if A had a 20% chance of winning on point X, for example, he might think it worth litigating – if he wins, he saves himself £100,000; and if he loses, he is no worse off than he would have been if he had not litigated.

Example 2 – a flexible rule: in the second case, a flexible rule says that the judge must make an order which is fair, taking into account all the facts of the case including X, Y and Z to the extent which they are relevant, but with no predetermined weight allocated to any one factor, and where the range of fair orders might be limited at between roughly £0 and £300,000. At a pre-trial negotiation, A offers B £100,000, and B demands £200,000. Because the rule places such discretion on the judge, if the parties litigate then the judge's view of what is fair may lead to a result which is either more or less than either of the existing offers. In other words, A may not only have to pay more than he is offering, but in fact pay more than B is asking for at the pre-trial negotiations. For B, on the other hand, litigation may end up with her getting less than she is asking for, but also less than A is offering. Both parties consequently have a strong incentive to settle.

So, if Harris is right, one of the great virtues of fairness in this context is its uncertainty. By telling people to be fair, but not giving too much detail about what that means in practical terms, the courts have promoted private settlements and reasonable negotiation, while preserving the possibility of judicial intervention in cases where an independent body is required to ensure that justice is done.

However, even if we are convinced by this argument, the question remains of whether fairness is nonetheless so uncertain that it cannot effectively secure practical justice in the family finance cases. When even the highest courts are using the term to mean quite contradictory things, one must ask whether clearer guiding principles should be found. That said, though, it is important to keep in mind that, although this chapter has focused on *judicial* statements of principle, it is not really the job of the judges to work out the principles of justice in this context. That task falls to Parliament and, while one might have hoped for more than a 'rag-bag of Parliamentary anxieties and statements of the obvious' as guiding principles[127] (or, indeed, in cohabitation cases, for any guiding principle at all), there is no reason to think that there is any political will to re-enter the fraught territory of divorce law reform. Given Parliament's evident disinterest in resolving these issues, the question to ask ourselves is whether we have done the best that we can within the existing legislative framework.

---

[127] Harris, 'The Miller Paradoxes', 1097.

7

The Values of Welfare

Key Questions

- Why does the law make children's welfare the paramount consideration in court disputes about their upbringing?
- How does the application of the welfare principle relate to the rights
  and interests of people other than the child concerned?
- Is the welfare principle applied consistently in different contexts?

The earliest origins of the welfare principle are hard to trace, but judicial
statements can be found from at least the mid-1870s which link clearly to the
modern law. A good example is a divorce case called *Symington*, where Lord
Cairns LC said:

> Parliament has given the Court the widest and more general discretion, and has
> purposely done so; and I think it must be the duty of the Court to consider all the
> circumstances of the case before it . . . and, above all, it should be the duty of the
> Court to look to the interest of the children.[1]

Just ten years later, the Court of Appeal came close to expressing the welfare principle in its modern form. In denying that there was any absolute rule
involved in deciding the case, Baggallay LJ said that 'all we have to consider
is whether it is established to our satisfaction to be for the benefit of the ward
that the application should be granted'.[2]

In 1925, the welfare principle gained statutory force, with courts instructed
to 'regard the welfare of the infant as the first and paramount consideration'
when deciding questions about custody or upbringing.[3] The formulation 'first

---

[1] *Symington v Symington* (1875) LR 2 Sc & Div 415 (HL), 420.
[2] *Re Callaghan* (1885) LR 28 Ch D 186 (CA), 189.
[3] Guardianship of Infants Act 1925, s 1.

and paramount' was introduced at a relatively late stage of the Parliamentary process: the Bill had originally proposed to make the child's welfare the 'sole consideration'.[4] The amendment was intended specifically to broaden the scope of judicial consideration, as the Lord Chancellor explained during the House of Lords debates:

> [W]e ought not to look solely at the welfare of the infant, because there may be other considerations which affect the welfare of the infant which should be taken into account. After all, the infant is a member of a social unit, the family.[5]

When s 1 of the 1925 Act came to be applied by the courts, it was consequently interpreted in line with these intentions – and, indeed, with the plain words of the Act. In a case often cited as being illustrative of this approach, Eve J looked at a full range of factors when determining a child's place of residence, including citing from a pre-1925 decision which made clear that a blameless parent who was capable of meeting the child's needs had an effective right to have the care of their child.[6] Eve J's decision was upheld on appeal, the Master of the Rolls stating explicitly that s 1 of the 1925 Act contained 'no new law' and instead 'merely enacts the rule which had up to that time been acted upon in the Chancery Division'.[7]

The movement away from seeing the child's welfare as merely the first of many relevant considerations can be seen by the early 1960s,[8] and culminated in the landmark House of Lords decision of *J v C* at the end of that decade.[9] The effect of *J v C* is taken to be that the child's welfare became, in effect, the court's only consideration, with the rights, wishes or interests of others (such as parents or other children) being considered only insofar as they affect the child's welfare.[10]

In its report which led to the Children Act 1989, the Law Commission recommended that the wording of the welfare principle be amended to reflect the *J v C* interpretation more explicitly by stating that 'the welfare of any child likely to be affected by the decision should be the court's only concern'.[11] This change was not adopted, but the word 'first' was dropped, making the child's welfare simply the paramount consideration, as seen in the extract from the 1989 Act set out in Box 7.1.

---

[4] See S Cretney, *Law, Law Reform and the Family* (Oxford, Oxford University Press, 1998) ch 7.

[5] Lord Haldane LC, Hansard, *House of Lords Debates*, vol 58, col 350 (9 July 1924), quoted in Cretney, *Law, Law Reform and the Family*, 177.

[6] *Re Thain* [1926] Ch 767 (Ch), 682.

[7] Ibid, 689.

[8] See, eg, *Re Adoption Application No 41/61* [1963] Ch 315 (CA), 329.

[9] *J v C* [1970] AC 668 (HL).

[10] See, eg, J Herring, *Family Law*, 5th edn (Harlow, Longman, 2011) 417.

[11] Law Commission, *Review of Child Law: Guardianship and Custody*, Report No 172 (London, HMSO, 1988) [hereafter, *Review of Child Law*, Report], [3.14].

> **Box 7.1: extract from the Children Act 1989, s 1(1) – the welfare principle**
>
> When a court determines any question with respect to –
>
> (a) the upbringing of a child; or
> (b) the administration of a child's property or the application of any income arising from it,
>
> the child's welfare shall be the court's paramount consideration.

THE WELFARE CHECKLIST

Before looking at the welfare principle in general, there are things to say about the welfare checklist which was added to the English law as part of the Children Act 1989 on the recommendation of the Law Commission. The checklist is set out in Box 7.2.

> **Box 7.2: extract from the Children Act 1989, s 1(3) – the welfare checklist**
>
> In the circumstances mentioned in subsection (4), a court shall have regard in particular to –
>
> (a) the ascertainable wishes and feelings of the child concerned (considered in the light of his age and understanding);
> (b) his physical, emotional and educational needs;
> (c) the likely effect on him of any change in his circumstances;
> (d) his age, sex, background and any characteristics of his which the court considers relevant;
> (e) any harm which he has suffered or is at risk of suffering;
> (f) how capable each of his parents, and any other person in relation to whom the court considers the question to be relevant, is of meeting his needs;
> (g) the range of powers available to the court under this Act in the proceedings in question.

As it says, the checklist does not apply to all cases which are governed by the welfare principle, but only to those mentioned in the next subsection. Subsection 4 lists disputed s 8 orders, special guardianship orders or care and supervision orders,[12] but judges are advised to regard the checklist as 'a most useful *aide-mémoire*' in other cases as well.[13]

It is important to appreciate the purpose and scope of the checklist, since misunderstanding seems all too easy. The danger can be illustrated with an example from a relocation case. The leading English case on relocation makes clear that one important factor in a judge's assessment of the application will be the effect on a primary carer of refusing the application, because if she will be adversely affected then this factor is likely to be an important factor in assessing the child's welfare.[14] By comparison, a recent draft international document, called the Washington Declaration, suggested an alternative approach to relocation applications which did not mention this consideration at all.[15] In the case of *Re AR (A Child: Relocation)*,[16] Mostyn J considered these rival approaches. His Lordship set out the welfare checklist, and then said this:

> It is noteworthy that while Parliament thought it appropriate to draw particular attention in [point (b) of the checklist] to the emotional needs of the child when making or refusing a s 8 order, it did not think it necessary to make an express statement as to the emotional impact on the parent were an order under s 8 to be made or refused. I doubt that this was an oversight. Perhaps this factor is to be read between the lines of (f). In seemingly relegating [the effect of refusing permission to relocate on the applicant parent] to a status of minor importance it may be remarked that the drafters of the Declaration are in fact mirroring the Parliamentary hierarchy of emphasis.[17]

With respect to the judge, this passage suggests a misunderstanding of the welfare checklist. The description of it as a 'hierarchy of emphasis', in particular, is difficult to reconcile with the Law Commission's intentions in proposing s 1(3). As Lady Hale (who, as a Law Commissioner, was one of the chief architects of the Children Act 1989) has explained extra-judicially, the checklist is intended to be a value-free list of relevant considerations,[18] and there is no indication given in the Act as to what weight any of the factors should have. It is true that the Law Commission referred to the checklist as 'a clear statement of what society considers the most important factors in the welfare of children',[19] but the same paragraph of the Report makes clear that the factors which prove to be significant in any particular case will vary. The intention of setting out the list in this way is simply to 'make clear to all what, as a minimum, would be considered by the court'.[20]

---

[12] Children Act 1989, s 1(4).
[13] *Re B (Change of Surname)* [1996] 1 FLR 791 (CA), 793.
[14] *Payne v Payne* [2001] EWCA Civ 166, [2001] 1 FLR 1052.
[15] Washington Declaration on International Family Relocation 2010. See also ch 3 above, 'International Family Law', text from n 80.
[16] *Re AR (A Child: Relocation)* [2010] EWHC 1346 (Fam), [2010] 2 FLR 1577.
[17] Ibid.
[18] Lady B Hale, 'Relocation', paper presented at the *International Child Abduction, Forced Marriage and Relocation Conference*, London Metropolitan University, July 2010.
[19] Law Commission, *Review of Child Law*, Report, [3.19].
[20] Ibid, [3.18].

It is particularly clear that this non-hierarchical approach was intended by Parliament if one compares similar sections of statutes from other jurisdictions. To give one example, the Australian Family Law Act 1975 (Cth), as amended, contains both 'primary considerations' and 'additional considerations' which guide a judicial assessment of the child's best interests. One of the primary considerations is 'the benefit to the child of having a meaningful relationship with both of the child's parents'.[21] While the assessment of the 'benefit' here is factual, the process demanded by the Act requires judges to consider as the first thing on the list whether promoting a 'meaningful relationship' is in the child's interests. If equal parental responsibility is ordered (which it presumptively will be),[22] there is a further requirement that the judge consider whether the child should spend 'equal time' or, failing that, 'substantial and significant time' with each parent.[23] By comparison with the welfare checklist, these considerations and processes can be seen to be directive, reflecting the law's view that it is presumptively in the child's interests to split his or her time between two households after parental separation.

Returning to *Re AR*, it is also worth commenting on Mostyn J's remark about the welfare checklist not making reference to the effect of making or refusing an order on the parent of the child in question. Again, an understanding of the aims of the checklist make this 'omission' unsurprising. Firstly, the checklist has to be applicable to many types of child case, both in private law and in public law.[24] It would be entirely inappropriate in a child protection case to consider, 'in particular', the effect of making a care or supervision order on the parent of the child allegedly being abused or neglected, rather than focusing the enquiry entirely on the child concerned. In part for this reason, and in part because of the factual differences between, say, a residence order and a specific issue order regarding a medical operation or religious upbringing, the Law Commission excluded any fact-specific considerations:

> [A] statutory checklist is only practicable if it is confined to the major points, leaving others to be formulated elsewhere. If a detailed checklist is provided, it cannot be appropriate to all types of decision and thus separate lists would be needed to deal with each issue.[25]

Consequently, the fact that an issue is not mentioned by the checklist says nothing about whether it is or is not relevant to a particular type of case. The Court of Appeal may well be right to say that, 'in most relocation cases the most crucial assessment and finding for the judge is likely to be the effect of the refusal of the application on the [applicant's] future psychological and emotional stability'.[26] But whether one agrees with the detail of this view or

---

[21] Family Law Act 1975 (Cth), s 60CC.
[22] Ibid, s 61DA.
[23] Ibid, s 65DAA.
[24] Children Act 1989, s 1(4).
[25] Law Commission, *Review of Child Law*, Report, [3.19].
[26] *Payne v Payne* [2001] EWCA Civ 166, [2001] 1 FLR 1052, [32].

not, there is no doubting that the Court of Appeal should be laying down guidelines about how welfare should be assessed in particular classes of case,[27] and the fact that a factor is not mentioned in s 1(3) says only that that factor is not a relevant consideration in *all* cases.

UNDERSTANDING THE WELFARE PRINCIPLE

We saw earlier that the summary version of the welfare principle is that the child's welfare is the court's sole consideration, with anyone else's rights, interests or wishes considered only if they have relevance to the child's welfare.[28] This approach has been subjected to many criticisms, one of which will be addressed here. That criticism is, essentially, that the welfare principle excludes consideration of the interests of people other than the child, such that 'the welfare of the child is . . . the single deciding factor, that is, paramount over, and in fact displacing, all other considerations'.[29] Similarly, it is said that the welfare principle requires the court to focus only on the child,

> regardless of the impact that such a course of action will have on the interest of the child's parents, any other children, or the wider community. Indeed, the principle appears to require the court to make an order which would very slightly improve the welfare of the child even where that would cause a huge level of harm to others.[30]

However, it might be questioned whether these criticisms are quite fair. Various authors make suggestions of ways in which the welfare principle should be changed, or replaced, but might some of the attacks be based on a parody of the welfare principle?

Part of the basis of these criticisms seems to be judicial statements about the relative unimportance of considerations such as the rights of parents. The courts frequently assert, for example, that they are 'concerned with the interests of the mother and the father only in so far as they bear on the welfare of the child'.[31] But is it fair to say that this means that the courts give no weight to the parents' rights in their own regard? The parents' rights are, it is true, being assessed in the context of the child's welfare, but that seems to be a

---

[27] *MK v CK (Relocation: Shared Care Arrangement)* [2011] EWCA Civ 793, [2012] 1 FLR forthcoming, [40].

[28] See, eg, Herring, *Family Law*, 417.

[29] S Choudhry and H Fenwick, 'Taking the Rights of Parents and Children Seriously: Confronting the Welfare Principle Under the Human Rights Act' (2005) 25 *Oxford Journal of Legal Studies* 453, 455.

[30] J Herring, 'Farewell Welfare?' [2005] *Journal of Social Welfare and Family Law* 159, 166.

[31] *Re O (Contact: Imposition of Conditions)* [1995] 2 FLR 124 (CA), 128.

different proposition from saying that the courts assess welfare 'without regard for' the rights, interests or welfare of others.[32]

It might more accurately be said that the welfare principle does not require these rights to be disregarded in their entirety, merely to be disregarded if they are entirely irrelevant to the child's welfare. Consequently, it might be suggested that these considerations are not 'displaced' by welfare,[33] but form part of it. And while the welfare principle might, on occasion, require an outcome which did indeed 'cause a huge level of harm to others',[34] such a solution will be exceptional, because the harm to others – particularly a parent or other family member – will in itself impact adversely on the child, which will be a significant factor to take into account when deciding what is in the child's best interests in the first place.

In *J v C* itself, the House of Lords explained that the welfare principle involved

> a process whereby, when all the relevant facts, relationships, claims and wishes of the parents, risks, choices and other circumstances *are taken into account and weighed*, the course to be followed will be that which is most in the interests of the child's welfare as that term has now to be understood. That is the first consideration because it is of first importance and the paramount consideration because it rules upon or determines the course to be followed. (emphasis added)[35]

The suggestion that the welfare principle requires the child to be viewed in isolation from his or her family and community would seem to ignore the first part of this explanation of the process. Issues like parents' rights are not irrelevant or excluded under the welfare principle; quite the contrary, they may be a very important part of the process of deciding which course is best for the child. In his somewhat neglected summary in *J v C*, Lord MacDermott explained that 'in applying section 1, the rights and wishes of parents, whether unimpeachable or otherwise, must be assessed and weighed in their bearing on the welfare of the child in conjunction with all other factors relevant to that issue'.[36]

J v C remains the leading explanation of the process involved in the welfare principle, and shows that only factors which have *no bearing whatever* on the child's welfare need be discounted. This approach is somehow morphed in some critics' analysis to suggest that welfare is a stand-alone factor, as if the child's welfare were unaffected by those around him or her. Of course some factors will be more important to the child's welfare than others, and part of the court's job is to assess the relevance of each factor – but factors which are of indirect relevance to welfare may still be important in the overall assessment of an individual case.

---

[32]   J Herring, 'The Human Rights Act and the Welfare Principle in Family Law: Conflicting or Complementary?' [1999] *Child and Family Law Quarterly* 223, 225.

[33]   Choudhry and Fenwick, 'Taking the Rights of Parents and Children Seriously', 455.

[34]   Herring, 'Farewell Welfare?', 166.

[35]   *J v C*, n 9 above, 710–11.

[36]   Ibid, 715.

All of this is not to say that there are not convincing arguments that the English courts currently give inadequate attention to the rights and interests of the parties when determining child law disputes.[37] There are also compelling arguments that the welfare principle allows for opaque decision-making because of the inherent indeterminacy of the best interests standard,[38] and allows patriarchal values to be imposed by the court on mothers and children.[39] Similarly, it is pointed out that there can be a 'darker' side to the welfare principle, which John Eekelaar has termed 'welfarism'; this view points out that the welfare principle allows paternalistic outcomes to be imposed on children and families in the name of their interests, where those outcomes promote a particular vision of the socially desirable family.[40] The point here is not to dispute these criticisms, but simply to say that those who want to criticise the welfare principle need to be careful to criticise its reality and not a caricature which fails to do justice to its subtlety.

APPLYING THE WELFARE PRINCIPLE: THE ROLE OF CONTEXT

One reason why the welfare principle has survived so long, and why it is used in so many countries despite such persistent criticism, may be its flexibility. Not only is it a single principle which can be applied to all public and private law child disputes, but the very indeterminacy which is criticised enables judges to take into account whatever peculiarities a case throws up. The process can also, crucially, be developed over time to adapt to changing social conditions. Indeed, this aspect of the welfare principle was noted explicitly in *J v C*. Lord Upjohn quoted from a number of authorities, which he said were

> valuable as showing the gradual development of the law and practice in relation to infants. They have developed, are developing and must, and no doubt will, continue to develop by reflecting and adopting the changing views, as the years go by, of reasonable men and women, the parents of children, on the proper treatment and

[37] See, eg, J Eekelaar, 'Beyond the Welfare Principle' [2002] *Child and Family Law Quarterly* 237; S Harris-Short, 'Family Law and the Human Rights Act 1998: Judicial Restraint or Revolution?' [2005] *Child and Family Law Quarterly* 329; Choudhry and H Fenwick, 'Taking the Rights of Parents and Children Seriously'; S Choudhry and J Herring, *European Human Rights and Family Law* (Oxford, Hart Publishing, 2010).

[38] See, eg, R Mnookin, 'Child-Custody Adjudication: Judicial Functions in the Face of Indeterminacy' (1975) 39 *Law and Contemporary Problems* 226; J Eekelaar, 'The Interests of the Child and the Child's Wishes: The Role of Dynamic Self-Determinism' [1994] *International Journal of Law and the Family* 42; H Reece, 'The Paramountcy Principle: Consensus or Construct?' (1996) 49 *Current Legal Problems* 267.

[39] See, eg, C Smart, *The Ties That Bind: Law, Marriage and the Reproduction of Patriarchal Relations* (London, Routledge & Kegan Paul, 1984).

[40] See, eg, J Eekelaar, *Family Law and Personal Life*, paperback edn (Oxford, Oxford University Press, 2007) 9 ff.

methods of bringing up children; for after all that is the model which the judge must emulate for . . . he must act as the judicial reasonable parent.[41]

These changes over time can be readily illustrated, as can be seen from the examples given in Box 7.3.

Box 7.3: Examples showing reinterpretation of the welfare principle by the English courts over time

- **Children's residence:** As we saw, the welfare principle gained statutory force in 1925.[42] However, before and after the Act entered force, some courts considered that an adulterous mother was generally unsuitable to have the custody of (and even sometimes access to) her child.[43] Stephen Cretney notes that not until the end of the Second World War was it 'fairly generally accepted that the fact that a mother had committed adultery was not necessarily inconsistent with her being a good parent to her children'.[44]

- **Contact with non-resident parents:** It is clear that the English law today will go to considerable lengths to promote contact between a child and a non-resident parent. The Court of Appeal has been clear that, '[w]hatever the difficulties, however scant the prospects of success, the courts must not relent in the pursuit of the restoration of what had been a natural relationship between father and [child]'.[45] This approach is adopted even if contact is opposed by the resident parent.[46] However, looking back it is not difficult to find that this view did not always prevail, and the fact that a resident parent opposed contact was once seen as a significant consideration in deciding whether to order contact or not. In 1981, the President of the Family Division explained that 'stress which would be caused . . . to a custodial parent through the children . . . having access to the other parent is a matter properly to be taken into consideration in relation to the question of whether access

---

[41] *J v C*, n 9 above, 722–23.

[42] Guardianship of Infants Act 1925, s 1.

[43] This thinking can be traced to well before 1925 (see, eg, *Seddon v Seddon* (1862) 2 SW & TR 639, 164 ER 1146 (Court of Probate)) but, a century later, little had changed for some judges: in *Re L (Infants)* [1962] 3 All ER 1 (CA), it was said that '[i]f a wife chooses to leave her husband, for no ground which she chooses to put forward, but because she has a fancy or passion for another man, . . . she must be prepared to take the consequences', meaning the loss of the children. This thinking was finally disapproved in *Re K (Minors) (Children: Care and Control)* [1977] Fam 179 (CA).

[44] S Cretney, *Family Law in the Twentieth Century: A History* (Oxford, Oxford University Press, 2003) 577.

[45] *Re S (Contact: Promoting Relationship with Absent Parent)* [2004] EWCA Civ 18, [2004] 1 FLR 1279, [46].

[46] The exception is if 'the mother's fears, not only for herself but also for the child, are genuinely and rationally held': *Re D (Contact: Reasons for Refusal)* [1997] FLR 48 (CA), 58.

should be granted'.[47] As recently as 1993, the Court
that 'the implacable hostility of a mother towards ʋ
a factor which is capable . . . of supplying a cogent reasʋ
ing from the general principle that a child should grow up in ʋ
ledge of both of his parents'.[48]

However, while this flexibility may account for the welfare principle's sur-
vival through time, it may also create difficulties in an increasingly globalised
family law world.[49] Just as conceptions of welfare change over time, so too they
vary between nations. Many countries use the welfare principle, but one might
wonder whether they all mean the same thing. Eekelaar explains that 'conceptions of children's best interests are strongly rooted in the self-images of world
cultures',[50] while Philip Alston cautions that the 'apparent commonality [of the
welfare principle in different countries] contrasts sharply . . . with the very
diverse interpretations that may be given to the principle in different settings'.[51]

This variation in the interpretation given to the welfare principle can be well
illustrated using research into relocation disputes in the courts of England and
New Zealand.[52] These two countries are often compared by legal scholars
because they share many background factors – the same language, the same
common law system, a similar constitutional set-up, and similar societies and
cultures. Given these commonalities, one might expect an analysis of a child's
welfare in a given case to be more or less the same in both countries. To test
this theory, legal practitioners in the two countries were given an identical
series of short hypothetical case studies involving relocation disputes. There
were 22 participants in each country, made up of trial judges, barristers, solicitors and court welfare advisers, all experienced in relocation disputes. They
were asked to assess which factors were relevant to the case, and what the
outcome was likely to be. Both England and New Zealand base decisions
about relocation on the welfare principle,[53] though the guidance from case law
in the two countries is different.[54] These differences can be seen by looking at

---

[47] *B v A (Illegitimate Children: Access)* (1982) 3 FLR 27 (HC), 32

[48] *Re D (A Minor) (Contact: Mother's Hostility)* [1993] 2 FLR 1 (CA), 7.

[49] See generally ch 3 above, 'International Family Law'.

[50] J Eekelaar, 'The Interests of the Child and the Child's Wishes: The Role of Dynamic Self-
Determinism' [1994] *International Journal of Law and the Family* 42, 57; see also J Eekelaar,
'Children Between Cultures' [2004] *International Journal of Law, Policy and the Family* 178.

[51] P Alston, 'The Best Interests Principle: Towards a Reconciliation of Culture and Human
Rights' [1994] *International Journal of Law and the Family* 1, 5.

[52] R George, 'Reassessing Relocation: A Comparative Analysis of Legal Approaches to
Disputes over Family Migration after Parental Separation in England and New Zealand'
(unpublished DPhil thesis, Oxford University: 2010); some of this work is published in R George,
'Practitioners' Views on Children's Welfare in Relocation Disputes: Comparing Approaches in
England and New Zealand' [2011] *Child and Family Law Quarterly* 178.

[53] Children Act 1989 (England), s 1(1); Care of Children Act 2004 (New Zealand), s 4(1).

[54] *cf Payne v Payne* [2001] EWCA Civ 166, [2001] 1 FLR 1052 and *D v S* [2002] NZFLR 116
(New Zealand Court of Appeal).

one of the hypothetical case studies, which concerns a boy called Tom and which is set out in Box 7.4.[55]

Box 7.4: Tom's case as presented to study participants

Tom's parents separated when he was 2 years old. Now aged 6, Tom lives with his mother. He has always had good contact with his father, which has been increasing since the parents separated and now includes overnight stays once or twice a fortnight. Although the parents' relationship has been reasonably amicable, Tom's father thinks the mother is indifferent about contact, and she has sometimes resisted increases in the amount of contact between Tom and the father. About a year ago, the mother married an American and is 4 months pregnant with their first child. The mother's husband is very keen to return to California to be nearer his family, to make a home there, and because he thinks it will provide better opportunities for his growing family. Tom's mother lived in California for a year when she was a student and strongly supports her husband's desire to move home. The father opposes the move because of the great difficulties of contact and otherwise maintaining his relationship with Tom. He is unconvinced by the mother's plans for webcam chat, thinking it more likely he will be sidelined, given Tom's age and the mother's history of indifference to contact generally. The father points out that the mother and Tom are both happy living in [the United Kingdom/New Zealand], and all of the mother's wider family and support networks are here. He is also worried that the mother was unable to tell him what she would do if Tom did not settle well in the USA. The mother counters that her husband's family will all be nearby if they move, and is worried that her husband would be very resentful if he were stopped from returning home because Tom could not be taken too. She also stresses her role as primary carer and the fact that Tom's father works long hours and is not well placed to care for Tom if she went to America anyway.

Think about the case, and consider Tom's welfare:

• Which factors seem significant in assessing Tom's welfare?
• If you were the judge, would you allow the mother's application to relocate to California?

Both of these questions divided English participants and New Zealand participants. The extracts from participant interviews quoted in Box 7.5 were typical of the two groups, and illustrate the different ways in which a welfare analysis can be used to assess Tom's case.

---

[55] The facts of this case study were based loosely on *Re B (Leave to Remove: Impact of Refusal)* [2004] EWCA Civ 956, [2005] 2 FLR 239.

Box 7.5: extracts from interviews with legal practitioners in England and New Zealand when discussing Tom's case, as set out in Box 7.4

English Barrister

If I am looking at Tom, I would say that there is a strong case here for removal. This boy is likely to go. What are the main factors? Firstly, there is a link to the place that the caring parent is seeking to go to: Californian husband, she lived in California for a year, so it is not a stab in the dark. Secondly, there is quite a strong connection to California because she is married to a Californian, and he has got family there, and he wants to work there, and she has been there for a year. The third factor is that the father in this case is only ever likely to be a contact father: he doesn't look as if it ever going to be a serious candidate for residence. He is having good contact, but it is a contact role, and that it is going to be his role. Fourthly, there is the aspect of the half siblings who is going to California, probably, and no court, I think, would want to separate siblings like that, so that is a significant factor. And the fifth factor is that the boy is very young, so he is actually very transportable because children that age, as long as they are with the person they love, which is their caring parent or their contact father, then they are happy. He would probably slot in very simply in California. So that is a strong case for removal. *Q: The father says that the mother is indifferent about contact – does that have any relevance?* A certain amount of indifference is to be expected in a situation like this. It is not a case of outright hostility. He has been having contact, so it is not as if she's actually stopping him having contact.

New Zealand Judge

I would want to know a lot more about California, more about the schools – more than just the fact that she happens to be married to an American. He is obviously [in New Zealand], so why is he suddenly wanting to go back? I would have to be convinced that they really have got no choice but to do that. Tom's mother lived in California for a year – well, that means nothing really. And of course, if I did eventually say that they could go, it would have to be set up so that Tom could see the father, so there would have to be pretty clear contact responsibilities. You would have to tease out of this business about the mother's lack of enthusiasm about contact, and whether that is genuine or whether the father is just saying that. [The father's] point about the mother's wider family and support networks being here may be a very good point. *Q: The mother says her husband will be resentful if he is not allowed to relocate – does that matter?* Yes, well, he will definitely be giving evidence, just to hear what he has to say about that, but of course that's nothing really – I mean, too bad. I think really he is the least of the issues. . . . I think my gut feeling would be to say no, unless they could convince me otherwise. But, being aware of the fact that the father is not a primary carer, and that they separated when he was two. . . . Mind you, he is still only six. And the father works long hours, which you would really be taking into consideration. There are so many issues to look at, but on those facts, no, Tom wouldn't go.

English Solicitor:

The remarriage, to me, is the key thing. Although she has not got any ties to America, it is clear that her husband has and perhaps it is unsurprising that he wants the child to grow up where he did, and that is the key aspect of it. It is a very standard separated care arrangement, nothing particularly special on that, and then comes the fact that if you say no, what is going to happen to the marriage? I would finish off in the evidence about the effect it would have, particularly on the husband, about how he would feel if he was forced to stay in this country – resentment is bound to come in there. [The father] would try and develop the 'indifferent about contact' bit, and to show that her motivation is going to be to decrease the relationship between Tom and his father, but it would be difficult to give convincing evidence about that because he is not saying that she is obstructing his contact, just that she is not very enthusiastic and imagining him in the witness box saying that, it is not going to come across as a very telling point. The key is going to be: what are the arrangements for Tom to come to this country and for his father to go to America to see him, and how long that would go on for? How are you going to pay for it? [If the case went to trial,] I think the mother would get permission. I think it is reasonably clear that she would. I struggle to see how she wouldn't be able to go. I think it would be sloppy work if she did fail.

New Zealand Solicitor:

The mother's history of indifference to contact - well, she is sunk before she starts. If I was the lawyer for child and I could get proof of that, 'sorry mum, you can't head off and be indifferent towards contact, that's not what it's about: you've got to promote, improve, maintain, and indifference is not enough'. So that's one thing. . . . I'm presuming Tom has a close relationship with his dad. He is a boy and he's six, and he needs his dad. Oh, this is the one where mum has a new boyfriend. He's American, but she is a New Zealander, so she's not going home and there are no mental health issues. She is so indifferent about [contact] – if it's true, I would be really concerned that this will be one of those cases where Tom goes off to America and that will be that. Is there any proof about whether she's able to afford contact? No, it is the indifference – she's not even trying. *Q: what about the mother's husband's resentment?* A: Well, he'll get over it. He should have thought of that before he decided to marry a Kiwi woman. It doesn't tell us what sort of relationship Tom has with the stepfather, but he has got his own father, and his mother's family – they seem to feature prominently here too. I bet his mother's family is very grateful the court turned down the relocation. . . . There are no mental health issues, and no obvious commitment to keeping Tom in contact with dad, so she's not going, no. There are no benefits aside from an un-grumpy stepfather so far as I can see.

The English participants here focused on the importance of the mother's well-being, and of the stability of her new relationship, to Tom's overall welfare, and thought that the relationship with the father could be adequately preserved through careful on-going contact arrangements after relocation. The New Zealanders, by contrast, questioned the motivation for the relocation and rejected the suggestion that refusing permission to move would have any serious consequences for the family; the mother's attitude to contact was seen as a crucial factor pointing against the relocation. As the diagram in Box 7.6 illustrates,[56] these attitudes were typical of participants in the study – English participants thought that Tom's welfare required the relocation to be allowed, while New Zealanders thought that the welfare analysis led to the opposite conclusion.

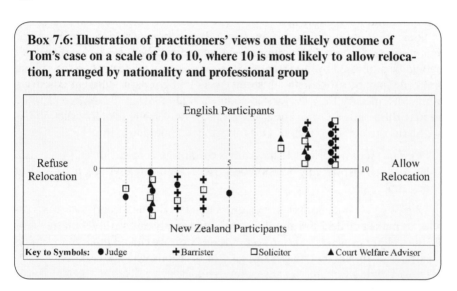

Box 7.6: Illustration of practitioners' views on the likely outcome of Tom's case on a scale of 0 to 10, where 10 is most likely to allow relocation, arranged by nationality and professional group

These findings demonstrate vividly that answers based on the welfare principle are capable of producing hugely varied results, depending on who is asked the question. Since decisions about children's welfare in most cases involve predictions about the future, rather than assessments of the past, there is an extent to which any decision in this field 'falls into the category of crystal ball gazing'.[57] But is this a reason to reject the welfare principle as the basis for decision-making in disputes concerning children?

---

[56] The diagram was previously published in George, 'Practitioners' Views on Children's Welfare in Relocation Disputes', 189. Thanks to Jordan Publishing for permission to reproduce it here.

[57] *Re H (A Child) (Removal from Jurisdiction)* [2007] EWCA Civ 222, [2007] 2 FLR 317, [27].

VALUING WELFARE

In this chapter we have addressed three main issues. We have looked at the origins of the welfare principle and at how it came to have its modern interpretation. We have suggested that a welfare approach to decision-making may not be as individualistic or as blinkered to the existence of others as is sometimes suggested. And we have seen that the welfare principle takes account of context, which leads to variation in how cases are assessed when they are put in different contexts. This contextual nature makes the welfare principle flexible, and therefore usable over time and in different social and cultural situations, but it also gives rise to questions.

Some of those questions are most significant for international family law.[58] For example, if one seeks an international agreement about how relocation cases should be addressed by family courts,[59] basing such an agreement on the welfare principle may be problematic: it seems likely that courts in different countries, being informed by their own social contexts, will interpret the requirements of welfare differently.[60] Other questions are more universally relevant when thinking about the welfare principle. One fundamental question is this:

• Does the welfare principle have any substantive content, or is it used as a label which justifies any decision because it can mean anything to anyone at any time?

One way to think about this question is to focus on the second part. Is it possible to make *any* decision about a child's upbringing and justify it on the basis of the welfare principle? The answer must be 'no'. We can all think of examples – extreme examples, horrible examples – of decisions which are so plainly contrary to a child's welfare that any claim to make such a decision on the basis of the welfare principle would be obviously untenable. But the law goes further in constraining decision-making within the welfare framework, for only 'reasonable' decisions are allowed. We know this because an appeal court may overturn a judge's decision if it is outside 'the generous ambit within which a reasonable disagreement is possible'.[61] This assessment can be based purely on the outcome reached by the trial judge, as Sir Mark Potter explained:

[d]espite the fact that the judge has on the face of it considered the correct principles, and had regard to the relevant factors in exercising his discretion, his conclusion is none the less 'plainly wrong'.[62]

---

[58] See further ch 3 above, 'International Family Law'.
[59] Washington Declaration on International Family Relocation 2010.
[60] George, 'Practitioners' Views on Children's Welfare in Relocation Disputes', 200–2.
[61] *G v G (Minors) (Custody: Appeal)* [1985] FLR 894 (HL), 899.
[62] *Re S (Children) (Relocation: Permission)* [2011] EWCA Civ 454, [2011] 2 FCR 356, [53].

The very fact that the court has this fall-back position of overturning a decision on the basis that the judge's view of what the child's welfare required was 'plainly wrong' says something about the welfare principle – it says that the range of outcomes which different people (even experienced professionals in the family courts) think will be in a child's welfare must be enormous. Presumably no judge who understands the applicable legal principles and who looks at all the relevant information then makes an order which she herself believes to be 'plainly' contrary to the child's welfare! Yet that is precisely what the appeal judges are saying has happened: the judge made no error in the legal principles, and the judge had in mind all the pertinent information, and none the less made a decision which the appellate judges consider so contrary to the child's welfare as to be 'plainly wrong'.

There must, therefore, be some limits to the range of outcomes which can be justified under the 'welfare' banner. Even accepting that, though, there is no denying that the welfare jurisdiction is discretionary, and in any case there will be a number of different options available, none of which can be said to be wrong.[63] Given this inherent variability, combined with the other criticisms which are made of welfare-based reasoning, is there any reason to favour keeping the welfare principle?

There are quite a few different reasons which might be suggested, but here is one to consider:[64]

> The welfare of the child is a better thing to argue about.

Cases about children's upbringing are, by their very nature, disputes. They are arguments. In private law cases, they are arguments between parents or others who are closely involved in the child's life. In public law cases, they are arguments between the state and the family – though they often involve arguments between family members as well. The greatest virtue of the welfare principle is not necessarily that it leads to the best possible outcome (though of course it aims to do so), but that it makes people think about the child. A parent is allowed to discuss the importance of their rights, their wishes, or their interests – but all such discussion has to be focused on the child. A parent is allowed to criticise the other parent's drug habit, bad manners or lack

---

[63] New Zealand's courts take a different view. There, it is said clearly that decisions about children's welfare are not discretionary: the High Court explained that views about children's welfare 'may vary with each Judge. But that is because the answers involve value judgments, which by their nature will never yield a definitive answer; it is not because the answers are discretionary': *B v B [Relocation]* [2008] NZFLR 1083 (New Zealand High Court), [42]. Consequently, New Zealand has a broader view of when an appeal court can overturn the original decision: 'If the appellate court's opinion is different from the conclusion of the tribunal appealed from, then the decision under appeal is wrong in the only sense that matters, even if it was a conclusion on which minds might reasonably differ': *Austin, Nichols & Co v Stichting Lodestar* [2008] 2 NZLR 141 (New Zealand Supreme Court), [16].

[64] This suggestion owes much to my many conversations with Mavis Maclean.

of parenting skills – but all such criticism has to be focused on its relevance to the child.

Does this stop parents from arguing with each other? No, of course not. There were 162,540 private law cases involving children in England and Wales in 2010, including nearly 37,000 private law residence disputes and nearly 100,000 private law contact disputes.[65] No, the welfare principle does not stop parents from arguing with each other. But nor is it meant to. The aim is to make the argument constructive, and to focus it on the person who has least say in the decision. The welfare principle stops parents from fighting over their own selfish interests, and forces them to construct their arguments in a way which at least nods towards someone else's interests. Family law disputes take place at times of crisis for families – no one litigates in the family court unless they have no choice. When things are tough, it is all too easy to think about yourself and forget about those around you. The welfare principle makes parents focus their attention on their children's needs. Those who would advocate abandoning the welfare principle should keep this important function in mind, for which of the alternative approaches offers this hope of a better argument?

---

[65] Ministry of Justice, *Judicial and Court Statistics 2010* (London, HMSO, 2011) 52 (Table 2.4).

8

Parental Responsibility, Parenting and Status

Key Questions

- What is parental responsibility used by the courts to do?
- How does this use of parental responsibility affect other court orders relating to children?
- Why is it important that the law regulate children's care arrangements, rather than leaving parents to make all arrangements privately?

There are many ways in which a society could organise the responsibility for the care and upbringing of children. At one end of the spectrum, adults who find themselves in control of children (usually because they are their parents) could be left alone entirely, to get on with parenting in whatever way they saw fit; at the other end, the state could take full responsibility for children's care and upbringing, with all children taken to state-run facilities at birth.[1]

Most societies adopt a position somewhere between these extremes. In English law, the primary responsibility for raising a child is placed on the

This chapter draws on P Harris and R George, 'Parental Responsibility and Shared Residence Orders: Parliamentary Intentions and Judicial Interpretations' [2010] *Child and Family Law Quarterly* 151. I am grateful to the Jordan Publishing for permission to reproduce parts of that article here, as well as to my friend and colleague Peter Graham Harris, Research Associate at the Oxford Centre for Family Law and Policy and formerly Assistant Secretary in the Lord Chancellor's Department, who helped me considerably in developing my thoughts on these issues.

[1] J Eekelaar, 'Foreword' in R Probert, S Gilmore and J Herring (eds), *Responsible Parents and Parental Responsibility* (Oxford, Hart Publishing, 2009) p v.

parents of that child,[2] and the state may interfere compulsorily in children's upbringing only where the child is suffering or is at risk of suffering significant harm.[3] The justification for having the state interfere with family life to protect children from serious harm at the hands of their parents is straightforward enough.[4] A more difficult question is what role the state, through the courts and the legal system, should have in purely private law disputes between parents about the upbringing of their child.

Chapter seven discussed the meanings and values of the welfare principle as the core focus of the law in England and Wales.[5] One of the two main areas where the welfare principle is applied is in disputes about children's upbringing between separated parents,[6] which is rightly described as 'one of the most important, difficult, sensitive and emotive areas of family law'.[7] Two key issues will be discussed in this chapter:

- parental responsibility
- day-to-day parenting

The aim of this chapter is to discuss these two issues with reference to some trends which have been emerging in the case law over recent years. In particular, we chart the shift from seeing parental responsibility and orders relating to children's care as being about practical, concrete issues which are important to children's lives, to seeing them as being focused on the status of parents, detached from the everyday lives of the children they are supposed to be about. We start with discussion of the meaning of parental responsibility in English law, before linking that to more practical aspects of everyday parenting, taking the example of shared residence orders. Finally, since there may be a temptation to think that the issues identified in this chapter could be resolved by removing the law from parenting disputes entirely, the chapter closes with a return to the theme of family justice discussed in chapter one.

PARENTAL RESPONSIBILITY

The starting point in understanding parental responsibility (or, PR) is the statutory definition, as set out in Box 8.1.

[2] See, eg, Law Commission, *Review of Child Law: Guardianship and Custody*, Report No 172 (London, HMSO, 1988) [2.1].

[3] Children Act 1989, s 31.

[4] The protection of children from serious harm, whether physical, sexual, psychological or emotional, is an inalienable function of the state in a just society.

[5] Children Act 1989, s 1(1).

[6] The other is in child protection law: see generally L Hoyano and C Keenan, *Child Abuse: Law and Policy Across Boundaries* (Oxford, Oxford University Press, 2007).

[7] D Norgrove (chair), *Family Justice Review: Final Report* (London, HMSO, 2011), [4.20].

> **Box 8.1: extract from the Children Act 1989, s 3(1)**
>
> In this Act, 'parental responsibility' means all the rights, duties, powers, responsibilities and authority which by law a parent of a child has in relation to the child and his property.

However, this definition simply begs the question: what *are* these rights, duties, powers, responsibilities and authority?

Some of the legal incidents of PR can be listed easily enough, as seen in Box 8.2,[8] though it is difficult to be sure whether the entire scope of the rights, duties, powers, responsibilities and authority can be captured by such a list:[9]

> **Box 8.2: Some of the legal incidents of parental responsibility**
>
> - naming the child
> - providing a home for the child
> - bringing up the child
> - having contact with the child
> - protecting and maintaining the child
> - administering the child's property
> - consenting to the taking of blood for testing
> - allowing the child to be interviewed
> - taking the child outside of the jurisdiction of the UK and consenting to emigration
> - agreeing to and vetoing the issue of the child's passport
> - agreeing to the child's adoption
> - agreeing to the child's change of surname
> - consenting to the child's medical treatment
> - arranging the child's education
> - determining the child's religious upbringing
> - disciplining the child and sometimes taking responsibility for harm caused by the child
> - consenting to the child's marriage
> - representing the child in legal proceedings
> - appointing a guardian for the child
> - disposing of the child's corpse

---

[8] This list is a combination of the suggestions in N Lowe and G Douglas, *Bromley's Family Law*, 10th edn (Oxford, Oxford University Press, 2007) 377 and the *Family Justice Review*, [4.6].

[9] See further R Probert, S Gilmore and J Herring (eds), *Responsible Parents and Parental Responsibility* (Oxford, Hart Publishing, 2009).

This kind of list of the legal consequences of having PR is, of course, a rather cold way of looking at parenting, and does 'no justice to the warmth and caring needed if parents are to nurture their children successfully'.[10] It does, though, start to give some insight into the importance of PR, and into why the *idea* of PR might be thought 'rather strange'.[11] To help in understanding PR, it is useful to look back at the origins of the concept – why it was introduced and what the aims of its inventors were – and then at how the courts have developed the idea over time.

Parliament introduced PR into the law in the Children Act 1989 on the recommendation of the Law Commission,[12] with the explicit aim of focusing attention on responsibilities for children as opposed to rights over them.[13] This socio-political aim (addressed both to parents and to agents of the state involved in children's care) was thought to be primarily rhetorical in its effect, with 'little difference in substance' in terms of everyday parenting.[14]

Before the 1989 Act, the key legal concept was *custody*, but the Law Commission was concerned that the effect of custody orders (or joint custody orders) on the rights and duties of parents was not clear.[15] The level of disagreement was such that a parent with day-to-day care who was concerned that joint custody would enable the other parent to interfere in that day-to-day care would be told not to worry because such orders were 'simply "a matter of words"' – yet at the same time, the other parent would be told that they should press for such an order because it was 'an important ratification of his continued parental role'.[16]

To exacerbate the difficulty, judges' views on, and uses of, joint custody orders varied widely. While some thought granting joint custody was unnecessary if the parents were co-operating and a source of further conflict if they were not, others thought that a joint custody order helped to keep the parent without day-to-day care involved in the child's upbringing. Unsurprisingly, research indicated a wide difference between courts in the use made of joint custody orders.[17]

---

[10] *Family Justice Review*, [4.7].

[11] Eekelaar, 'Foreword', p v.

[12] See Law Commission, *Review of Child Law: Guardianship and Custody*, Report No 172 (London, HMSO, 1988) [hereafter, *Review of Child Law,* Report) and Law Commission, *Review of Child Law: Custody*, Working Paper No 96 (London, HMSO, 1986) [hereafter, *Review of Child Law*, Working Paper].

[13] *Review of Child Law*, Report, esp [2.1] and [2.4].

[14] Ibid, [2.4].

[15] Ibid, [4.3].

[16] J Priest and J Whybrow, 'Custody Law In Practice in the Divorce and Domestic Courts' (1986) Supplement to the *Review of Child Law*, Working Paper, [8.4], discussed in *Review of Child Law*, Report, [4.3].

[17] Ibid.

It was in response to these and other difficulties[18] that the Law Commission adopted as a 'fundamental principle' the proposition 'that the primary responsibility for the upbringing of children rests with their parents' and that the courts should intervene 'only where the child is placed at unacceptable risk'.[19] Accordingly, the Commission recommended (and the subsequent legislation created) the concept of *parental responsibility*. Moreover, PR was conferred not only on the child's parents,[20] but also on guardians of the child, on those with whom the child resides under a court order, and even on local authorities into whose care children are committed by the courts.

As Peter Graham Harris and I have charted in our work,[21] the courts have used their interpretative powers to shift the perception, and consequently the role, of PR in the years since the Children Act entered force.[22] The courts initially gave full weight to the substantive content of PR, as illustrated by cases where fathers who did not automatically have PR sought it from the courts. For example, in *Re H (Minors) (Local Authority: Parental Rights) (No 3)*, Balcombe LJ pointed out that the reason for not granting all fathers parental responsibility as of right was that 'the position of the natural father can be infinitely variable', ranging from the married father, to the case where there was 'only the single act of intercourse (possibly even rape)' to connect the father to the child.[23] His Lordship said that '[c]onsiderable social evils might have resulted if the father at the bottom end of the spectrum had been automatically granted full parental rights and duties'.[24]

The Court of Appeal therefore suggested that certain criteria ought to be met by an applicant father before parental responsibility would be granted; in *Re H*, criteria which might be relevant were said to be: '(1) the degree of commitment which the father has shown towards the child; (2) the degree of attachment which exists between the father and the child, and (3) the reasons of the father for applying for the order'.[25] This approach demonstrates a construction of parental responsibility which involves substantive rights and

---

[18] See P Harris and R George, 'Parental Responsibility and Shared Residence Orders: Parliamentary Intentions and Judicial Interpretations' [2010] *Child and Family Law Quarterly* 151, 153–57.

[19] *Review of Child Law*, Report, [2.1].

[20] At the time, this meant mothers, marital fathers, fathers who entered a parental responsibility agreement with the mother, or fathers who obtained a court order granting them such responsibility: Children Act 1989, s 4. The routes for fathers to obtain parental responsibility were broadened by the Children and Adoption Act 2002 to include fathers registered on the child's birth certificate.

[21] Harris and George, 'Parental Responsibility'.

[22] See also the excellent analysis by H Reece, 'The Degradation of Parental Responsibility' in R Probert, S Gilmore and J Herring (eds), *Responsible Parents and Parental Responsibility* (Oxford, Hart Publishing, 2009).

[23] *Re H (Minors) (Local Authority: Parental Rights) (No 3)* [1991] 1 FLR 214, 218. This case was decided under the Family Law Reform Act 1987, with the Court of Appeal discussing the 1989 Act's provisions some months before they entered force.

[24] Ibid.

[25] Ibid.

powers, hence the need for care to be taken in its allocation to people who would not otherwise have it.

In more recent years, though, there has been a steady trend in judicial remarks suggesting that PR is more a matter of status recognition than of substantive rights, responsibilities, etc.[26] Indeed, Helen Reece describes the courts' approach as seeing 'parental responsibility as legitimation' of fathers, attempting to reinforce their symbolic importance to their children.[27] The first major step in this direction can be seen in *Re S (Parental Responsibility)* in 1995, where Ward LJ said that it was

> wrong to place undue and therefore false emphasis on the rights and duties and powers comprised in "parental responsibility" and not to concentrate on the fact that what is at issue is conferring upon a committed father *the status of parenthood* for which nature has already ordained that he must bear responsibility. (emphasis added).[28]

A few years later, Ward LJ reaffirmed this view, saying that 'it should be understood by now that a parental responsibility order is one designed not to do more than confer on the natural father *the status of fatherhood*' and that 'it is important that, wherever possible, the law should confer on a concerned father that *stamp of approval*' (emphasis added).[29]

With respect, these comments seem misconceived. How can it be 'wrong' to place emphasis on the rights and duties and powers of parental responsibility when those are the precise terms in which the Children Act defines PR? It would, in a sense, be wrong if one overlooked the responsibilities and authority also encompassed in parental responsibility, but somehow one does not think that was what Ward LJ meant, given his dichotomy between 'rights and duties and powers' on the one hand, and 'the status of parenthood' on the other. Parental responsibility was designed to separate out parenthood as a question of *fact* from parenting as an on-going child-raising *act.*[30]

However, the Court of Appeal continued this approach over the following years. Ward LJ criticised one judge for giving 'no consideration whatever [to] that fundamental aspect of the parental responsibility order, which is that it is a matter of status'.[31] In that case, in which direct contact between the children and the father had been refused, his Lordship continued the conflation of parenthood and parental responsibility: 'it is essential for the well-being of the children . . . to begin to know that their father was concerned enough to

---

[26] See Harris and George, 'Parental Responsibility', 161–64.

[27] Reece, 'The Degradation of Parental Responsibility', 101.

[28] *Re S (Parental Responsibility)* [1995] 2 FLR 648 (CA), 657

[29] *Re C and V (Contact and Parental Responsibility)* [1998] 1 FLR 392 (CA), 397.

[30] See generally A Bainham, 'Parentage, Parenthood and Parental Responsibility: Subtle, Elusive, Yet Important Distinctions' in A Bainham, S Day Sclater and M Richards (eds), *What is a Parent? A Socio-Legal Analysis* (Oxford, Hart Publishing, 1999).

[31] *Re M (Contact: Family Assistance: McKenzie Friend)* [1999] 1 FLR 75 (CA), 80.

make an application *to be recognised as their father*, and that his *status* as their father has the stamp of the court's approval' (emphasis added).[32]

Lest it be thought from these quotations that Ward LJ is alone in taking this view, note that other judges have taken the same line. In *Re H (Parental Responsibility)*, Butler-Sloss LJ said that '[p]arental responsibility is a question of status . . . The grant of the application declares the status of the applicant as the father of that child'.[33] Thorpe LJ has similarly argued that 'the development of caselaw in this area . . . has been, and continues to be, towards the grant of what is essentially an acknowledgement of status . . . This is essentially an acknowledgement and declaration of [the father's] parental status'.[34]

So it seems that the courts have changed the meaning of PR so that, at least in some cases, the focus has moved away from the practical effect of having rights, duties, responsibilities and so on, and towards seeing PR as a label, a badge, representing a desired status. We see here the law recreating a status seen to be 'an important ratification of [a person's] continued parental role', which is how custody orders were described before the Children Act 1989 was enacted.[35] In other words, as Harris and I argue, the law has come full circle and re-created problems very similar to those which the 1989 reforms were intended to resolve.[36]

Indeed, similar concerns can be seen with regard to the more 'concrete' and practical aspects of parenting with which the courts are concerned. In the next section, we turn to issues about children's upbringing and their relationships with their parents and other important people in their lives, asking how those provisions of the Children Act have fared over time.

DAY-TO-DAY PARENTING: THE EXAMPLE OF SHARED RESIDENCE

In the terminology of the Children Act 1989, the orders under consideration here are primarily *residence orders* and *contact orders*, though it is worth considering the interface between these orders and *specific issue orders* and *prohibited steps orders*, as set out in Box 8.3.

---

[32] Ibid. It is curious that in all these cases the court talks of the importance of the child knowing that the father was concerned enough *to apply for* parental responsibility, when what actually seems to matter in the courts' conception is that the father *is given* parental responsibility.

[33] *Re H (Parental Responsibility)* [1998] 1 FLR 855 (CA), 858.

[34] *Re H (A Child: Parental Responsibility)* [2002] EWCA Civ 542, [2002] All ER (D) 64 (Apr), [15] and [16].

[35] Priest and Whybrow, 'Custody Law In Practice in the Divorce and Domestic Courts', para [8.4], discussed in *Review of Child Law, Report*, [4.3].

[36] Harris and George, 'Parental Responsibility', 170.

Box 8.3: extracts from the Children Act 1989

Section 8(1)

In this Act –

'a contact order' means an order requiring the person with whom a child lives, or is to live, to allow the child to visit or stay with the person named in the order, or for that person and the child otherwise to have contact with each other;

'a prohibited steps order' means an order that no step which could be taken by a parent in meeting his parental responsibility for a child, and which is of a kind specified in the order, shall be taken by any person without the consent of the court;

'a residence order' means an order settling the arrangements to be made as to the person with whom a child is to live; and

'a specific issue order' means an order giving directions for the purpose of determining a specific question which has arisen, or which may arise, in connection with any aspect of parental responsibility for a child.

Section 11(4):

Where a residence order is made in favour of two or more persons who do not themselves live together, the order may specify the periods during which the child is to live in the different households concerned.

The focus here will be on children's living arrangements and their relationships with their parents and other important people in their lives. A particularly illustrative example is the courts' changing approach to shared residence orders. Shared residence can mean an arrangement where the child splits his or her time equally between two households,[37] or where the time is divided less equally but still involves the child living in two places (rather than living in one place and sometimes staying in another).

As with parental responsibility, the terminology of *residence* and *contact* was devised by the Law Commission. The old terms of *custody* and *access* were swept away,[38] and the focus was placed on concrete and practical issues about the child's place of residence and his or her relationships with people not living in that household. The Law Commission stressed that orders should be about the realities of children's lives, and this overarching policy was reflected both on the face of the Act and by Ministers when introducing

---

[37] Precise arrangements vary, but include daily changeovers, weekly changeovers, or more elaborate swaps like 4:4:3:3 or 5:5:2:2.

[38] Despite being gone for more than 20 years, the terms *custody* and *access* appear to remain in common use outside the legal profession: *Family Justice Review*, [4.56].

the Bill in Parliament. Lord Mackay, the Lord Chancellor, said in the House of Lords debates that:

> the approach of the Law Commission's report and the Bill is to focus attention away from the theoretical and arguably undefinable nature and content of parental authority [and] parental rights . . . and to focus the attention of the courts and the parties on the concrete issues that arise about children . . . not on abstract ideas like custody and so on, but on concrete issues as to where the child should live and whether the child should have association with a particular person.[39]

The Minister of State, David Mellor, echoed that policy in the House of Commons debates when he said that '[t]he new orders will seek to concentrate the minds of the parties and of the court on the concrete issues relating to the day-to-day care of the child'.[40]

Because of this focus on practical realities, it was envisaged that the vast majority of cases would involve the child having a single main home, and so consequently most court orders would be for residence with one parent and contact with the other.[41] What is more, it was clear both from the Parliamentary debates[42] and from the wording of the Act[43] that *contact* might include overnight stays away from the child's main home, and that this did not require the order to be called 'shared residence'.[44]

When the Children Act entered force, the courts initially defended this approach. In 1996, in response to some trial judges' inclination to make shared residence orders to indicate that the parents had equal status, the Court of Appeal stressed that it was the child's perspective that mattered,[45] and suggested that the appropriate order 'depend[ed] on the child's answer to a practical question: "Where do you live?"'.[46]

A similar view could still be seen some years later. In *D v D (Shared Residence Order)*,[47] for example, Hale LJ stated that she would not place any gloss on the wording of the Children Act,[48] but stressed that a shared resi-

---

[39] Hansard, *House of Lords Debates,* vol 502, col 1153 (19 December 1988).

[40] Hansard, *House of Commons Debates*, vol 151, col 1114 (27 April 1989).

[41] Hansard, *House of Lords Debates*, vol 501, cols 1217 and 1218 (19 December 1988); see also Department of Health, *The Children Act 1989: Guidance and Regulations, Volume 1* (London, HMSO, 1991) [2.28].

[42] Hansard, *House of Lords Debates*, vol 501, cols 1217 and 1218 (19 December 1988).

[43] Look at the definition of a contact order in s 8: 'to allow the child to visit *or stay with* the person'.

[44] *Review of Child Law*, Report, [4.12].

[45] Children's wishes and feelings 'ought to be particularly important in shared residence cases, because it is the children who will have to divide their time between two homes and it is all too easy for the parents' wishes and feelings to predominate': *Holmes-Moorhouse v Richmond Upon Thames London Borough Council* [2009] UKHL 7, [2009] 1 FLR 904, [36].

[46] S Gilmore, 'Court Decision-Making in Shared Residence Order Cases: A Critical Examination' [2006] *Child and Family Law Quarterly* 478, 483, quoting *Re P (Minors)* (unreported, 12 February 1996, Neill and Ward LJJ). Ward LJ later re-affirmed this 'practical test' of 'ask[ing] the children, where do you live?': *Re H (Children)* [2009] EWCA Civ 902, [13].

[47] *D v D (Shared Residence Order)* [2001] 1 FLR 495 (CA).

[48] Ibid, [32].

dence order was appropriate only where it 'reflects the reality of [the] children's lives'.[49] Hence while there may have been pressure to make shared residence orders for symbolic reasons even where in fact the child had its home with only one of its parents, it was resisted, presumably to avoid the law falling back into the state of confusion that existed in respect of the old joint custody order.

Following *D v D*, the emphasis was placed firmly on the reality in which the children lived. Building on her earlier judgment, Hale LJ went to some effort to remind judges what the purpose of residence orders was in *Re A (Shared Residence)*.[50] The trial judge had made a shared residence order in relation to the three children involved, including one child who was unwilling even to see his mother. On appeal, Hale LJ said:

> I completely appreciate why the recorder wished to make a shared residence order in this case. He wanted to recognise the equal status of each parent in relation to all three of these children. He may, although he does not say so, have been afraid that the father would not recognise this if he did not make a shared residence order in relation to all three children. But the law is that the parents already have shared parental responsibility for their children. They have equal and independent power to exercise that parental responsibility. A residence order is about where a child is to live.[51]

This case might be seen to demonstrate an attempt at restraint in the use of shared residence, and a reminder to judges to look back at the Act and use its provisions appropriately.[52]

However, as the courts increasingly turned parental responsibility into a label marking mere parental status, pressure started to mount on residence orders. The problem was that if PR could be given to a father who was to have virtually no relationship with his child – and who might, indeed, might be positively dangerous to the child[53] – it was hard to justify not giving something more to good, committed parents who were strongly involved in their children's lives. While it is hard to be sure, it seems likely that this pressure was the cause of the increasing use of shared residence orders to reflect parental status rather than the realities of children's living arrangements.[54] PR was being used to reaffirm a person's *core status* as a parent, and shared residence started to be used as a further accolade to show a person's *equal status* as a good parent alongside the person providing the bulk of the day-to-day care. Consider these judicial statements:

---

[49] Ibid, [34].

[50] *Re A (Shared Residence)* [2001] EWCA Civ 1795, [2002] 1 FLR 495.

[51] Ibid, [17].

[52] See also *Re A (Children) (Shared Residence)* [2002] EWCA Civ 1343, [2003] 3 FCR 656, [16] (Thorpe LJ); Gilmore, 'Court Decision-Making in Shared Residence Order Cases'.

[53] See, eg, *Re S (Parental Responsibility)* [1995] 2 FLR 648 (CA): the father had convictions for child pornography offences and had been refused any direct contact with his daughter, but was still given PR.

[54] See further Harris and George, 'Parental Responsibility', 166–69; Reece, 'The Degradation of Parental Responsibility', 94.

- **Sir Mark Potter P:** 'a shared residence order may be regarded as appropriate . . . where, in a case where one party has the primary care of a child, it may be psychologically beneficial to the parents in *emphasising the equality of their position* and responsibilities' (emphasis added).[55]
- **Wall LJ:** 'shared residence . . . as a concept is designed to show that parents are *equals in the eyes of the law*' (emphasis added).[56]
- **Wilson J:** 'to make a shared residence order to reflect the arrangements here chosen by the judge is to choose one label rather than another. Her chosen arrangements for the division of the [children's] time could also have been reflected in orders for sole residence to the mother and for generous defined contact with the father. But labels can be very important. . . . [W]ill an order for shared residence be valuable to [the children] as a setting of the court's seal upon an assessment that the home offered by each parent to them is of *equal status and importance* for them?' (emphasis added)[57]
- **Wall LJ:** '[a shared residence order] emphasises the fact that both parents are *equal* in the eyes of the law, and that they have *equal duties and responsibilities* as parents' (emphasis added).[58]

In a sign of awareness of the oddity of this approach, some judges have sounded notes of caution. Lady Hale took the opportunity presented by a judicial review case concerning public housing to point out that family court orders are 'meant to provide practical solutions to the practical problems faced by separating families. They are not meant to be aspirational statements of what would be best in some ideal world which has little prospect of realisation'.[59] Even more direct were subsequent comments by Black LJ in *T v T (Shared Residence)*,[60] as seen from the extract given in Box 8.4.

Box 8.4: extract from *T v T (Shared Residence)* [2010] EWCA Civ 1366, [2011] 1 FCR 267 (Black LJ)

[26] In *Re AR (A Child: Relocation)*,[61] Mostyn J said (at [52]) that a joint or shared residence order 'is nowadays the rule rather than the exception even where the quantum of care undertaken by each parent is decidedly unequal'. That, in my view, is to go too far. Whether or not a joint or shared residence order is granted depends upon a determination of what is in the best interests of the child in the light of all the factors in

---

[55] *Re A (Joint Residence: Parental Responsibility)* [2008] EWCA Civ 867, [2008] 2 FLR 1593, [66].

[56] *Re T (A Child)* [2009] EWCA Civ 388, [6]. Note that this was a leave to appeal application, not a full appeal.

[57] *Re F (Shared Residence)* [2003] EWCA Civ 592, [2003] 2 FLR 397, [32] and [35].

[58] *Re P (Shared Residence Order)* [2005] EWCA Civ 1639, [2006] 2 FLR 347, [22].

[59] *Holmes-Moorhouse v Richmond Upon Thames LBC* [2009] UKHL 7, [2009] 1 FLR 904, [38].

[60] *T v T (Shared Residence)* [2010] EWCA Civ 1366, [2011] 1 FCR 267.

[61] *Re AR (A Child: Relocation)* [2010] EWHC 1346 (Fam), [2010] 2 FLR 1577.

the individual case. However, it has certainly been established that it is not a pre-requisite for a shared residence order that the periods of time spent with each adult should be equal and nor is it necessary that there should be co-operation and goodwill between them and shared residence orders have been made in cases where there is hostility . . .

[27] What is profoundly disappointing is to see how, in practice, instead of bringing greater benefits for children, shared/joint residence can simply serve as a further battlefield for the adults in the children's lives so that even when the practicalities of how the child's time should be split are agreed or determined by the court, they continue to fight on over what label is to be put on the arrangement. This can never have been intended when shared/joint residence orders were commended by the courts as a useful tool.

Similar criticisms of the status-driven approach to residence orders can be seen in the Family Justice Review. In explaining the proposal to abandon the terms *residence* and *contact* in favour of a single *child arrangements order*, the Review suggests that this approach 'would aim to move discussion away from loaded terms such as residence and contact to focus on the practical issues of the day to day care of the child'.[62] In other words, the Review suggests that a single order of this kind covering all issues about the child's living arrangements would help parents to focus on 'the details of a child's day to day arrangements and care, rather than on status in relation to residence and contact'.[63]

One would certainly not want to take issue with the aim of preventing arguments about status and instead focusing discussion on positive issues to do with the child's life. It will be recalled, for instance, that this was said to be one of the main strengths of the welfare principle in child law.[64] However, it is worth remembering that the exact same aim underpinned the Law Commission's work which led to the Children Act in the first place.[65] The Commission was concerned 'to "lower the stakes" so that the issue is not one in which "winner takes all" or more importantly "loser loses all"'.[66] The intention was to 'reduce rather than increase the opportunity for conflict and litigation in the future'.[67] The Commission therefore recommended that, where both parties had parental responsibility, the court be limited to dealing

---

[62] *Family Justice Review*, [4.15].
[63] Ibid, [4.51].
[64] See ch 7 above, text from n 64.
[65] Given this, it is unsurprising that Lady Hale is able to say that the Review's proposal 'would restore the original vision underlying the 1989 Act': *Family Justice Review*, [4.60].
[66] *Review of Child Law*, Report, [4.5].
[67] *Review of Child Law*, Report, [4.5].

with concrete and practical issues about with whom the child should live, what contact she should have with others, and any disputed matters relating to the exercise of parental responsibility.[68] The Commission aimed to remove the need to argue over rights and statuses, which is why the confusing terminology of *custody* (which was used to mean both parental rights and physical possession of the child) and *access* was abolished. The terms *residence* and *contact* were specifically intended to avoid loaded connotations, and were meant to be used as a purely factual description of the reality of the child's life.

Given this history, one might wonder whether changing the terminology again will help. There will still be a practical need to distinguish between different roles which a parent might play in a child's life, and one wonders whether judges, lawyers and individual litigants will be able to resist adding layers of meaning to whatever orders are being made which were not intended by those who crafted the law.

A separate concern is whether having a single *child arrangements order* (rather than separate residence and contact orders) will lull the courts into becoming ever more involved with the minutiae of children's living arrangements. One serious deficiency with the law before 1989 was the perception that the courts interfered unnecessarily in making arrangements about the details of children's upbringing.[69] This was why the Law Commission adopted as a 'fundamental principle' the proposition 'that the primary responsibility for the upbringing of children rests with their parents' and that the courts should intervene 'only where the child is placed at unacceptable risk'.[70] The whole tone of the reform was to stop courts making unnecessary orders which interfered unduly with parental autonomy.[71]

It was a reflection of this aim that the Commission considered but expressly rejected the option of having a single 'care and control order' under which the court would allocate the child's time between his or her parents. Their rejection of that option was based largely on the expectation that exercising such a power would likely involve the court determining in detail the time the child was to spend with each parent. In the Commission's view, the better solution where the child's day-to-day care was being provided primarily by one parent was to state that the child should live with that parent and have reasonable contact with the other, leaving the details of when, where and for how long, for the parents to work out as time went on and circumstances changed.[72] That approach chimed with their policy of bolstering the primacy of parental responsibility by discouraging the use of the courts to settle matters that are

---

[68] *Review of Child Law*, Report, [4.2]–[4.11].
[69] See further Harris and George, 'Parental Responsibility', 153.
[70] *Review of Child Law*, Report, [2.1].
[71] *Review of Child Law*, Report, [3.2].
[72] *Review of Child Law*, Report, [4.12].

y for parents to decide, and with the policy of reducing the scope for
s and litigation. Consequently, if parental responsibility continues to
alued and used as a meaningless label – and so cannot serve the pivotal
.ion for which it was intended – there is every reason to think that the
changes which the Family Justice Review suggests would follow a similar
path to that taken by the Children Act's original ideas of residence and
contact.

FAMILY LAW AS JUSTICE

So far, this chapter might be seen to imply that the law is making things worse
for families rather than better, by creating unnecessary statuses for parents to
fight about after separation. The idea that the law's attempts to make things
better might actually make them worse is certainly not new – this was the
principal charge made against the law before the 1989 reforms.[73] Moreover,
the note of caution seen in the previous section as to the likelihood of a *child
arrangements order* improving matters could be seen as strengthening that
view. From all of this, there may be a temptation to wonder whether the law
should withdraw from parenting disputes altogether. Perhaps the law should
simply leave parents to get on with being parents as best they can, so long as
the child is not put at undue risk of harm.[74]

One version of this argument was encountered in chapter one when we
considered the UK coalition government's opposition to family litigation in
general.[75] We might extrapolate from those views to see all parenting disputes
as 'unnecessary litigation' and, indeed, to say that 'generally [it will not] be in
the best interest of the children involved for these essentially personal matters
to be resolved in the adversarial forum of a court'.[76] Consider the version of
this argument presented in Box 8.5.

---

[73] *Review of Child Law*, Report, [1.2].
[74] The line would presumably be drawn by reference to child protection law: Children Act
1989, s 31.
[75] See ch 1 above, 'Family Law and Family Justice'.
[76] Ministry of Justice, *Proposals for the Reform of Legal Aid in England and Wales*,
Consultation Paper 12/10, Cm 7967 (London, HMSO, 2010) [2.11] and [4.210].

Box 8.5: A polemical argument against court orders in private law parenting disputes

Most separated parents make their own arrangements for their children's residence and contact – in fact, only around 10 per cent of separated parents ever litigate over these issues.[77] Those cases which are in the 10 per cent are the hard cases – they often involve intractable high-level conflict, allegations of domestic violence, or issues which start to border on public law, including mental health problems and concerns over drug and alcohol abuse.[78]

Thinking about domestic violence as an example, it is reasonably clear that children are harmed both when they are the direct victims of violence and when they witness violence towards others.[79] In one study of separated parents, 56% reported that there had been domestic violence while 78% said that they feared violence;[80] however, the court makes orders for contact more than 95% of the time.[81] Now, some of those reports of violence may be untrue, but since it is hard to know how many it may be worth thinking about a range of possibilities. Table 8.1 provides hypothetical calculations for how many children would be made to have contact in cases involving domestic violence in five alternative situations, where between 25% and 75% of allegations of domestic violence turn out to be true.[82]

The numbers in Table 8.1 are purely hypothetical, but the calculations work like this. In each case, work across the table from left to right. All the calculations start from the fact that 56% of parents allege that there is domestic violence. Now, in column 1 make an assumption about how

---

[77] J Hunt with C Roberts, *Child Contact with Non-Resident Parents*, Family Policy Briefing Paper 3 (Oxford, University of Oxford, 2004) 1.

[78] J Hunt and A Macleod, *Outcomes of Applications to Court for Contact Orders After Parental Separation or Divorce* (London, HMSO, 2008); R Aris and C Harrison, *Domestic Violence and the Supplemental Information Form C1A*, Ministry of Justice Research Report 17/07 (London, HMSO, 2007) 24.

[79] M Hester, C Pearson and N Harwin, *Making an Impact: Children and Domestic Violence*, 2nd edn (London, Jessica Kingsley, 2006). 'Harm' includes seeing or hearing the ill-treatment of another: Children Act 1989, s 31(9).

[80] A Buchanan, J Hunt, H Bretherton and V Bream, *Families in Conflict* (Bristol, Policy Press, 2001) 15. A study of court files found allegations of domestic violence in 94% of cases, three quarters of which were supported by additional evidence within the file: Aris and Harrison, *Domestic Violence and the Supplemental Information Form C1A*, 23.

[81] In 2010, there were 95,460 cases about contact in England and Wales, affecting 46,350 children. Of those 95,460 cases, 96.51% ended with a contact order being made – 2.29% of cases were withdrawn by the applicant, 0.88% ended with an order for 'no order', and only 0.31% ended with a specific refusal of contact: Ministry of Justice, *Judicial and Court Statistics 2010* (London, HMSO, 2011) 52 (Table 2.4), author's calculations from raw data.

[82] The numbers in Table 8.1 are purely hypothetical, since almost all the information going into the calculations is likely to be wrong. In particular, it is not clear whether the 56% allegation rate is the right number to use, since that is for all separating parents. The calculations also assume that all cases of withdrawal, refusal and 'no order' involve violence, which is unlikely to be true.

many of those allegations are true; the five examples I have used are 25%, 35%, 50%, 65% and 75%. In column 2, use the 56% allegation rate and the number in column 1 to calculate what percentage of contact cases actually involve violence. So, for the first example, if 25% of the allegations are true, then 0.56 x 0.25 = 0.14, or 14% of cases. Now, contact is not ordered in 3.5% of cases, so that is noted in column 3, and 3.5% is deducted from the number in column 2 to get the percentage of cases where contact is ordered and where domestic violence exists. So, in the first example, 14% − 3.5% = 10.5% of cases. Finally, in column 5 this percentage is turned into an actual number. There were 46,350 children involved in contact cases in 2010. For simplicity, assume that they were equally divided amongst all cases, so calculate 46,350 x 0.105 = 4,867 children.

Table 8.1: Table showing number of children likely to be involved in court-ordered contact in cases involving domestic violence if given proportions of allegations of domestic violence in contact cases were to be true, assuming that 56% of separating parents involve allegations of violence and given that contact occurs in 96.5% of litigated cases

Proportion of the DV allegations assumed to be true (given that 56% of cases allege DV)	% of contact cases involving DV if assumption is true (ie 56% multiplied by column 1)	% of contact cases where contact does not occur, as taken from court statistics	% of contact cases where contact occurs despite DV (ie column 2 minus column 3)	Approx no of children in court-ordered contact despite DV (ie 46,350) multiplied by the % in column 4)
0.25	14	3.5	10.5	4,867
0.35	19.6	3.5	16.1	7,462
0.5	28	3.5	24.5	11,356
0.65	36.4	3.5	32.9	15,429
0.75	42	3.5	38.5	17,845

If any of the assumptions used in column 1 of Table 8.1 turn out to be close to the reality, then we might venture to suggest that something between 4,800 and 17,800 children have their cases heard in court and are made the subject of contact orders despite the presence of domestic violence every year. Given the harm which we know children suffer when exposed to domestic violence, is this a good thing?

So, the following points might be made:

- most parents manage to sort out residence and contact by themselves anyway
- litigation is widely recognised as being bad for children (and adults!)
- most of the cases which reach the courts involve serious problems which potentially put the children involved at serious risk of harm
- the law itself seems to be creating issues for parents to fight about.

So given all that, would it be better to stop courts from hearing these cases at all?

The answer to this argument is essentially the same as that found in Chapter 1 for why family law in general needs to be seen as a matter of justice. Family law involves questions of people's rights, most significantly in this context the right to respect for private and family life.[83] Families involve power dynamics which call for state regulation to prevent the strong from exerting undue control over the weak. In Chapter 6, we saw that when it comes to financial issues, men are typically the stronger parties, which makes the law crucial to protect women's financial interests from abuses of power by men. In private law children's cases, the power dynamics are different. Women typically have more direct control over children's time, since they tend to be the main care-givers.[84] This enables women to perform a goal-keeping function, thereby creating the possibility of abuses of power to prevent men from having continuing relationships with their children.[85] At the same time, though, people can abuse power in the form of violence and intimidation (physical, emotional or psychological), and those who use this power tend to be men.[86] These varied power dynamics, coupled with the importance of recognising the existence of people's rights with regard to their personal lives, all call for the involvement of the law in what might seem like purely private matters.

As we saw in Chapter 1, justice is about fairness in the allocation of basic rights and in the division of the advantages and disadvantages which arise over time from social cooperation.[87] Family interactions are not exempt from

[83] European Convention on the Protection of Human Rights and Fundamental Freedoms 1950, Art 8.

[84] See, eg, J Hunt with C Roberts, *Child Contact with Non-Resident Parents*, Family Policy Briefing Paper 3 (Oxford, University of Oxford, 2004) 1.

[85] See, eg, M Lamb and J Kelly, 'Improving the Quality of Parent Child Contact in Separating Families with Infants and Young Children: Empirical Research Foundations' in R Galatzer-Levy, J Kraus and J Galatzer-Levy (eds), *The Scientific Basis of Child Custody Decisions*, 2nd edn (Hoboken, NJ, John Wiley, 2009) 195–96.

[86] Buchanan, Hunt, Bretherton and Bream, *Families in Conflict*.

[87] J Rawls, *Justice as Fairness: A Restatement* (Cambridge MA, Harvard University Press, 2001) § 4.1.

the principles of justice – indeed, since families are such a core part of society, justice in families is vital.[88] Power is frequently distributed unevenly within families,[89] and in a society based on justice it is unacceptable to leave the outcomes of life to be determined only according to which individual is more powerful. The purpose of the law, and in particular of courts, is to provide a framework and a forum for the fair adjudication of disputes on a level playing field.

All of this is not to say that parents should not be encouraged to compromise and negotiate with a view to reaching cooperative, mutually satisfactory outcomes to parenting disputes. They should, just as anyone considering whether to assert a right should ask themselves whether the better, more responsible course of action is to refrain from asserting that right.[90] However, in the event that these alternative options are not successful for whatever reason, or in the event that they are not a suitable way to resolve the dispute in question (because, for instance, the power dynamics make negotiation too open to abuse of power), the dispute must still be resolved and people's rights given their due respect. That means that family law, administered within an effective family justice system with judges and lawyers (paid for with legal aid if the individuals cannot reasonably afford to pay the fees themselves) cannot be withdrawn from families. For all their flaws, family law and the family courts are essential parts of a just society.

---

[88] Ibid, § 50.4.

[89] J Eekelaar, 'Family Justice: Ideal or Illusion?' (1995) 48(2) *Current Legal Problems* 191, 210.

[90] J Eekelaar, *Family Law and Personal Life*, paperback edn (Oxford, Oxford University Press, 2007) 127–31; see also ch 2 above, 'Rights and Responsibilities', text from n 37.

Bibliography

Allen, C, 'Status and Capacity' (1930) 46 *Law Quarterly Review* 277

Alston, P, 'The Best Interests Principle: Towards a Reconciliation of Culture and Human Rights' [1994] *International Journal of Law and the Family* 1

Aris, R and Harrison, C, *Domestic Violence and the Supplemental Information Form C1A*, Ministry of Justice Research Report 17/07 (London, HMSO, 2007)

Bailey-Harris, R, 'The Paradoxes of Principle and Pragmatism: Ancillary Relief in England and Wales' [2005] *International Journal of Law, Policy and the Family* 229

Bainham, A, 'Parentage, Parenthood and Parental Responsibility: Subtle, Elusive, Yet Important Distinctions' in A Bainham, S Day Sclater and M Richards (eds), *What is a Parent? A Socio-Legal Analysis* (Oxford, Hart Publishing, 1999)

Barlow, A, 'Regulation of Cohabitation, Changing Family Policies and Social Attitudes: A Discussion of Britain Within Europe' (2004) 26 *Law and Policy* 57

Barlow, A, Burgoyne, C, Clery, E and Smithson, J, 'Cohabitation and the Law: Myths, Money and the Media' in A Park, J Curtice, K Thomson, M Phillips, M Johnson and E Clery (eds), *British Social Attitudes: The 24th Report* (London, Sage Publishing, 2008)

Barlow, A, Burgoyne, C and Smithson, J, *The Living Together Campaign: An Investigation of its Impact on Legally Aware Cohabitants* (London, HMSO, 2007)

Barlow, A, Duncan, S, James, G and Park, A, *Cohabitation, Marriage and the Law: Social Change and Legal Reform in the 21st Century* (Oxford, Hart Publishing, 2005)

Beaumont, P and McEleavy, P, *The Hague Convention on International Child Abduction* (Oxford, Oxford University Press, 1999)

Bottomley, A and Wong, S, 'Changing Contours of Domestic Life, Family and Law: Caring and Sharing' in A Bottomley and S Wong (eds), *Changing Contours of Domestic Life, Family and Law* (Oxford, Hart Publishing, 2009)

Bridgeman, J, Keating, H and Lind, C (eds), *Regulating Family Responsibilities* (Farnham, Ashgate, 2011)

——, (eds), *Responsibility, Law and the Family* (Farnham, Ashgate, 2008)

Buchanan, A, Hunt, J, Bretherton, H and Bream, V, *Families in Conflict* (Bristol, Policy Press, 2001)

Buck, T, *International Child Law*, 2nd edn (Abingdon, Routledge-Cavendish, 2010)

Burgoyne, C and Sonnenberg, S, 'Financial Practices in Cohabiting Heterosexual Couples', in J Miles and R Probert (eds), *Sharing Lives, Dividing Assets: An Interdisciplinary Study* (Oxford, Hart Publishing, 2009)

Cane, P, *Atiyah's Accidents, Compensation and the Law*, 7th edn (Cambridge, Cambridge University Press, 2006)

——, *Responsibility in Law and Morality* (Oxford, Hart Publishing, 2002)

Choudhry, S and Fenwick, H, 'Taking the Rights of Parents and Children Seriously: Confronting the Welfare Principle under the Human Rights Act' (2005) 25 *Oxford Journal of Legal Studies* 453

Choudhry, S and Herring, J, *European Human Rights and Family Law* (Oxford, Hart Publishing, 2010)

Collins, L, Morse, C, McClean, D, Briggs, A, Harris, J and McLachlan, C (eds), *Dicey, Morris and Collins on the Conflict of Laws*, 14th edn (London, Thompson Reuters, 2010)

Cooke, E, 'Miller/McFarlane: Law in Search of Discrimination' [2007] *Child and Family Law Quarterly* 98

Crawford, C, Goodman, A, Greaves, E and Joyce, R, *Cohabitation, Marriage, Relationship Stability and Child Outcomes: An Update*, IFS Commentary C114 (London, Institute for Fiscal Studies, 2011)

——, *Family Law in the Twentieth Century: A History* (Oxford, Oxford University Press, 2003)

Cretney, S, *Law, Law Reform and the Family* (Oxford, Oxford University Press, 1998)

Daly, M and Rake, K, *Gender and the Welfare State: Care, Work and Welfare in Europe and the USA* (Cambridge, Polity Press, 2003)

Davis, G, Cretney, S and Collins, J, *Simple Quarrels: Negotiating Money and Property Disputes on Divorce* (Oxford, Clarendon Press, 1994)

Deech, R, 'The Case Against Legal Recognition of Cohabitation' (1980) 29 *International and Comparative Law Quarterly* 480

Department of Health, *The Children Act 1989: Guidance and Regulations* (London, HMSO, 1991) vol 1

Dewar, J, 'The Normal Chaos of Family Law' (1998) 61 *Modern Law Review* 467

Diduck, A, 'Fairness and Justice for All? The House of Lords in White v White' (2001) 9 *Feminist Legal Studies* 173

——, 'Family Law and Family Responsibility' in J Bridgeman, H Keating and C Lind (eds), *Responsibility, Law and the Family* (Aldershot, Ashgate, 2008)

——, 'Relationship Fairness' in A Bottomley and S Wong (eds), *Changing Contours of Domestic Life, Family and Law: Caring and Sharing* (Oxford, Hart Publishing, 2009)

——, 'What is Family Law For?' (2011) 64 *Current Legal Problems* 1

Diduck, A and Kaganas, F, *Family Law, Gender and the State*, 3rd edn (Oxford, Hart Publishing, 2012)

Douglas, G and Perry, A, 'How Parents Cope Financially on Separation and Divorce: Implications for the Future of Ancillary Relief' [2001] *Child and Family Law Quarterly* 67

Duff, RA, *Answering for Crime* (Oxford, Hart Publishing, 2007)

Duncan, W, 'Children's Rights, Cultural Diversity and Private International Law' in G Douglas and L Sebba (eds), *Children's Rights and Traditional Values* (Farnham, Ashgate, 1998)

Eekelaar, J, 'Beyond the Welfare Principle' [2002] *Child and Family Law Quarterly* 237

——, 'Children Between Cultures' [2004] *International Journal of Law, Policy and the Family* 178

——, 'Family Justice: Ideal or Illusion?' (1995) 48(2) *Current Legal Problems* 191

——, *Family Law and Personal Life*, paperback edn (Oxford, Oxford University Press, 2007)

——, *Family Law and Social Policy*, 2nd edn (London, Weidenfeld and Nicolson, 1984)

——, 'Foreword' in R Probert, S Gilmore and J Herring (eds), *Responsible Parents and Parental Responsibility* (Oxford, Hart Publishing, 2009)

——, 'The Interests of the Child and the Child's Wishes: The Role of Dynamic Self-Determinism' [1994] *International Journal of Law and the Family* 42

——, '"Not of the Highest Importance": Family Justice under Threat' [2011] *Journal of Social Welfare and Family Law* 311

——, 'Personal Obligations' in M Maclean (ed), *Family Law and Family Values* (Oxford, Hart Publishing, 2005)

——, 'Why People Marry: The Many Faces of an Institution' (2007) 41 *Family Law Quarterly* 413

Eekelaar, J and Maclean, M, 'Marriage and the Moral Bases of Personal Relationships' (2004) 31 *Journal of Law and Society* 510

——, 'The Significance of Marriage: Contrasts between White British and Ethnic Minority Groups in England' (2005) 27 *Law and Policy* 379

Eekelaar, J, Maclean, M and Beinart, S, *Family Lawyers: The Divorce Work of Solicitors* (Oxford, Hart Publishing, 2000)

Elizabeth, V, 'Managing Money, Managing Coupledom: A Critical Examination of Cohabitants' Money Management Practices' (2001) 49 *Sociological Review* 389

Fehlberg, B and Maclean, M, 'Child Support Policy in Australia and the United Kingdom' [2009] *International Journal of Law, Policy and the Family* 1

Fehlberg, B, Smyth, B, Maclean, M and Roberts, C, 'Legislating for Shared Time Parenting After Separation: A Research Review' [2011] *International Journal of Law, Policy and the Family* 318

Fineman, M, *The Autonomy Myth* (New York, New Press, 2004)

Fraser, N, 'Mapping the Feminist Imagination: From Redistribution to Recognition to Representation' (2005) 12 *Constellation* 295

——, 'Reframing Justice in a Globalising World' (2005) 36 *New Left Review* 69

Freeman, M, 'In the Best Interests of Internationally Abducted Children? Plural, Singular, Neither or Both?' [2002] *International Family Law* 77

Galanter, M, 'Worlds of Deals: Using Negotiation to Teach about Legal Process' (1984) 34 *Journal of Legal Education* 268

Gardner, J, 'Hart and Feinberg on Responsibility' in M Kramer, C Grant, B Colburn and A Hatzistavrou (eds), *The Legacy of HLA Hart: Legal, Political and Moral Philosophy* (Oxford, Oxford University Press, 2008)

——, 'On the Ground of Her Sex(uality)' (1998) 18 *Oxford Journal of Legal Studies* 167

Gardner, S, *An Introduction to Land Law*, 2nd edn (Oxford, Hart Publishing, 2009)

Gardner, S and Davidson, K, 'The Future of Stack v Dowden' (2011) 127 *Law Quarterly Review* 13

Geekie, C, 'Relocation and Shared Residence: One Route or Two?' [2008] *Family Law* 446

Genn, H, *Paths to Justice* (Oxford, Hart Publishing, 1999)

George, R, 'Cohabitants' Property Rights: When Is Fair Fair?' [2012] *Cambridge Law Journal* 39

——, 'Practitioners' Views on Children's Welfare in Relocation Disputes: Comparing Approaches in England and New Zealand' [2011] *Child and Family Law Quarterly* 178

——, 'Reassessing Relocation: A Comparative Analysis of Legal Approaches to Disputes over Family Migration after Parental Separation in England and New Zealand' (unpublished DPhil thesis, Oxford University: 2010)

——, 'Regulating Responsibilities in Relocation Disputes' in J Bridgeman, H Keating and C Lind (eds), *Regulating Family Responsibilities* (Farnham, Ashgate, 2011)

——, review 'Responsibility, Law and the Family, edited by Jo Bridgeman, Heather Keating and Craig Lind' (2009) 72 *Modern Law Review* 147

George, R, Harris, P and Herring, J, 'Pre-Nuptial Agreements: For Better or For Worse?' [2009] *Family Law* 934

Gilmore, S, 'Court Decision-Making in Shared Residence Order Cases: A Critical Examination' [2006] *Child and Family Law Quarterly* 478

Glendon, M, *Rights Talk: The Impoverishment of Political Discourse* (New York, Free Press, 1991)

Hale, B, 'Equality and Autonomy in Family Law' [2011] *Journal of Social Welfare and Family Law* 3

——, 'Families and the Law: The Forgotten International Dimension' [2009] *Child and Family Law Quarterly* 413

——, 'Family Responsibility: Where Are We Now?' in C Lind, H Keating and J Bridgeman (eds), *Taking Responsibility, Law and the Changing Family* (Farnham, Ashgate, 2011)

——, 'Relocation', paper presented at the *International Child Abduction, Forced Marriage and Relocation Conference*, London Metropolitan University, July 2010

Hale, B, Pearl, D, Cooke, E and Monk, D, *The Family, Law and Society*, 6th edn (Oxford, Oxford University Press, 2009)

Harris, P, 'The Miller Paradoxes' [2008] *Family Law* 1096

Harris, P and George, R, 'Parental Responsibility and Shared Residence Orders: Parliamentary Intentions and Judicial Interpretations' [2010] *Child and Family Law Quarterly* 151

Harris, P, George, R and Herring, J, 'With This Ring I Thee Wed (Terms and Conditions Apply)' [2011] *Family Law* 367

Harris-Short, S, 'Family Law and the Human Rights Act 1998: Judicial Restraint or Revolution?' [2005] *Child and Family Law Quarterly* 329

Harris-Short, S and Miles, J, *Family Law: Text, Cases and Materials*, 2nd edn (Oxford, Oxford University Press, 2011)

Hart, HLA, *Essays in Jurisprudence and Philosophy* (Oxford, Clarendon Press, 1983)

——, 'Varieties of Responsibility' (1967) 83 *Law Quarterly Review* 346

Haskey, J, and Lewis, J, 'Living Apart Together in Britain: Context and Meaning' (2006) 2 *International Journal of Law in Context* 37

Henaghan, M, 'The Normal Order of Family Law' (2008) 28 *Oxford Journal of Legal Studies* 165

Herring, J, *Family Law*, 5th edn (Harlow, Pearson, 2011)

——, 'Farewell Welfare?' [2005] *Journal of Social Welfare and Family Law* 159

——, 'The Human Rights Act and the Welfare Principle in Family Law: Conflicting or Complementary?' [1999] *Child and Family Law Quarterly* 223

——, 'The Meaning of Domestic Violence' [2011] *Journal of Social Welfare and Family Law* 297

——, 'Why Financial Orders on Divorce Should Be Unfair' [2005] *International Journal of Law, Policy and the Family* 218

Herring, J, Harris, P and George, R, 'Ante-Nuptial Agreements: Fairness, Equality and Presumptions' (2011) 127 *Law Quarterly Review* 335

Herring, J and Taylor, R, 'Relocating Relocation' [2006] *Child and Family Law Quarterly* 517

Hester, M, Pearson, C and Harwin, N, *Making an Impact: Children and Domestic Violence*, 2nd edn (London, Jessica Kingsley, 2006)

Hibbs, M, Barton, C and Beswick, J, 'Why Marry? Perspectives of the Affianced' [2001] *Family Law* 197

Hodson, D, *A Practical Guide to International Family Law* (Bristol, Family Law, 2008)

Hohfeld, W, *Fundamental Legal Concepts as Applied in Judicial Reasoning* (New Haven, Yale University Press, 1928)

Hoyano, L and Keenan, C, *Child Abuse: Law and Policy across Boundaries* (Oxford, Oxford University Press, 2007)

Hunt, J and Macleod, A, *Outcomes of Applications to Court for Contact Orders After Parental Separation or Divorce* (London, HMSO, 2008)

Hunt, J with Roberts, C, *Child Contact with Non-Resident Parents*, Family Policy Briefing Paper 3 (Oxford, University of Oxford, 2004)

Hutchinson, A-M, Roberts, R and Setright, H, *International Parental Child Abduction* (Bristol, Family Law, 1998)

Ingleby, R, *Solicitors and Divorce* (Oxford, Oxford University Press, 1992)

Inglis, D, *New Zealand Family Law in the 21st Century* (Wellington, Thompson Brookers, 2007)

Irvine, C, 'John Cleese: Marriage Should be Renewed "Like Dog Licence"', *The Telegraph* (31 October 2008)

Kamerman, S and Kahn, A, *Family Change and Family Policies in Great Britain, Canada, New Zealand and the United States.* (Oxford, Clarendon, 1998)

Katz, S, *Family Law in America* (Oxford, Oxford University Press, 2003)

Lamb, M and Kelly, J, 'Improving the Quality of Parent Child Contact in Separating Families with Infants and Young Children: Empirical Research Foundations' in R Galatzer-Levy, J Kraus and J Galatzer-Levy (eds), *The Scientific Basis of Child Custody Decisions*, 2nd edn (Hoboken NJ, John Wiley, 2009)

Law Commission, *Cohabitation: The Financial Consequences of Relationship Breakdown*, Consultation Paper No 179 (London, HMSO, 2006)

——, *Cohabitation: The Financial Consequences of Relationship Breakdown*, Report No 307 (London, HMSO, 2007)

——, *Review of Child Law: Custody*, Working Paper No 96 (London, HMSO, 1986)

——, *Review of Child Law: Guardianship and Custody*, Report No 172 (London, HMSO, 1988)

Lewis, J, *The End of Marriage? Individualism and Intimate Relations* (Cheltenham, Edward Elgar Publishing, 2001)

Lind, C, Keating, H and Bridgeman, J, 'Taking Family Responsibility, or Having It Imposed?' in C Lind, H Keating and J Bridgeman (eds), *Taking Responsibility, Law and the Changing Family* (Farnham, Ashgate, 2011)

Loader, I and Sparks, R, *Public Criminology? Studying Crime and Society in the Twenty-First Century* (Abingdon, Routledge, 2010)

Lord Chancellor's Department, *Looking to the Future: Mediation and the Ground for Divorce, A Consultation Paper* (London, HMSO, 1993)

Lowe, N, 'Where in the World Is International Family Law Going Next?' in G Douglas and N Lowe (eds), *The Continuing Evolution of Family Law* (Bristol, Family Law, 2009)

Lowe, N and Douglas, G, *Bromley's Family Law*, 10th edn (Oxford, Oxford University Press, 2007)

Lowe, N, Everall, M and Nicholls, M, *International Movement of Children: Law, Practice and Procedure* (Bristol, Family Law, 2004)

Lucas, J, *Responsibility* (Oxford, Clarendon Press, 1993)

Maclean, M and Eekelaar, J, *Family Law Advocacy: How Barristers Help the Victims of Family Failure* (Oxford, Hart Publishing, 2009)

——, 'Family Justice' [2011] *Family Law* 3

——, 'The Obligations and Expectations of Couples Within Families: Three Modes of Interaction' [2004] *Journal of Social Welfare and Family Law* 117

——, *The Parental Obligation: A Study of Parenthood across Households* (Oxford, Hart Publishing, 1997)

Maclean, M, Eekelaar, J, Lewis, J, Arthur, S, Finch, S, Fitzgerald, R and Pearson, P, 'When Cohabiting Parents Separate: Law and Expectations' [2001] *Family Law* 373

Maclean, M, Hunter, R, Wasoff, F, Ferguson, L, Bastard, B and Ryrstedt, E, 'Family Justice in Hard Times: Can We Learn From Other Jurisdictions?' [2011] *Journal of Social Welfare and Family Law* 319

Maclean, S, *Legal Aid and the Family Justice System* (London, Legal Aid Board Research Unit, 1998)

Marmor, A, 'On the Limits of Rights' (1997) 16 *Law and Philosophy* 1

Masson, J, Bailey-Harris, R and Probert, R, *Cretney's Principles of Family Law*, 8th edn (London, Sweet and Maxwell, 2008)

McCarthy, F, 'Cohabitation: Lessons from North of the Border?' [2011] *Child and Family Law Quarterly* 277

McGlynn, C, *Families and the European Union: Law, Politics and Pluralism* (Cambridge, Cambridge University Press, 2006)

McLellan, D, 'Contract Marriage: The Way Forward or Dead End?' (1996) 23 *Journal of Law and Society* 234

Miles, J, 'Charman v Charman (No 4): Making Sense of Need, Compensation and Equal Sharing After Miller/McFarlane' [2008] *Child and Family Law Quarterly* 378

——, 'Responsibility in Family Finance and Property Law', in Bridgeman, J, Keating, H and C Lind (eds), *Regulating Family Responsibilities* (Farnham, Ashgate, 2011)

Millbank, J, 'The Role of the "Functional Family" in Same-Sex Family Recognition Trends' [2008] *Child and Family Law Quarterly* 155

Ministry of Justice, *Judicial and Court Statistics 2010* (London, HMSO, 2011)

——, *Proposals for the Reform of Legal Aid in England and Wales: Consultation Paper 12/10* (London, HMSO, 2010)

——, *Reform of Legal Aid in England and Wales: The Government Response*, Cm 8072 (London, HMSO, 2011)

Mnookin, R, 'Child-Custody Adjudication: Judicial Functions in the Face of Indeterminacy' (1975) 39 *Law and Contemporary Problems* 226

Mnookin, R and Kornhauser, L, 'Bargaining in the Shadow of the Law: The Case of Divorce' (1979) 88 *Yale Law Journal* 950

Mossman, M, 'Gender Equality, Family Law and Access to Justice' [1994] *International Journal of Law and the Family* 357

Mostyn, N, 'What Is Marriage? What Should It Be?', online at www.familylawweek. co.uk/site.aspx?i=ed70850

Norgrove, D (chair), *Family Justice Review: Final Report* (London, HMSO, 2011)

O'Neill, O, 'Children's Rights and Children's Lives' (1994) 8 *International Journal of Law and the Family* 24

Office for National Statistics, *Statistics Bulletin: Divorces in England and Wales 2010* (Newport, Office for National Statistics, 2011)

Pahl, J, 'Individualisation in Couple Finances: Who Pays for the Children?' (2005) 4 *Social Policy and Society* 381

——, *Money and Marriage* (Basingstoke, Macmillan, 1989)

Parker, S, 'Rights and Utility in Anglo-Australian Family Law' (1992) 55 *Modern Law Review* 311

Pearce, N, 'Forced Marriage Protection Orders: Practice and Procedure under FPR 2010' [2011] *International Family Law* 602

Polikoff, N, *Beyond (Straight and Gay) Marriage: Valuing All Families Under the Law* (Boston, Beacon Press, 2008)

Price, D, 'Pension Accumulation and Gendered Household Structures', in J Miles and R Probert (eds), *Sharing Lives, Dividing Assets: An Interdisciplinary Study* (Oxford, Hart Publishing, 2009)

Priest, J and Whybrow, J, 'Custody Law In Practice in the Divorce and Domestic Courts', supplement to Law Commission, *Review of Child Law: Custody*, Working Paper No 96 (London, HMSO, 1986)

Probert, R, '*Hyde v Hyde*: Defining or Defending Marriage?' [2007] *Child and Family Law Quarterly* 322

——, *Marriage Law and Practice in the Long Eighteenth Century: A Reassessment* (Cambridge, Cambridge University Press, 2009)

Probert, R, Gilmore, S and Herring, J, (eds) *Responsible Parents and Parental Responsibility* (Oxford, Hart Publishing, 2009)

Rawls, J, *Justice as Fairness: A Restatement* (Cambridge MA, Harvard University Press, 2001)

Raz, J, *The Morality of Freedom* (Oxford, Oxford University Press, 1986)

Reece, H, *Divorcing Responsibly* (Oxford, Hart Publishing, 2003)

——, 'The Degradation of Parental Responsibility' in R Probert, S Gilmore and J Herring (eds), *Responsible Parents and Parental Responsibility* (Oxford, Hart Publishing, 2009)

——, 'The Paramountcy Principle: Consensus or Construct?' (1996) 49 *Current Legal Problems* 267

Schuz, R, 'Habitual Residence of Children Under the Hague Abduction Convention: Theory and Practice' [2001] *Child and Family Law Quarterly* 1

——, 'The Influence of the UN Convention on the Rights of the Child on the Implementation of the 1980 Hague Child Abduction Convention' (paper presented at the *International Child Abduction, Forced Marriage and Relocation Conference*, London Metropolitan University, July 2010)

——, 'In Search of a Settled Interpretation of Article 12(2) of the Hague Child Abduction Convention' [2008] *Child and Family Law Quarterly* 64

Scott, K, 'Standing in the Supreme Court: A Functional Analysis' (1972) 86 *Harvard Law Review* 645, 674

Sen, A, *The Idea of Justice* (London, Penguin, 2010)

Smart, C, 'The Ethic of Justice Strikes Back: Changing Narratives of Fatherhood' in A Diduck and K O'Donovan (eds), *Feminist Perspectives on Family Law* (Abingdon, Routledge-Cavendish, 2006)

——, *The Ties That Bind: Law, Marriage and the Reproduction of Patriarchal Relations* (London, Routledge & Kegan Paul, 1984)

Spaventa, E, 'Seeing the Wood Despite the Trees? On the Scope of Union Citizenship and its Constitutional Effects' (2008) 45 *Common Market Law Review* 13

Taylor, N, Tapp, N and Henaghan, M, 'Respecting Children's Participation in Family Law Proceedings' (2007) 15 *International Journal of Children's Rights* 61

Thorpe, M, 'Relocation Development' [2010] *Family Law* 565

——, 'The Work of the Head of International Family Law', online at www.familylaw-week.co.uk/site.aspx?i=ed1865

Trinder, E, 'Shared Residence: A Review of Recent Evidence' [2010] *Family Law* 1192

United Nations, 'Trends in Total Migrant Stock: The 2008 Revisions', 1, available online at www.un.org/esa/population/migration/UN_MigStock_2008.pdf

Vogler, C, 'Managing Money in Intimate Relationships: Similarities and Differences Between Cohabiting and Married Couples' in J Miles and R Probert (eds), *Sharing Lives, Dividing Assets: An Interdisciplinary Study* (Oxford, Hart Publishing, 2009)

Waite, L and Gallagher, M, *The Case for Marriage* (New York, Broadway Books, 2000)

Warriner, C, 'Do We Need to Worry About an Anti-Gay Marriage Amendment?', online at www.sosogay.org/2011/opinion-do-we-need-to-worry-about-an-anti-gay-marriage-amendment

Williams, Z, 'So We Can't Afford Legal Aid? Look at the Costs Without It', *The Guardian* (23 June 2011)

Worwood, A, 'International Relocation: The Debate' [2005] *Family Law* 621

Index